UP OFF THEIR KNEES
A Commentary on the
Civil Rights Movement in
Northern Ireland

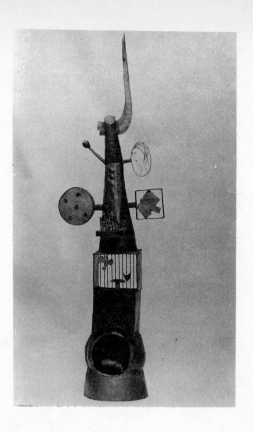

My sculpture 'Derry, October 5th' was exhibited using the name Constantin Cluskey during 1985, with Independent Artists in the Arts Council Gallery, Belfast and the Guinness Hop Store, Dublin. It is a celebration of the Civil Rights movement.

At the base the emerging chrysalis of minority protest on the spines of reaction. Behind the bars is the suggestion of a prisoner or a casualty or a dead body. The book and sheets represent civil rights publicity. Opposite this the round panel at the front represents the good emerging, at the back evil retreating. The club at the top represents the intimidation for over sixty years. I suppose Burntollet was also in the mind. The female head is to celebrate the part women have played in civil rights. The unconscious produced the two lances reaching for the sky in prayer and defence.

CONN McCLUSKEY

Up off their Knees

A Commentary on the
Civil Rights Movement in
Northern Ireland

Foreword by P.J. McCooey

Conn McCluskey
and associates

First published in the Republic of Ireland by
Conn McCluskey and Associates in 1989

© Conn McCluskey 1989

Cover Design: John McEvoy

Photography: John Searle

Editor and indexer: Bridget Lunn
Production: Mairead Peters

ISBN 0 9514837 0 6 hardback
       0 9514837 1 4 paperback

Print origination by Irish Typesetting & Publishing Co. Ltd., Galway

Printed and bound by Camelot Press, Southampton

To all those who agitated for
Civil Rights in Northern Ireland,
whether anonymously or publicly,
and to the people who kept the
Campaign for Social Justice afloat
by their generous cash contributions.

CONTENTS

FOREWORD

SINCERE and altruistic people suffer many disabilities, suspicion of their motives, disbelief in their probity, criticism and vilification. Their final penalty, and the most difficult to bear, is to be misunderstood, even by friends and associates. Thus it was with the progenitors of civil rights in Northern Ireland.

There is a modicum of injustice in all societies. Sometimes it is unintentional, even inevitable; then again it may be inbuilt, planned and consistently applied. The Northern Ireland of the sixties had all these shades of injustice in fair measure, yet it ambled along as it had done for more than three decades, and nobody took much notice. Most intelligent people realised that many things were wrong but what was there to do? That was just the way it was and what cannot be cured must be endured or, as the Tyrone woman put it, 'What bees, biz.' Those who suffered the injustices smouldered on, their resentment unchannelled and made even keener by their very impotence. (The knowledge that a considerable body of opinion held that they had contributed to their own plight did little to help.)

If there was an occasional howl of protest at the hustings or a stuttering speech in Stormont, sure wasn't that only to be expected? Didn't politicians have to say something to justify their existence and their big pay? The pundits knew it would never change—no, nay, never.

Then, to the confusion of punditry, something began to change, a new approach emerged. Quietly, almost surreptitiously at first, the hard, grinding, unspectacular work of gathering *facts* had begun. Where there had formerly been only vague generalisations, now there was *evidence*, uncontestable,

1

incontrovertible, painstakingly laid out for all to see. This development, the foundation of the Campaign for Social Justice in Northern Ireland, was the single most important one in the genesis of the civil rights movement.

Those who formed the Campaign were an unlikely lot. What was in it for them? Not money, because most of them had that in fair abundance. Certainly, compared with those they sought to help, they were affluent. Not fame, because they must have known that they would be scorned and jeered at as a collection of middle-class busybodies. Could it possibly be, then, that it was actual dedication to some abstruse, un-native ideal—fair play, equity, or even justice?

The twitching, nose-tapping, winking pundits had it all taped as usual, however: *she* was *after the seat*. *That* was the glittering prize, a position in the gilded halls of Stormont or Westminster! Some prize indeed, but it was the goal of many who looked on *the seat* as the ultimate attainment, the apex of human endeavour.

Who was *she* or, more properly in the then almost entirely male-dominated society of Northern Ireland, why was it *she*? To find out we must go back to the middle of that decade called The Hungry Thirties, in Scotland.

It was in the rumbustious No Mean City, Glasgow, that the young, newly qualified Patricia McShane first came up against the appalling effects of man's inhumanity to man. In the Gorbals and in other less salubrious districts, where Razor Kings terrorised every 'close' in the narrow streets, she carried out her social work, storing up the experiences which would later benefit more rural but similarly deprived people.

After marriage to a general practitioner, she settled down to a period of mainly genial domesticity in Dungannon. With three daughters reared, and in those more mature years when the creature comforts would normally beckon, she began to feel unease at the plight of many young married mothers. Her husband, Dr Conn McCluskey, had told her about these women, with their stories of the impossibility of getting housing accommodation, who crowded his surgery every day. He had begun to despair of treating these harassed young women medically while their elementary social needs went unsatisfied. This despair was communicated to his wife, who decided that something must be done about it.

It is told later in this book how Mrs Patricia McCluskey then started the group with the inspired title of The Homeless Citizens' League. When, in her wide-brimmed hat and striking costume, she headed a parade of homeless young mothers, their babies and prams, through Dungannon, she strode right into the conscience of a people and into the history of our times. There, indeed, all unknowing, walked the Juno, the veritable Mother of Civil Rights in Northern Ireland.

Beside this Juno, in the stirring years that followed, the dashing figure of her husband always appeared. It would be straining the O'Casey analogy too far to describe him as the Paycock (though some might claim that his sartorial rectitude and general elegance would qualify him for just such a title!). Here was no dithering, foostering, ineffective character like the Paycock in the play. Instead, there was a sometimes sardonic, sometimes outrageous, frequently stimulating and entertaining, always *concerned*, family doctor.

It is surely no discourtesy to the other dedicated members of the Campaign to mention that the McCluskeys worked ceaselessly—annotating, checking, querying, often encouraging, cajoling and bullying others to greater efforts. During all those years of intense community activity Conn McCluskey carried on a busy medical practice, frequently going far beyond the call of duty in the interests of his patients. And when the Northern Ireland Civil Rights Association commenced, he continued urging his new associates ever onward and upward. Excelsior!

Who, then, better to write a history of civil rights in Northern Ireland than one who had been so deeply involved in the game before the others had even heard the starting whistle?—*a* history, not *the* history, because this is not the definitive story of the civil rights movement and its genesis —nor does it pretend to be. It is a highly individual account of a period, written by an artist, for artists can usually see right to the centre of things.

An artist as well? Yes, under the name of Constantin Cluskey he has sculpted many widely acclaimed pieces which were, and are, exhibited in various parts of the world. It is most appropriate that some of his larger works have been put on display in the wide open spaces of parkland, exhibition centre and airport where the public can enjoy them. Such figures as Lugh Lamh Fhada, Excelsior, Coquette, Laocoon and the smaller pieces: Icarus, The Underdog, The Prisoner, Derry, and others, illustrate the depth of his sympathy and understanding which probe close to the heart of the human condition.

Life in Northern Ireland would have been different if tolerance and understanding had prevailed—or had even been given a fair trial. The members of the Campaign for Social Justice and of the original N.I. Civil Rights Association (all decent, reasonable, ordinary people) asked—pleaded for—tolerance and understanding. It was not to be, however, though some more liberal representatives of the Unionist establishment tried hard, even if for merely selfish reasons, to inaugurate a more equitable system. They were pursued and dragged down to ruin by the baying hounds of intolerance and bigotry which have bedevilled Irish society for centuries.

Up off their Knees is an insight into a traumatic period when many people were tested in the crucible of peace and justice. It will cause hair to stand on end. Some will chuckle, others rage and curse. Others still will threaten, but that will not be a new experience for the author. His book will, of course, be misunderstood, for it seems there can never be an end to misunderstanding in our Northern Irish society.

Two things will be established by this book—*she* was not *after the seat*, and (to expand Robert Burns) 'a chiel has been amang ye takin' notes an', feth, he has *printed* them'.

P.J. McCooey
June 1989

INTRODUCTION

'See how these Christians love one another'
> Quintus Septimus Florens Tertullianus, AD 160–230

IF THERE is any truth in the theory advanced by a small
minority of American psychologists that the minds of babies
can be influenced before birth by what goes on in the outside
world, my involvement in civil rights matters must have
received a very early push. Shortly after my parents were
married, and I was on the way, they rented Cohannon House
near Dungannon as their first home. Until then the house
always had Protestant tenants, so the local Orangemen
assembled at the gates to beat their enormous drums in
protest. My parents were forced to leave and find a quiet,
mainly nationalist, area at Warrenpoint, Co. Down in which
to live.

In the same way, when she was a girl, iron must have
entered the soul of a certain Patricia McShane, living on the
main street of a notably 'black' town, Portadown, where her
father owned a drapery shop.

Over the years the house came in for a lot of Protestant
attention, drumming, plate glass window smashing and
general intimidation. It became so bad during the July
marching season that the young McShane family, year after
year, had to be sent away for safety.

Eventually we two were married and ended up in a general
medical practice in Dungannon.

When Brian Gregory prevailed upon me to put a book about
civil rights in Northern Ireland between covers, I warned him
that it would be 'a warts and all' production. Nevertheless,

5

should anyone feel cross with me about what I have said about them they might console themselves with the knowledge that I have been applying the old journalist's adage throughout the whole volume, 'when in doubt, leave out'.

It angers me greatly when I think of all the terrible things that have happened since the mid-sixties. The various Unionist Governments and their masters at Westminster allowed things to go so far that the reputation of our beautiful little country has been sullied in the eyes of the world. They delayed reform so long that odious violence came to the surface—violence which is part of the make-up of us all, but hopefully lies buried in our unconscious minds. For many young men it surfaced and led to ruined lives. The first intimation I had that things might go from bad to worse was after we had presented our case, and there was time for it to sink in. Gerry Fitt, on an Independent Television programme, using charts and statistics on a blackboard, clashed with Mr Roy Bradford, MP, reputed to be a moderate Unionist. The discussion was about the Derry voting gerrymander. Mr Bradford argued with seeming conviction that there was nothing wrong with the voting situation in Derry.

I am afraid that some, perhaps most, Protestants who might read this book will label me a bigot. I must counter by claiming that I have only presented what I believed the situation to be. I would welcome it if some Protestant apologist for Unionist policy were to produce a reply, backed up, of course, with documentation and statistics.

I hasten to add that, being born and bred in Northern Ireland, I have always loved the place and, what is more, being a Christian, I must love everyone in it (Catholics are Christians too!). The only people I would exclude from this sentiment are those who indulge in violence, or support it.

When I say that I loved everyone in Northern Ireland this especially applied to my Protestant patients. How I appreciated these intelligent, direct and reliable people, and how I admired their Nonconformist conscience that made them such pleasant contacts. I appreciated their sterling worth in staying with me against what I am sure were considerable pressures.

I have always felt hurt when the impression surfaces, as it

does from time to time, that many Protestants, deep down, regard us Catholics as non-persons. They do not consider us as individuals but are content to discount us all equally. Here are some examples of what I mean:

1. Many Protestants continue to assert that all people interested in civil rights are republicans. This is quite untrue, as the reasonably well-informed among them must know.

2. The dismissive attitude to Father Denis Faul disturbs me. I know him well. He is a very special person. What sets him apart is his desire to serve 'the least brethren'. His concern for Caitlín ní h-Ullacháin is a very secondary one. I remember once asking him in the early days why he involved himself so deeply. It was during the time of Internment. 'If you could see', he said, 'the sheer misery of the mothers going in the station wagons to see their imprisoned relatives, and their unhappy children, you would understand.'

3. Some years ago, after he resigned, Patricia and I travelled down alone in a lift at a hotel in London's Knightsbridge with Captain Terence O'Neill. He did not show even the slightest sign of recognition of two people who should surely have given him many times 'furiously to think'.

4. When Lord Grey was to open a new wing at South Tyrone Hospital I demonstrated with a group against religious discrimination in employment at the hospital. After the Governor had passed in, I handed my placard to someone else and went in after him as a local general practitioner to attend the opening. I was told afterwards that two burly Protestants had been positioned behind me in order to lift me to my feet if I did not rise for the Anthem. That the Dungannon people should not have the sense to know that my kind of Catholic would never dream of offering a discourtesy to the Queen is disturbing.

This book could never have begun but for the work of my secretary in Dungannon, Rita McQuaid, née Corrigan. Her filing, duplicating and general secretarial work was indispensable and of a very high standard. My appreciation goes also to Kathleen McGovern who deciphered my dreadful handwriting and typed from my longhand. Thanks also to my daughter Darine Gleeson who read the proofs.

May I end with an appeal. Firstly to my Protestant fellow countrymen: have a titter of wit and realise that you will never get the genie back into the bottle; and to nationalists: I beg them to undertake the slower but more hopeful approach of bridge-building—try to achieve every day the unity of feeling we only experience when Ireland plays England in Rugby football at Landsdowne Road or when Irish boxers meet foreign opponents—there is no other way.

Conn McCluskey
Belfast, June 1989

1.
THE DUNGANNON AFFAIR

IF ON the morning of Tuesday 28 August 1963 the citizens of Dungannon had known the implication and the upshot of what had happened the night before in their town, the temptation would have been, either to have pulled the bedclothes over their heads and stay where they were or to think of changing their place of residence forthwith. As it was, they arose for the day and gradually picked up some very odd vibrations from the community. It happened like this.

In the centre of the province of Ulster, Dungannon was an average country town with, at that time, a population of around seven thousand, half Protestant, half Catholic. There were two textile factories, both Protestant owned, and the upper echelons of the workforce were virtually all Protestant. The larger shops were mainly Protestant owned and staffed. A few Catholic owners were in business in a smaller way. The best and largest farms were owned by Protestants. There were four Protestant banks and one Catholic. Protestants dominated the health services and the hospital, the Ministry of Labour, Post Office and Electricity Board. Most lower-status nurses, lesser artisans and labourers were Catholic. There was a reasonably mixed spread of schoolteachers, solicitors, and medical practitioners in private practice, but no Catholic accountants. Only in the Golf Club did the middle class of both persuasions associate as equals. Boys going to the famous Dungannon Royal School, founded in 1615, could look forward to a more promising future than the students of the corresponding Catholic grammar school. Needless to say the outcome of all this was that Catholics were inferior creatures and felt themselves to be 'second class citizens'. During the emotive annual July marching season Catholics withdrew further into their shells, and were frequently reminded by the Orange brethern of their subordinate position.

The most crushing handicap of working-class Catholics at that time was the housing shortage. The town's gerrymandered electoral system consisted of three wards, two of which were controlled by the Unionists (Protestants). There was no points system for housing allocation, tenancies being assigned in the Unionist ward by the Unionists, and in the one anti-Unionist ward by the Nationalist (Catholic) councillors. Since no new houses had been built in the Catholic ward, the only houses on offer there were re-lets. This arrangement invited abuse because there was no local government election of anti-Unionist councillors. They were merely selected by the local Nationalist MP to the Stormont Parliament, the late Joe Stewart. The position was that, to control voting strength, no Catholic family had been allocated a permanent house for thirty-four years. Young newly-weds were compelled to move in with in-laws and keep their wedding presents under the bed. This usually worked until the second child arrived, when family tensions began to mount. In some cases families had been waiting as long as twelve years for a home. As a medical practitioner myself, I had close contact with several of these people and could clearly observe their suffering. There was one particularly bad case of overcrowding in the town where a large private house had been indifferently converted into eight flats. In one of these, ten people were living in one room. The strain on young mothers trying to maintain order and a degree of quiet, where most facilities had to be shared, was very great. Men on night shift work found it impossible to sleep. One young mother took a drug overdose and was removed to hospital. Something had to be done. A few married women called a meeting which was chaired by a local curate. Banded together as the Homeless Citizens League, a committee was formed, led by a dynamic and personable young woman, Mrs Angela McCrystal. It was agreed that statistics should be assembled and a further public meeting should take place in a week's time. The gathering assembled but neither the curate nor the public representatives turned up. After a delay of an hour, by which time the mothers were becoming distraught, my wife, Patricia, fearing that the impetus of the new movement might be lost, decided to take a hand. She had

10

attended the meeting only as a concerned person and never spoken before in public. In a state of righteous anger she mounted the stage and called the meeting to order. A new era of public protest was born!

The sixty-seven members of the Homeless Citizens League began to mount pressure against the Council. First there was a picket outside the Urban Council offices, placards were carried, television and newspaper reporters were on hand, the police did not interfere and the atmosphere was cordial. A deputation from the League was heard by the Council but was refused any of the 142 council houses just completed in a Unionist ward. These were subsequently allocated mainly to Protestant newly-weds. There was nothing for it but to begin protest marches around the town. The first of these took place in June 1963. They were sad but impressive turnouts, the women in their Sunday best, children walking and in prams. Stragglers were marshalled by Patricia. Here and there was the odd husband looking hangdog in his unwelcome notoriety. Police permission had been obtained and the demonstrators were led by the Irish National Foresters brass band. Regrettably the marches were not supported by the Catholic middle class. They obviously could not bring themselves to associate closely in those testing times with the 'lumpenproletariat' of the housing estates.

By now Ireland, North and South, was aware of the problem but still the Council stubbornly resolved—no houses for Catholics. This could no longer be borne.

At this stage it was being put about by hardline Unionists that the Homeless Citizens League was a bunch of ragamuffins. The Unionist local newspaper, the *Tyrone Courier*, on 6 June 1963 published an interview with the eight committee members and included a large photograph where it was plain to see that these were dignified and attractive women.

There was an estate of pre-fabricated bungalows at Fairmount Park, just vacated by those who had been allocated new houses. The 'prefabs' were to be dismantled and sold as outhouses or henhouses, although they were in a reasonable condition, neatly painted and papered inside. There was water laid on with a back boiler in some. In fact they were in as good condition as hundreds of similar ones occupied by families in Derry, Belfast and many other towns. The League

11

held a late-night meeting on 27 August, chaired by Patricia, at which a decision was taken to do nothing. At about two o'clock the following morning Brian Morrison, a Nationalist councillor rang Patricia, 'Mrs McCluskey, Mrs McCluskey, the whole town is on the move!' The next morning when we awoke we were told that seventeen families had squatted in the 'prefabs'. Horror, astonishment, elation!

The Council cut off electricity and water supplies but the latter was reconnected when the illegality of this action was pointed out. Relatives of the squatters rallied round and also a small number of middle-class people provided food, blankets, bedding and oil heaters, the last being very necessary since there were small children and a few infants amongst the new tenants. Soon the squatters, looking youthful and tidy, were joyously explaining their position to the newspapers and television interviewers. During the following fortnight, under cover of darkness, groups of two or three families loaded their belongings on vans and lorries and moved in by the light of candles. They carried children and furniture into the first real home most of them had possessed since they were married. The Unionist Council chairman, the late Senator William Stewart, blustered and threatened to remove the squatters from the housing list. The Council contemplated ejectment proceedings. At this juncture the Stormont Government agreed to become involved, and a delegation from the squatters was invited to the Parliament buildings to meet the Minister of Health and Local Government, Mr William Morgan. The delegation consisted of Maurice Byrne a local dentist, the late Christopher Mallon, solicitor, and myself. We were armed with a detailed and carefully researched dossier.

To satisfy the press and more especially to reassure the squatters we took a formal departure from the Fairmount Park estate. All the new residents and their friends were assembled to see us on our way. There was an intense sense of occasion to be savoured and relished by Patricia and the three delegates. The shining eyes of the mothers showed that they were aware they were being swept along into an entirely new situation. Even the older children knew that something different was in train, while the younger ones were strangely quiet. The men, standing closely together, were talking and smoking furiously. Also present was an occasional sombre grandparent. As we drove off a cheer went up.

Meanwhile the number of houses taken over had risen to thirty-five, accommodating 120 people. The *Belfast Telegraph*, a Unionist evening newspaper, which had recently become more liberal, produced a leader supporting the squatters. Mr Morgan could do nothing but allow them to remain. A new housing estate in the Nationalist ward was to be hurried to completion and the squatters were promised houses there.

Shortly after the 'prefabs' were taken over I had occasion to bring one of the local hospital consultants to visit a patient. It was a measure of the fear and distrust existing between the two communities in the town that he seemed fearful of entering the area—afraid to go amongst what were in reality a group of gentle matriarchs and their inoffensive families.

There was a happy sequel to the squatting operation when the Homeless Citizens League held a social to which Patricia and I were invited; Patricia was presented by them with an inscribed silver plate tea service, which, needless to say, she has come to regard as a valued possession.

General resentment had now built up, especially amongst the younger people, about the absence for the past forty years of any opportunity for the anti-Unionists to choose their councillors by election. Patricia went to see a resident of the town, Patsy McCooey, known even in those early days for his integrity. He suggested John Donaghy, a telephone engineer, and secondary school teachers Bríd McAleer and Peter Finnegan, as potential councillors. A public meeting was called in St Patrick's Hall where a strong impulse for change was indicated. The following were chosen to contest the seven seats in the anti-Unionist ward at the forthcoming election—Patricia, John Donaghy, Bríd McAleer, Patsy McCooey, James Corrigan outgoing member, Peter Finnegan and Angela McCrystal. The candidates selected as their slogan—'Vote for justice, vote for the team'. Opposing them were the Nationalists and Northern Ireland Labour.

The election itself, held in May 1964, was the most exciting and heartwarming event that Dungannon had seen for many a year. Turnout was just 97 per cent of the total voting population, Catholic and Protestant. As a man on a stretcher

13

was being carried past her, Sergeant Owens of the local RUC remarked to Patricia: 'There are as many miracles here as during biblical times!'

McCooey, Donaghy, Corrigan and Patricia were elected, as were James Donnelly and P.G. McQuaid, for the Nationalists, and John Murphy, Independent Labour. From then on, ordinary meetings of the Urban Council were to prove tempestuous affairs, with the Unionists using their gerrymandered majority, and not conceding a quarter of an inch in the matter of housing and council jobs. For example, by January 1967 only thirty-four Catholic families, compared with 264 new Protestant families, had been accommodated in permanent houses by the Urban Council since the last war. A points system for housing allocation was repeatedly rejected.

Bias at times bordered on farce. The newly elected Council met in 1965 to choose the members of the various Committees. Patricia's colleagues, indeed everyone else locally, were aware that she and I had done a reasonable amount of foreign touring, thus they proposed her name as the Council's representative on the Tourist Development Body for Northern Ireland. The Unionists rejected her, appointing instead a man whose claim to suitability was that he was an employee of Ulsterbus, and was involved in running the half-day Mystery Tours from Dungannon.

There was one very dramatic incident. Some houses were to be let. A large crowd had gathered outside the Council offices which were located on the first floor of a building in Dungannon Market Square. Police and the army were present. Senator William Stewart rose to propose an all-Unionist letting, and as he stood he was taken ill with an apoplectic seizure, and collapsed to the floor. Councillors rushed to throw open the window to give him air. This was done with such vigour that the glass shattered and fell to the street below. The public thought a fight had broken out. An ambulance arrived and removed the Senator to hospital.

2.
THE CAMPAIGN FOR SOCIAL JUSTICE IN NORTHERN IRELAND

IN THE weeks following the squatting operation in Dungannon, we were approached from many parts of the North with requests for help with housing problems. Letters approving of our activities arrived, asking us to continue. It was obvious that we could never influence the Unionist Government. Our only hope lay in letting the outside world know of our problems—a daunting task but we felt we might make a dent if we hit hard enough and often enough. The first thing needed was a properly constituted organisation, preferably with only a handful of members because large groups of Irish people are prone to discuss matters too fully without making final decisions, and eventually split up.

We found four wise advisers in Belfast: J.J. Campbell, a lecturer in Queen's University, Brian McGuigan, a solicitor, J.C. May, a leading businessman and James Scott, professor of dentistry in Queen's University. They suggested that we should try to involve some liberal Protestants and that we should not become involved with Members of Parliament. They themselves were not disposed to join us. We wrote to three moderate Protestants well known in the public life of Northern Ireland, but we had no success. They approved of our aims, very warmly and generously, but could not accept our idea of publicity outside Ireland. Their response was 'Let us try to sort out our problems amongst ourselves.'

We began a search amongst our 'own kind', gaining experience all the time. Many were too nationalist to be of use. Fifty years of the same sort of agitation by the Nationalists had achieved nothing. Heated discussions about the 'border' would be a waste of time and energy. Our idea was, since we lived in a part of the United Kingdom where the British remit ran, we should seek the ordinary rights of British citizens which were so obviously denied us.

We went to see a group in Derry city but it was not a profitable visit. They were older men, wedded to Nationalist party thinking and seemed horrified that we should propose such a novel approach. Why, we asked them, should they allow the Lord Mayor alone to allocate all council housing, in a city where the Unionists were relatively so few in number? Their reaction was a leaden resignation, so different from the effervescent working people of Dungannon.

We also called on Eddie McAteer, the Stormont MP and leader of the Nationalist Party. Again we made little progress but he did offer us a very interesting dictum about the people of the Republic of Ireland—'We are the bastard children of the Republic, sometimes they must needs acknowledge us, but generally speaking they try to keep their distance.'

There was an important get-together in the house of Peter Gormley, chief eye and ENT surgeon in the Mater Hospital, Belfast. Nearly all the people who were later to form our committee were present. We were deeply conscious of how the quiet drip of discrimination had stifled initiative and dampened the fires of dissent in our community. Someone declared, 'We must do everything we can to get the people up off their knees.' Obviously this was to be one of our main aims. The ideas of our new organisation had begun to coalesce. A name was chosen, 'The Campaign for Social Justice in Northern Ireland'. Good brains had been selected, people whom we judged to be entirely reputable, and who had in their personalities that essential thread of steel.

This was our Committee: Brian Gregory, an architect, a shrewd contributor from the first day; Peter Gormley, an ear, nose and throat surgeon with a province-wide reputation for reliability; Conor Gilligan, a general surgeon and a completely dependable helper at all times; Maurice Byrne, a dentist, who had been one of the three members of the deputation for the squatters; J.J. Donnelly, an Enniskillen councillor, whose dogged singlemindedness we had often cause to appreciate; Hugh McConville of Lurgan, an experienced committee man in his school-teacher association; Tom McLaughlin of

16

Armagh, a wealthy business man well used to negotiation in his public service activities; Leo Sullivan, a science professor from Omagh and myself. There were three women, Olive Scott, warm-hearted and a fervent nationalist; Maura Mullally, whose quiet English voice smoothed many a heated discussion; and Patricia, whom the group at our first meeting made chairperson.

It was decided to hold a press conference in the Wellington Park Hotel, Belfast on 14 January 1964. A press release was prepared, part of which read:

> The Government of Northern Ireland's policies of apartheid and discrimination have continued to be implemented at all levels with such zeal that we, whose names are set out below, have banded ourselves together to oppose them. We intend to call our organisation 'The Campaign for Social Justice in Northern Ireland', with address, 3 Castlefields, Dungannon, Co. Tyrone.
>
> Our first objective will be to collect comprehensive and accurate data on all injustices done against all creeds and political opinions, including details of discrimination in jobs and houses and to bring them to the attention of as many socially minded people as possible.
>
> A booklet will be published for the widest circulation in which we will feel no need to select or slant our facts for the best effect, our case being so strong that the presentation of the unvarnished truth will be sufficient.
>
> We will make as full use as funds allow of newspaper, poster and leaflet publicity outside Ireland, availing of the services of an advertising consultant. In this way we will force all the disturbing details of life here to the attention of the British and American people so that it can never again be said that they were unaware of what was happening in Northern Ireland.
>
> The aims of our Association transcend party politics but we feel free to approach, from time to time, any political party anywhere which we think is likely to help us. Ultimately, if all this fails, we intend to present our case to the Commission for Human Rights in Strasbourg, and to the United Nations.
>
> Whilst we know that the majority of Northern Ireland

people, both Protestant and Catholic, are warm-hearted and humane, a minority continues to make life difficult and embarrassing for the rest and to repress continued appeals for fair play by men of good will. Our aim is, we think, both basic and Christian but nevertheless has not been realised here for hundreds of years, namely—equality for all.

The night before the press conference when all our nerves were on edge, a trade unionist from Derry and a County Down medical practitioner, whom we had chosen as committee members, rang up to withdraw. We faced the press that morning and they treated us gently. This was our first and somewhat bewildering experience of a press conference, the intimidating television lights, the untidy microphones, the lisping cameras, the watchful indolence of the newsmen, being questioned closely by Cal McCrystal and others like him. However, the next day we had a good press and we all felt blooded, and very pleased and relieved.

When our Campaign met we were all agreed on one thing. The facts we proposed to present to the world must be scrupulously correct. Too often in the past inaccurate claims were easily disposed of by a much more sophisticated opposition. A number of questionnaire forms on such matters as jobs and housing were prepared. Each set was presented in a special envelope to our carefully selected agents. Circulation had to be discreet because a person found collecting statistics might suffer in his or her job prospects. Indeed we found it was something of a cloak and dagger operation, returned forms being often printed or typed, not just handwritten. A packet would arrive with a plop on our doormat and a shadowy figure would be seen retreating in the darkness.

As time went on, we had the satisfaction of knowing that in only one case, in the reams of documentation we supplied, did we make an error. In giving a housing discrimination fact, we mistook one man for his brother. Fortunately they were decent Protestants and there was no litigation, although we were very uneasy for a time.

Our first publication was *Northern Ireland—the Plain Truth*. This was a pamphlet which contained a short resumé of the position and a set of statistics on job and housing discrimination in Derry and Dungannon. One of our claims was that the

18

British taxpayer was subsidising Northern Ireland to the tune of £46 million. This infuriated the Unionists who were so blinkered that they counterclaimed that taxes collected in Northern Ireland more than covered the amount of the grant from the British Exchequer—which was nonsense! In 1964 Stormont received £81 million from Whitehall and £165 million in 1965 (*Belfast Telegraph* 26 October 1966). In the year 1987 Westminster spent an incredible £4,810 million on Northern Ireland.

At this time we received annoyance from an unexpected source. We had telephone messages and letters from fervent nationalists objecting to our using the word 'Londonderry' instead of 'Derry' in our publications. This single fact encapsulated the difference between ourselves and those who had gone before. 'Londonderry' it was on the maps that our foreign readers would consult. We had no wish to confuse them.

A bombshell burst on the British readership of the *Sunday Times*. An article by Cal McCrystal entitled 'John Bull's political slum' (3 July 1966) exposed with awe-inspiring clarity the way Ulster politics operated. From then onwards cover-ups were impossible.

In time the Unionists issued a spate of documents such as *Ulster, the facts*, and *Northern Ireland, the facts at your fingertips*. Needless to say none of our allegations was disproved, most were not even tackled. There were vague generalisations about the good things in Northern Ireland, with which we would not attempt to disagree.

Our *Plain Truth* was only a first effort and not nearly comprehensive enough. The second edition, produced in 1969, was much better. It is reproduced in full in an Appendix. It became our main organ of publicity and over 100,000 were produced and circulated. They were requested and willingly supplied to the various civil rights organisations, British and foreign parliamentarians, groups of supporters in Britain, Europe, USA and Australia. Even the Government of the Republic of Ireland acquired a supply for a publicity drive they were undertaking at ambassadorial level.

I had an agitated phone call from a London supporter. He was at Speakers' Corner in Hyde Park where he saw an old and decrepit man selling *Northern Ireland, the Plain Truth* at a mark-up of over 200 per cent. Another time I was told that our pamphlet was being distributed free in London, over-stamped in red by the Communist Party. Some of our committee were horrified, my feeling was that our case was being presented, and as long as the wording was not interfered with, it was alright.

When this book was projected, Brian Gregory suggested that not much space should be devoted to the matter of religous discrimination, because everyone was well aware of the position. True, but *The Plain Truth* is included in full in case, within ten or twenty years, people should have forgotten much of the detail. In the end it might even be suggested that discrimination never happened. The booklet sets out the outrageous statements made by the Unionist leaders and the squalid things they did. And it is worth noting that, as reprint followed reprint, not one fact in it was ever contradicted or disproved. It must be emphasised that the facts given were those of the time the booklet was issued. They do not relate to the position now, since many improvements have taken place. Just how necessary it is to include *The Plain Truth* at the back of this book was shown when J.J. Keating of Blacon, Chester, England, sent a copy to the Minister of Home Affairs at Stormont, Mr William Craig, and asked for his comments. On 21 April 1964 Mr Craig wrote to J.J. Keating: 'This pamphlet is typical of the scurrilous propaganda put out by a small section of the community whose avowed intention is to overthrow the Constitution of Northern Ireland.'

Conditions were so bad in Derry that our committee decided that a separate leaflet should be issued giving more detail than was previously available. *Londonderry one man, no vote* was prepared and included in all our mailings.

When Sir Alec Douglas Home, MP, visited Northern Ireland in March 1964 he stated in reply to questions at a Belfast press conference, and later on television, that recourse could be had to the courts in matters of complaint regarding religious discrimination. We wrote to Sir Alec. The British have many fine qualities but one besetting sin, hypocrisy. In letters which followed, five in number, there was a series of evasions from his department and from the Home Secretary's Department. This correspondence was printed by the Campaign as a leaflet *Northern Ireland, Why Justice can not be done* (see

Appendix). It is likely that Sir Alec, whom most Westminster politicians describe as a decent man, had reason to regret not supervising his civil servants more closely. At every by-election when he was Prime Minister we sent copies of this leaflet with our other publicity material to leading citizens in the town where the by-election was taking place.

Our last leaflet was *Northern Ireland, Legal Aid to oppose discrimination, not likely*. It will be detailed later in the appropriate chapter.

The next production to go into print on the Campaign's behalf was a joint booklet written by Father Denis Faul of Dungannon and myself called *Northern Ireland, the mailed fist*. It was a record of army and police brutality from 9 August till 9 November 1971. There were detailed records of events on the streets as well as statements by detainees and one by Amnesty International. We had an illustration on the cover of the booklet of soldiers dragging away Hugh Logue by his hair. He was later to become a member of the Northern Ireland Assembly. A most impressive preface was written by Mr Tony Smythe of the London National Council for Civil Liberties.

It is only fair to say that since then police attitudes and methods have greatly changed, the RUC now making serious efforts to be appreciated by the minority community. At that time it was essential also that key people such as members of Parliament and Dáil deputies, as well as politicians in the USA and leading newspaper editors and correspondents, should be continually reminded that injustices here were still common events, and that little was being done by Britain as the supreme power.

At intervals the Campaign issued a Newsletter, at first printed by a Gestetner duplicator and later as a very well finished production by the Bethlehem Abbey Press, Portglenone. The Newsletter consisted of a commentary on events and photostat copies of newspaper cuttings. There were up to forty pages in each. In all, seventeen issues were printed and sent to all parts of the world where there was interest in things Irish.

In the early days of our publicity drive we discovered that it was the law of the land in the United Kingdom that all printed matter should be lodged with the Home Office Library of the British Museum. This we did as well as sending everything we produced to the Linenhall Library, Belfast, to the Public Record Office of Northern Ireland, to the Bodleian Library, Oxford, and to the Library of the United States Congress.

We were concerned that, after the adequate coverage of the Dungannon squatters, nothing was appearing in the Southern papers about discrimination in Northern Ireland. Patricia and I wrote to and received appointments with the editors of both the *Irish Independent* and the *Irish Press*. When we met them we explained that we would not expect banner headlines about our troubles, but that if the press recorded, on an inner or even the back page, acts of injustice as they occurred, it would gradually enlighten the people in the South about our problem. Both editors replied in almost the same words to the effect that they were sorry they could not help since these matters were not newsworthy.

At our initial press conference we had promised that we would attempt to present our case to the Commission for Human Rights in Strasbourg and to the United Nations. Accordingly, we wrote to the Minister for Foreign Affairs in the Republic, sending copies of our pamphlets, and asking for an interview. Mr Frank Aiken, the Minister, welcomed Tom McLaughlin, Patricia and me most warmly in July 1964. He had with him at the interview a highly placed legal authority. I think it was the Attorney General, but, unfortunately we forgot to take a note of this gentleman's name. They produced the Charter of the United Nations and other documents and assured us that there was no way in which our disabilities could be aired.

Our members were puzzled when some time later we were sent a press cutting by an English supporter recording Mr Aiken's address to the plenary meeting of the fifth special session of the United Nations General Assembly at the United Nations headquarters in New York at which he appealed for justice for the Territory of West Africa. The lady felt that 'Mr Aiken should have first agitated for his own kith and kin.' About that time we also met Brian Lenihan, TD, George Colley, TD, and Senator Eoin Ryan. They could not have been friendlier and more concerned, but they tended to avoid suggestions on the Northern problem.

As time progressed the press became more and more

interested in our story, first the *Irish News*, then later the Dublin dailies. Finally many of the leading reporters of the international press arrived. The sophistication of these men and women was a revelation to us. We enjoyed their close questioning because our case was watertight. They did not make use of the statistics we supplied, but went off and made their own enquiries. Whether it was the late David Holden's extroverted approach or Mary Holland's quiet probing, the result was the same: another story for the papers.

Once when Mr Holden visited us we knew he was after something special. We realised in the end he was anxious to find out what violent outburst was going to happen next. He spent an hour and a half questioning us but found out nothing because we knew nothing. We never had contact with violent men or even knew who they were. And we kept it that way. Leon and Jill Uris visited and eventually became for us much more than investigative journalists. Their joint *Ireland, a terrible beauty* included Jill's wonderful photography. Later there was a full-length novel *Trinity* by Leon with a contemporary Irish background.

We always found pressmen to be courteous and friendly. We never had a cross word with one of them. They were helping our cause, indeed the free press must be one of the most important assets the USA and Western Europe possess.

But by now we had begun to develop healthy suspicions. We judged that a couple of visitors claiming to be reporters were not really reporters. They had a significantly different approach, but we humoured them and answered their questions and allowed them to take our photographs.

At that time, too, we were pretty sure our telephone was tapped. The sound volume varied and there were an inordinately large number of clicks on the line when we were speaking. Again, with nothing to hide, we chatted on unconcerned. There was the time too, when we came home from holiday to find the bedroom window swinging open, not even secured by the hasp, but the thing that really took us to the fair was the matter of the passport.

One day I went to the 'travel drawer' in our lounge to make sure that our passport was not out of date. It was gone. Both of us searched through the papers in the drawer and the drawers next to it. I even took out the drawers and looked between them, but the passport was not to be found. Two weeks later when I was looking for something else in the same drawer, the passport was back again. Patricia was furious, obviously it annoys women when people trespass in their home. For my part, with nothing to hide and nothing missing, I was unmoved.

We were puzzled when a close associate of a Unionist Minister rang up and came to see us at our home. He talked to us for an hour but gave no real indication of why he visited us. We presumed that this was a 'buying off' contact, but, if it was, his mission was a failure. Twice Mr Colin Wallace called on us. By now we were thanking our lucky stars that our convictions were well in place before we started on our civil rights journey.

The organisation, National Unity, arranged a weekend meeting and invited our Campaign to send a speaker. Tom McLaughlin was nominated. His theme was abolition of 'second class citizenship' by giving everyone equal rights. He made the important point that discrimination resulted in a lessening of civic responsibility. He denied that Catholics 'were trying to destroy the image of Northern Ireland by drawing attention to discrimination' as a Unionist newspaper had just alleged. The meeting went smoothly because he was speaking to the converted. Our next expedition to speak to a group in a hotel at Larne did not go so well. Some of those present were abusive and descended to sectarianism. Conor Gilligan was reviled by a questioner. The subject was employment in the Mater Hospital. We concluded that local speaking engagements were not likely to be fruitful, and we decided not to involve ourselves in them.

Our next engagement was a very different one.

The NCCL Conference

On 13 March 1965 the British National Council for Civil Liberties decided to hold a conference on Northern Ireland in London. The venue was the Conway Hall, Red Lion Square, a famous building where many key meetings had been held in the past. When we went into the hall the first thing to catch my eye was a huge slogan permanently painted high above our heads: 'To thine own self be true'.

The speakers invited from Northern Ireland were: Mr

24

Charles Brett, Chairman of the Northern Ireland Labour Party, Patricia, representing the Campaign for Social Justice, Miss Betty Sinclair, Secretary of the Belfast Trade Union Council, a doughty warrior and a lovable woman, who was a member of the Communist Party, Mr S. Caughey, Republican Six County Election Directorate, Austin Currie, MP, Nationalist Party, Mr John Taylor, B.Sc., Unionist Party, Mr S. Egan, Working Committee on Civil Rights, Miss S. Murnaghan, MP, Liberal Party. Individual members and a number of delegates from organisations affiliated to the NCCL attended.

After the Chairman, Eric Lubbock, now Lord Avebury, made his opening remarks, the first speaker was Charles Brett. He agreed that there was undoubted manipulation of boundaries, plural voting and religious discrimination in housing and employment in appointments made to public bodies and private firms. He was against a Royal Commission of Enquiry. He did not think that a solution of the province's problems could possibly be imposed from outside. As things turned out he was very wrong in this.

Mr Taylor denied that there was discrimination in public bodies in Northern Ireland, and claimed that the province was already solving its own community problems. We could not see his justification for this point of view or for his claim that discrimination occurred only in private firms. He complained that the Connolly Association played a big part in NCCL affairs. In fact they are only one of the many bodies affiliated to it. Betty Sinclair, unfortunately no longer with us, supported the Campaign's findings and complained that mail to working-class organisations and people active in politics was being continually examined by the authorities. Halls for conferences or meetings were difficult to obtain, she added.

Sean Caughey explained that his party, under its proper name Sinn Féin, was a banned organisation. He complained of the various repressive measures of the Ulster Government. Austin Currie, like many of the other speakers, welcomed the proposal for a Commission of Enquiry. He supported the Campaign's findings on discrimination.

Patricia presented a very full dossier of Northern Irish discrimination. Miss Murnaghan was against a Commission of Enquiry, 'Let us deal with discrimination ourselves.' From

25

the floor, Mr James McCartney of the Faculty of Law, Queen's University, who was later to become one of our Committee members, gave the meeting a well researched dissertation on electoral law and franchise arrangements. He also gave details of discrimination in jobs, housing and education. Martin Ennals, the secretary of NCCL, gave a summing up which again helped the case the Campaign was presenting.

This was a most useful Conference and we are eternally indebted to the NCCL for setting it up. At last we had a platform in England. Whilst the British press ignored the Conference, the *Guardian* being the only newspaper to mention it (four lines on the back page) the Irish newspapers, including the Unionist ones, were impelled to report it and to present some of the relevant facts to their readers.

After their successful Conference, the NCCL did not abandon us. A spate of literate and well produced documents, pamphlets and news sheets followed. *Speak Out* was one such news sheet. It dealt with the various unsavoury events in Northern Ireland, and even had a bibliography and a list of organisations and parties involved both inside and outside Northern Ireland. There was also *Civil Liberties 1969* with a section on Northern Ireland. *Crisis in Northern Ireland 1971* contained the representations of the National Council for Civil Liberties to HM Government, dealing with discrimination, administration of justice, internment, treatment of detainees. Finally it made recommendations. The NCCL Bulletin dated May 1972 had statements on the Widgery Report and the Scarman Investigation. Then in June 1972 came the NCCL news release to which was attached a commentary on the Widgery Report on Bloody Sunday. This commentary was again issued as a forty-eight page booklet entitled *Justice Denied*. It was a thorough analysis for world consumption of what was, sad to say, another example of British hypocrisy, indeed the Report was generally regarded as a whitewash of a sordid, brutal event.

The Campaign for Democracy in Ulster
The build-up of pressure against the Northern Irish state continued. We had been steadily plying the Labour Party backbenchers with documentation. The result was the

26

formation of an important new group called the Campaign for Democracy in Ulster. The driving force of this movement was Paul Rose, MP for Blackley, Manchester. In the beginning he had the signatures of sixty MPs. This later rose to over one hundred, and included Lord Soper, a minister of the Methodist Church; local Councillors and constituency Labour Party officials were also associated with it. The president was the venerable Fenner Brockway, later Lord Brockway, well-known civil rights activist. The secretary was Bill O'Shaughnessy, the treasurer Mike Melly. Paddy Byrne was an extremely active back-room boy.

The aims of the Campaign were to secure an impartial enquiry into the administration of government in Northern Ireland, to bring electoral law into line with the rest of the United Kingdom, to press for the application of the Race Relations Bill to be extended to Northern Ireland and to include religious discrimination and incitement.

On 2 July 1965 the inaugural meeting was held in the House of Commons. Patricia was asked to address it. In her speech she publicised the four pamphlets she distributed and gave many details of discrimination. She was scathing on the recently announced plan to build the new city, Craigavon, when there were four thousand people out of work in Derry city. She pressed all to read Jim McCartney's paper on the electoral system, which he had presented to the NCCL Conference. About Sir Frank Soskice, a Labour minister who had recently visited Northern Ireland and expressed himself satisfied with the position there, she said, 'If Sir Frank were to be told there was dry rot in the attic of his home he would surely not shrug his shoulders and say, "I have been out looking at the roof, it is perfect." The Unionist members of Parliament at Westminster repeatedly claim that there is no discrimination because nobody takes legal action under the 1920 Act. We have tried to take legal action. It is impossible.'

Paul Rose in his speech said, 'What riles us above all is that when we question injustices in the Six Counties we are accused of interfering, yet there is no question of any constitutional limit on the voting powers of the Unionist members in the House.' Lord Brockway said 'It is not for us to raise the issue of the border in this Campaign. The Irish people themselves will solve the border problem in time.'

Sam Napier of the Northern Ireland Labour Party sent a message of support.

Bill O'Shaughnessy emphasised the importance of gaining the support of the trade unions in order to get resolutions through at the Annual Conference of the Labour Party.

On the preliminary agenda of the Labour Party Conference there were six resolutions concerning Northern Ireland. The Campaign approached every member of the National Executive for support and 740 personal letters of appeal with accompanying documentation went out to the secretaries of each trade union and individual constituency secretaries of the Labour Party. No resolution was debated.

The CDU began to move of its own accord, responding to requests from constituency parties for speakers on 'Ulster', and found it hard enough to meet demand. In a letter to our Campaign, Paddy Byrne reported that the CDU was getting demands for literature even from Australia and New Zealand. Recently there had been a request from Bangkok!

In a letter to the *Universe*, Paul Rose pointed out that 'the Campaign had grown up as a response to spontaneous demands from within Northern Ireland itself and from among Irish people living in England'. He continued: 'The only difference is that this group is better organised; it has restricted its demands to those things which are practicable. At a time when there is a good deal of rethinking, even among Unionists, and when so many new enthusiastic MPs are showing their concern about electoral laws and religious discrimination surely it is appropriate to harness this new mood.'

The CDU was still going strong in October 1971 when Labour was in opposition, and this time the National Executive allowed a resolution to be discussed at the Labour Party Conference. The speakers at a fringe meeting sponsored by the CDU, expressed severe disappointment with this debate. The speech of Mr James Callaghan, the Shadow Home Secretary, was described as 'disgraceful' because he supported the internment policy. Paul Rose, Kevin McNamara and Sid Sidwell were trenchant speakers.

Paul Rose said that Mr Faulkner and Mr Maudling (the Tory Home Secretary) had taken Northern Ireland to the abyss by their ill-conceived and clumsily-executed internment policy. He was disappointed that the Conference platform had failed to condemn it.

I was asked to speak and said 'The British Government and the British people have reduced the minority community to the conclusion which they now hold that they will get nothing without violence. When the B-Specials and the RUC turned their machine guns on the Catholic people of Belfast in 1969 the Catholics could muster perhaps ten guns. Now there are dozens and more every day because of the way you British are bungling things. You let us down in 1969 and we are afraid of it happening again.'

The CDU, in April 1967, sent a fact-finding delegation to Northern Ireland consisting of four MPs: Gerry Fitt, Dr Maurice Millar, Stan Orme and Paul Rose. They visited Derry, Dungannon, Strabane and Coalisland. Dr Millar who, with his wife, had recently visited India, said, 'With all its problems and difficulties there is more democratic right in India than in Northern Ireland.' Other comments were, from Paul Rose: 'On my last visit to Dungannon I saw segregated housing estates which would have done credit to South Africa.' Stan Orme: 'We have come to Derry to confirm the facts. The injustices stood out in Derry and these injustices were the focal point of our fight at Westminster.'

Some members of the Campaign for Social Justice had a very happy and convivial meal with the MPs and their associates in a Dungannon restaurant. The outcome of the visit was an open letter to the Stormont Premier, Captain O'Neill, requesting that a Royal Commission be set up to enquire into allegations against the Unionist administration. This request was in reply to Captain O'Neill's statement that the Campaign had made scurrilous and wholly baseless assertions about conditions in Northern Ireland. When they returned to London the MPs gave a full report to Mr Harold Wilson and Mr Roy Jenkins, the Home Secretary.

There was a CDU rally in Manchester on 25 November 1966. In her speech Patricia set out the essentials of action required of Captain O'Neill. They were the usual ones of changes in electoral law and an independent body to deal with discrimination in housing and jobs: 'I am absolutely certain that without the intervention of our good friends in the Campaign for Democracy in Ulster and without continual

29

pressure by the British Government this will never happen'. She continued, 'We have become a little tired in the North of Ireland of watching the anti-Tory politicians oppose each other whilst the Unionist walks over their fighting bodies to success at the polls. Finally, I want to impress on you, ladies and gentlemen, that this Campaign for Social Justice does not think, and I do not think, that all the Ulster Protestants are to be condemned. There are thousands of fine Protestants whose emotions have been so worked upon that they are a frightened people. We want to change all this. We want to live with our Protestant neighbours as equals, as fellow Christians and as fellow Irishmen and women.'

Paul Rose, writing in the *Belfast Telegraph* on 3 August 1967, continued his work of pointing out to the Unionists that there was another view as well as their own. He said, 'History and bad memories are the curse of Northern Ireland. When I read of a veteran Orangeman being expelled because of a simple act of human decency in attending the wedding of a Roman Catholic friend it is apparent that the commandment of 'Love thy neighbour' has no meaning. I have been accused of being an agent of Dublin and even, extraordinarily, of Rome!' Speaking of attitudes reflected in much of the Unionist press he said, 'In their eyes the Mater Hospital is the medical and surgical department of the Church of Rome in Belfast'. He also said, 'People in Northern Ireland must realise that if they want to be treated as loyalists, they must stop flag-waving and act like loyalists in their everyday lives . . . The eleven sheep in sheep's clothing which Ulster sends to Westminster are in direct contrast to Gerry Fitt, who in spite of the attacks on him by the Northern Irish press, has brought a breath of fresh air into the House of Commons as the authentic voice of the Belfast working class, whether Protestant or Catholic.' We in the Campaign for Social Justice would except from this criticism of the Unionist press the *Belfast Telegraph*.

The Campaign for Democracy in Ulster remained in being until early 1973, giving lectures and holding dances and other fund-raising activities and using its publicity sheet 'Spotlight Ulster'. However, it was eventually wound up, mainly because it was infiltrated and in danger of being taken over by extreme left-wing elements.

The 'Convention'

I think the activity of the CDU which pleased us most was their continual attacks on the 'convention' which provided that matters delegated to Stormont by the Government of Ireland Act 1920 could not be subject to parliamentary questions. While this was happening Ulster Unionist MPs voted in 1965 and 1966 against proposed legislation like the Housing Subsidies Bill, the Rent Bill and other measures which related not to Northern Ireland but to the rest of the United Kingdom. This infuriated Labour MPs.

This 'convention' went back as far as 1922 when a question by Joe Devlin about attacks on people in Belfast was ruled out of order by the Speaker.

In all our publicity material we quoted a Section of the 1920 Act, Clause 75, which says, 'Notwithstanding the establishment of the Parliament of Southern Ireland and Northern Ireland or anything contained in this Act, the supreme authority of the Parliament of the United Kingdom shall remain unaffected and undiminished over all persons, matters and things in Ireland and every part thereof.'

Paul Rose and his Labour colleagues, and later Gerry Fitt, when he became a Westminster MP, tried again and again to ask for an enquiry into the working of the 1920 Act, passed by their own Parliament, and were refused.

The Campaign for Social Justice had been pursuing a parallel course over a considerable time, writing to Labour leaders about various Northern Ireland problems, and receiving replies from their secretaries thus:

Mr A.L. Williams, secretary of the Labour Party, 12 February 1965: 'I was sorry to hear of the difficulties at the Home Office [re the Mater Hospital, Belfast, left out of the Medical Scheme] about which you recently wrote to the Prime Minister, but you will realise, I am sure, that I cannot comment on a matter of this kind.'

Mrs Castle, Minister of Overseas Development, 18 June 1965: 'I cannot intervene. The only constitutional course is for the matters to be taken up with the appropriate authorities in Northern Ireland.'

Secretary to Mr Harold Wilson, Prime Minister, 19 August

31

1965: 'The matters about which you allege discrimination are falling within the field of responsibility of the Northern Ireland Government and Parliament. This being so, he thinks it would be wrong for him to seek to intervene.'

Secretary to Mr Roy Jenkins, Home Secretary, 10 February 1966: 'It would be improper for him to comment on the institution of the legal proceedings to which you refer [litigation against Dungannon Urban District Council for discrimination in housing].'

And again Mr Jenkins, 21 November 1966: 'The provision of Legal Aid in Northern Ireland is, I am afrad, a matter solely for the Northern Ireland authorities. United Kingdom funds could not be used to finance legal proceedings in Northern Ireland.'

Alice Bacon, MP, of the Home Office, in a letter to Alf Morris, MP, 13 February 1967, wrote: 'The matters about which allegations on religious discrimination are made in Northern Ireland fall in general within the field of responsibility of the Northern Ireland Government and Parliament.'

Harold Wilson, Prime Minister, 12 September 1967: 'The constitutional relationship of the Northern Ireland Government cannot, and should not, be ignored and it is a fact that under the Government of Ireland Act 1920, the matters you have raised fall clearly within the competence of the authorities in Northern Ireland.'

Secretary to Mr James Callaghan, Home Secretary, 14 February 1968: 'Mr Callaghan cannot comment on the matters you raised as under the Constitution of Northern Ireland these are matters which fall solely within the field of responsibility of the Northern Ireland Government and Parliament . . . '

Harold Wilson, Prime Minister, 21 July 1968 (concerning the Race Relations Bill): 'The Northern Ireland authorities have been consulted on whether the Bill should apply to Northern Ireland and have decided that it should not, since race relations is a field in which Northern Ireland would prefer to legislate itself should the need arise.'

Secretary to Mr Harold Wilson, 16 July 1968: 'Mr Wilson cannot comment on the matters you raise since under the Constitution of Northern Ireland they fall solely within the field of responsibility of the Government and Parliament of Northern Ireland.'

In fact, the Westminster Government intervened in the affairs of Northern Ireland three times of which we are aware. It intervened when an attempt was made by the Unionists to reduce children's allowance for third and subsequent children [to discriminate against Catholics who have larger families], again when attempts were being made to vest Catholic Church property; and thirdly the Westminster Government expressly applied the Prices and Incomes Act despite the fact that the Act deals with matters within the powers delegated to Stormont.

The Society of Labour Lawyers' Enquiry

In April 1967 a London group, the British Society of Labour Lawyers, announced that they intended to hold an Enquiry into the working of the Government of Ireland Act 1920, with particular reference to allegations of religious discrimination. The intention of the Enquiry was to receive written evidence. Heading the Committee was Mr Sam Silkin, QC, MP, Recorder of Bedford and Chairman of the Consultative Assembly of Europe. The secretary of the Committee was Cedric Thornberry, a barrister and university lecturer. The Committee's other members were: Lord Gifford, Peter Archer, MP, and Ivor Richards, MP. The Unionists were very displeased. A former Attorney General, Mr Edmund Warnock, QC, said 'Tell them to mind their own business. They are only a lot of busy-bodies. The whole thing is a political cod.' The Enquiry aroused opposition in the Northern Ireland Labour Party where one of their leading lights, Mr Harry Calvert, a lecturer in law at Queen's University, resigned the Party. The secretary of the Northern Ireland Labour Party, Mr Sam Napier, supported the Enquiry.

Eddie McAteer, leader of the Nationalist Party, held a very different point of view from the Campaign—'How much simpler it would be, and how much more helpful all round, if we could wash our dirty linen at home, rather than in the glare of Westminster.'

The Campaign for Social Justice felt that since the Enquiry had not the power to compel people to give evidence it could be regarded mainly as an opportunity for the Unionists to examine their consciences and it would interest further groups in the whole matter of Northern Ireland Government methods. For example, Cedric Thornberry was a lecturer in international and constitutional law at the London School of Economics, well known for its egalitarian perspectives. Therefore we made a very big effort to supply the Enquiry with every well-documented fact we possessed concerning housing, job discrimination and electoral malpractice. Our submission consisted of 208,000 words in forty-five separate papers.

Applying pressure to the Unionists, the Labour Lawyers, in August 1968, supplied them with twenty questions on the franchise in Stormont and local elections and on discriminatory and segregationist policies operated by local authorities in housing allocations, and also on the number of Catholics employed in the public service. The Enquiry wanted to know from the Unionists whether reform of local authority policies or practices was desirable, and what plans or proposals the Unionist Party had for reform.

The Enquiry reported, at that stage, that it had considered more than fifty submissions of evidence, many of them substantial. The Ulster Unionist Council in their reply stated that it 'did not accept the right of any body to interfere with the Constitution of Northern Ireland'. It 'emphatically refused to accept the implications of discrimination and irregularities contained in this tendentious document'.

The Labour Lawyers published a later report in August 1968; concerning voting practices they said 'Prima facie, we find it anomalous that such differences between Great Britain and Northern Ireland should exist.' They condemned variations in the ward sizes as between Unionist and non-Unionist councils, giving example in various towns. They drew attention to 'ghetto' type housing, again giving examples. They detailed examples of discrimination in employment on public boards. The Unionists rejected the report out of hand.

About this time, not to be outdone, the Northern Ireland Society of Labour Lawyers produced a booklet, *Discrimination—pride for prejudice*. The executive council of this body was: chairman Brian Garret, secretary Vincent Hanna, and treasurer Turlough O'Donnell, QC (later Judge O'Donnell). This booklet covered the usual ground by way of introduction and called for legislation to outlaw incitement and discrimination, racial or religious. The approach was socialist but the Society called for all-party support:

> This legislation should cover goods facilities and services, employment and housing and should have teeth, the legislation to bind the Crown, public bodies, firms and individuals. Discriminatory advertisements and notices to be unlawful. Separate private (including maintained schools) religious education not to constitute discrimination. Police code to be revised accordingly. An Anti-Discriminatory Practices Board to be established.

In all, a fine project, but hard to realise in the Northern Ireland of the time.

Some details of all these various initiatives are included in this book to show how pressures were building up from various directions to change what had been up till then an immovable situation.

The Washington Hearings

A dedicated, patriotic group, whose individual generosity we found to be overwhelming, the American Committee for Ulster Justice, whose members included Paul O'Dwyer, Dermot Foley, Frank Durkin and Tom Enright, working with Senator Ted Kennedy, managed to set up a series of hearings on 28 and 29 February and 1 March 1972 before the sub-committee in Europe of the Committee on Foreign Affairs of the USA House of Representatives. The hearings were held in Washington. They were written and oral, and everything that was said is contained in a US Government Printing Office Report which runs to 638 pages.

For me at least it was a frenetic expedition. I flew over with Father Faul and landed in New York where we stayed for a couple of days, being whisked around to various little interested groups and to meet pressmen. Apparently in New York it is the thing to be at least an hour late for everything, because of delays at the last assignments and the awful traffic congestion. We had hardly our coats off after arrival when a television interviewer was asking us questions. One reporter stumped me completely when he asked why it was that the Jewish community, with its large population in the United

States, especially in New York, retained numerous articulate representatives whereas the Irish, also very numerous, had only a small group of activists.

Father Faul and I stayed with Tom Enright at Queens. It was a pleasure, after the challenge of keeping up with the bustling Dinny Faul, to return in the evenings to the warmth and hospitality of Tom and his wife.

Subsequently we went on the shuttle to Washington DC—a real shuttle where planes queued up on the tarmac—were filled, and flew off... When we arrived for the hearings at Rayburn House in Washington I was astonished to discover the large number of witnesses from Ireland that the American Committee for Ulster Justice had assembled, people that I had no idea were coming. There was not time to hear all those people's evidence. Thus the non-Unionists had made comprehensive statements which are contained in full in the Report.

Father Faul and I had the customary meeting with Senator Ted Kennedy who later opened the hearings with a substantial speech. From Ireland came Michael Canavan, Father (later Bishop) Edward Daly, the priest whom everyone remembers seeing on television on Bloody Sunday, with his blood-stained handkerchief used as a flag, bent almost double as he accompanied a dying man to first aid. Then there were Brian Duddy and Nell McCafferty, at that time a retiring little creature, now more contentious. These people were all from Derry. Austin Currie, Thomas Conaty, Father Denis Faul, Sean Hopkins, and Kevin McCorry of the Northern Ireland Civil Rights Association were also there. I was deputed to speak for the Campaign for Social Justice in Northern Ireland.

Representing the Unionists were Mr Patrick Macrory, Mr Bill Henderson, publisher of the *Belfast Newsletter* and Mr David Smyth, a lawyer. Twenty-two members of Congress submitted statements. The chairman of the Enquiry was the Hon. Benjamin Rosenthal.

Father Faul dealt with the Special Powers Act, brutality in the interrogation centres and he included a very telling segment of his submission on the administration of justice in Northern Ireland.

On internment he said that 3,357 persons had been arrested under the Special Powers Act, thirty to forty per cent were brutally treated and 793 had been imprisoned without trial: 'I would like the Committee to note the practice of herding men. This is a sophisticated form of torture organised at the highest level in Belfast and London, whereby men are taken away for six or seven days, herded together, placed against a wall, deprived of food and drink and inflicted with a form of sensory deprivation which has caused long term effects.' Father Faul's evidence runs to eleven closely printed pages in the Report.

My contribution is contained in ten pages of the Report. I specially emphasised how the Unionists controlled the non-Unionists members of the population. I dealt fully with discrimination in employment, the bias against the non-Unionist majority west of the Bann river, the lack of effective protective legislation and the spurious reforms which at that time were being produced by the Unionist Government.

I compared Northern Ireland with Rhodesia where the difference in discrimination was one of degree only. For example, there was job discrimination in both places. Both Mr Faulkner and Mr Ian Smith claimed that their governments 'enjoyed the support of the majority of decent law-abiding Africans' (Catholics in Northern Ireland). Both claimed that agitation was Communist-led. Both operated a ghetto system. Detention without trial operated in both places. I even drew the parallel of the support in Rhodesia of tribal chiefs with the recent appointment for the first time of a 'Castle Catholic', Mr G.B. Newe, as Minister of State to the Prime Minister's office in Northern Ireland. I pointed out that Rhodesian blacks have now achieved much more than the minority in Northern Ireland. They must be very happy that their hopes have been fulfilled so soon.

It is noteworthy that, whilst Mr Wilson made a few lunges at Mr Smith, it was only when the Tories came to power that worthwhile results accrued there. One is tempted to wonder whether, had the Labour Party been still in power in Britain, we would have made the headway we have in Northern Ireland. Would it still have been a case of concerned, sympathetic backbenchers and a timid executive?

About the Protestant Churches: I suggested that they should have given a firmer and earlier lead. I noted that when Protestant divines pray for peace they rarely pray for peace with justice. 'To indicate the atmosphere in Northern Ireland, you may have seen or heard of the David Frost show. In it there was reference to the thirteen shootings in Derry (referred to amongst Catholics as "Bloody Sunday"). These shootings were welcomed by some members of the Protestant panel on the Show, one of whom said the day should have been called "Good Sunday". The view expressed on that occasion was that not enough Catholics had been shot. A Methodist minister, a Presbyterian and a Church of Ireland minister were members of the panel and none disavowed these blood-thirsty statements.'

In extenuation of all this I referred to the pressures on Protestant ministers because of the attitude of their Protestant congregations in Northern Ireland. I quoted from the moderate Unionist *Belfast Telegraph*, 'I know of several of my brother ministers,' said an eminent local Presbyterian theologian a month after the civil rights explosion in Londonderry three years ago, 'who had to leave congregations because they spoke out courageously about housing conditions, voting rights and discrimination.' Much more recently an outside observer has noted with dismay 'the ease with which eight Presbyterian ministers have been quietly forced to emigrate as a result of economic pressures effected by congregations who disapproved of their support for social justice for the minority.'

Kevin McCorry of NICRA made a short statement of two and a half pages. He gave a historical resumé of the beginning of the Northern Ireland state. He claimed that direct rule was no solution. We could not agree with this since many more Catholic opportunities have been provided on the jobs front since then. He supported an improved Race Relations Bill. A Bill of Rights was also required. He demanded that all internees and detainees should be released and that the British Army should be progressively withdrawn.

We were interested to hear what the Unionists would say, and particularly whether they would attempt to rebut our claims about Unionist misdeeds. Their first speaker was Mr Bill Henderson, vice-chairman of the Unionist Party's executive committee. In his submission of 25 pages there was little of substance. He attempted to justify internment but it is now generally agreed that internment was a huge blunder, out-of-date information being used to select the internees. These unfortunate people were mainly old-style republicans and some civil right activists. Mr Henderson made no attempt to justify discrimination. If it is felt that this is a biased opinion of his contribution, the full Report of the Hearings should be consulted.

In a seven-page deposition Mr Patrick Macrory commenced with a detailed statement of his family background, which had surely little to do with the subjects under study in Washington. He detailed the Northern Ireland Government's five-point reform programme produced in November 1968. It covered house allocation, investigation of citizens' grievances, a development commission for the city of Londonderry, reorganisation of local government and an associated review of local government franchise, and the withdrawal of those special powers in conflict with international obligations when this could be done without hazard:

> Affirmation of the Government's decisions on these points was made in the Downing Street declaration of August 1969 to which both the United Kingdom and Northern Ireland were signatories, and further changes affecting the police, community relations, employment discrimination, incitement to hatred, housing organisation and local government reorganisation were set out in the joint communiqué following meetings in Belfast between the then British Home Secretary, Mr James Callaghan and the Northern Ireland Cabinet in October 1969.

If I may explain, the position was chaotic in Northern Ireland. Mr Wilson summoned the then Prime Minister, Major Chichester-Clark to London and under intense pressure by Wilson and Home Secretary Callaghan, on 20 August 1969 the Downing Street Declaration was made. In it the existence of the border was confirmed as was 'responsibility for affairs in Northern Ireland a matter for domestic jurisdiction'. This was followed by the 'benefits', as detailed above by Mr Macrory. The minority was not impressed.

The planned changes, which were written up in August 1971 by the Government in a pamphlet called *A Record of Constructive Change* were as follows:

They decided that by 1971, that is after two years' delay, various councils were to be grouped into larger units. The minority suspected that the boundaries of the enlarged councils would probably be gerrymandered. The statement did not undertake, by excluding gerrymander and by offering fair boundary delineation, to give just and fair representation to those who opposed the Unionist Party. The Special Powers Act was altered by what could only be described as a stop-go programme. There was no undertaking to end it. The abolition of the business vote would involve only a small number of votes in all of Northern Ireland. The Ombudsman proposed would have no power to investigate the root causes of discrimination and it would not be physically possible for him to investigate the thousands of injustices and individual cases of discrimination.

Some councils had already refused to operate the points system for housing allocation. The notorious Derry Corporation was not to be replaced by a democratic one selected by the voters but by a Commissioner. There was no word in the *Record of Constructive Change* of reforms of the legal system although this was largely mistrusted by the minority.

The London-based National Council for Civil Liberties issued a statement in April 1970 when they had fully digested the data on the reforms. They pointed out that these did not include a repeal of the Special Powers Act, legislation to outlaw religious discrimination and incitement or the guarantee of fair electoral boundaries. The resolution also noted the recent additions to the Public Order Act and the increasing influence of extremist elements within the Unionist Party. The NCCL called for a Bill of Rights so as to write civil rights into the Constitution of Northern Ireland.

A most reputable group called the New Ulster Movement issued a statement on 23 April 1970 claiming that at least eleven firm promises in the communiqué issued by the Government in October 1969 had still to be implemented.

In the matter of the Ombudsman may I point out here that in April 1971, when this gentleman, a Mr John Benn, issued his first Annual Report, he stated that he had 1,195 complaints referred to him and his team of fifty. Only eighty-one complaints alleging discrimination were among the total, of which he had investigated fourteen, and in none did he find evidence of discrimination. Could a more absurd situation be imagined?

Back to Mr Macrory.

He made much of the Incitement to Hatred Act, a measure

badly needed, but the Act was so imperfectly drafted that when the first case was taken it failed, and no case had ever been taken since. (Here one is reporting the position in 1972.) The fact that these so-called 'reforms' were superseded, in as far as this was done, at a later date when the Tories came to power, shows them to have been inadequate.

Mr David Smyth, whose contribution runs to thirteen pages, carefully emphasised the lesser improvements which had occurred in Northern Ireland in response to British Government pressure. He pointed out that Northern Ireland had now a Catholic Minister in the Cabinet, but was reminded by Congressman Rosenthal that he was the first in fifty years. Mr Smyth denied Mr Rosenthal's suggestion that Stormont had been a dismal failure. Apparently Mr Macrory found it necessary to rescue Mr Smyth because he insisted at intervals on putting in his oar. Mr Smyth attacked the IRA but admitted that the British Army was a blunt weapon. He of course attempted to justify internment.

May I again suggest that anyone who wishes to fully comprehend the hearing should read the Government's printed report.

Whilst we were all applying ourselves to this project in Washington, the considerable resources of the British Embassy were working with the Unionists in the presentation of their case.

The Legal system and the Judiciary
The first indication from the records of the Campaign for Social Justice that all was not well with the legal system came in November 1966 when the Senior Catholic member of the Northern Ireland Bar, Mr James McSparran, QC, took to task the Minister of Home Affairs, Mr William Craig. Replying to Harry Diamond, MP, in the Stormont Chamber concerning religious discrimination at the Senior Bar, Mr Craig said that it was composed of five Catholics and nineteen of other denominations. Mr Craig then said, 'No doubt there were social and educational reasons for this proportion.' He went on to state that these reasons also applied to the alleged discrimination in other legal appointments. After pointing out that Mr Craig gave wrong figures—there are five Catholics and fourteen of other denominations in the Senior Bar, Mr

McSparran went on, 'Calls to the Inner Bar are at the discretion of the head of judiciary. Non-Catholics who apply know that members of the Inner Bar frequently progress to other offices filled by senior counsel. These jobs are rarely given to Catholics, thus there is less incentive for Catholics to become senior counsel.' Mr McSparran continued:

> One is entitled to ask, was the Attorney-General, the head of the Bar and protector of all its members, aware, when he furnished these figures, that they would be used to advance this deplorable argument by the Minister of Home Affairs. I note that another member in the course of the debate rushed into the fray to state that out of fourteen Crown prosecutors six were Catholic. The whole of the six Crown prosecutors would not in an average year equal the fees and emoluments of one of the two senior Crown prosecutors in the city of Belfast, or the annual salary of one of the six clerks of the Crown and Peace. The members' contribution to the debate is typical of the methods adopted by the apologists in the Northern Ireland Government when confronted with charges of discrimination—specious allegations and half truths which on analysis only highlight the justice of the Catholic minority's complaints.

In 1969 there were outspoken criticisms of the way in which the Northern Ireland judicial system worked, including the political affiliations of the magistracy and judiciary and the effects of the restrictive property qualification for jury service. To this could be added the way in which police and the Attorney General exercised their discretion on whether to prosecute or not and the apparent immunity of some members of the 'B' Specials and some Protestant extremists from prosecution. Most magistrates and judges were appointed from the ranks of active supporters of the Unionist Party.

Father Denis Faul of Dungannon set the cat among the pigeons when he delivered a lecture to the Study Group in which he said among other things:

> The Northern judges are felt to have to all appearance acquiesced in, perhaps actively promoted, systematic discrimination against the Catholic minority, and to have been rewarded for this and other services to Unionists by seats on the Bench. It is difficult to see how a Unionist

politican turned judge can earn the trust of the Minority. Twenty-one judges have been appointed to the High Court since 1921. Fifteen have been connected with the Unionist Party. Of the twenty-four County Court judges, fourteen have had connections with the Unionist Party.

He suggested that new judges should serve a five-year apprenticeship in England.

The right of prosecutors of unlimited challenge of jurors, whilst the defence had only twelve challenges without showing cause, operates against cases with a political tinge. All Crown solicitors are Protestants at present . . . A property qualification is also necessary. To be a resident property owner with a certain valuation is necessary before one's name is entered on the jury list. At present the men of property are sitting in judgment on the men of no property.

In High Court, County Court, and Resident Magistrate cases, experience shows that the Bench, almost without exception accepts the evidence of the police force. And yet the police force had been shown to have within its members some people who are anti-Catholic and who have attacked the people of Bogside [a reference to the Devenney case]. How can people believe that those men will give untinged evidence?

These are indisputable, though almost unbelievable, facts, but to everyone's astonishment and, indeed, chagrin, Cardinal William Conway rebuked Father Faul. In a short statement he said that he 'deprecated the remarks which he considered both unfortunate and unwanted'. This statement was entirely out of character in a man who had taken the greatest interest in the struggle for equal rights, and who, like many very large men, was gentle and calm. What probably happened was that Cardinal Conway was visited and pressurised by a Castle Catholic or a group of them who were, most likely, members of the legal profession.

The Campaign for Social Justice issued a statement supporting Father Faul in which we said:

British and Northern Ireland politicans have often drawn attention to provisions of the Government of Ireland Act 1920 which they alleged permitted discriminated-against citizens to appeal to the courts. We in the Campaign were surprised that these legal people had not pushed harder up till now to test the Act. In 1964 we approached a solicitor who engaged a barrister, to help take a case against Dungannon Urban Council for religious discrimination in housing. The barrister informed us that there were no provisions in the 1920 Act that could be used and therefore nothing could be done to help. The Campaign issued an information sheet setting out the position, but the barrister would not allow his name to be mentioned in it.

After a very informative lecture by Mr Harry Calvert at Queen's University, Belfast, on the relevant section of the Government of Ireland Act 1920, we tried again, making use of a different legal team and trying to exploit what appeared to be a small loophole in the Act.

The Law Society, which administers the Legal Aid Scheme, would not give the penniless man, who was taking the case, finance to fight it. It would have cost up to £20,000. Surely this was a deficiency in the law.

Some Catholic solicitors refused to handle civil rights cases, although they were prepared to defend the most sordid cases of other kinds. We have been informed that, when Republicans have been before the courts for political or semi-political offences, their legal advisers are often forced to seek adjournments, thereby perhaps prolonging their clients' terms in prison.

We observe that Miss Bernadette Devlin employs English barristers. The Civil Rights Association decided to take on an English barrister to watch its affairs at the Scarman tribunal. An English barrister, the present Attorney General, was defending counsel in the Talbot and Mallon case.

In 1968 several people, discriminated against, who wished to take their cases to the Council of Europe Human Rights Division asked for our advice. By this time we had decided that some Catholic legal people must be under pressure and lacked trust, and we therefore advised the litigants to employ a non-Irish advocate, remote from political pressures. This man required help about details of Northern Irish law and two Ulster solicitors agreed to provide this, but only if their names were not mentioned.

During these years Mrs Patricia McCluskey was slandered on one occasion and libelled on another. If these cases had occurred in Britain she would have secured substantial damages, whereas she was obliged to settle out of court because she was advised that if the case were heard in Belfast, since she was considered to be anti-Unionist and a 'trouble maker', the jury would not be favourably disposed.

On the subject of judges, Mr E.W. Jones, QC, then Attorney General, on 29 October 1966 asserted that there was no religious discrimination in Northern Ireland, nor had there ever been any. We know what the Cameron Report said about religious discrimination.

Gerry Fitt, MP, found it necessary to report Judge Lowry to the Lord Chancellor of England, Lord Gardiner, for saying, about Derry on 5 October 1966, 'most of the trouble in the city originated not among the citizens of Derry but from undesirable outside elements'.

The Northern Ireland Civil Rights Association issued a statement at the time which contained the following observations:

> It is a good and proper convention that the impartiality of the law, and in particular its administration, should not be questioned without due cause. But by the same token, judges and other law officers should refrain from comments on current political controversies, and should not, by word or deed, display a too close affinity with the ruling political party which has a voice in their appointment. The Northern Ireland judiciary has on many occasions broken that convention, and they cannot then expect, because of their office, to be immune from criticism.
>
> Examples of recent judicial statements can be given as follows:
>
> Mr Justice Lowry at Derry Assizes etc. [see above].
>
> In May of this year at the Armagh Assizes Mr Justice Curran said 'When I hear criticism of the police I know what to think.' This comment flatly contradicted a statement of a lower court judge in Armagh who described RUC behaviour in certain incidents as 'disgraceful'.
>
> The involvement of persons who hold the office of Justice of the Peace in violent or near-violent political conflicts had

not served to make that judicial office respected or trusted in the community. The actions of Mr William Douglas, JP, present in Limavady Town Hall during a civil rights meeting last May, may be mentioned.

On 17 April 1971 a 'Catholic lawyer' who of course dare not sign his name, wrote to the *Irish News* as follows: 'At Belfast City Commission yesterday Lord Justice Curran enquired from Defending Counsel whether or not his client in an arms charge was a Protestant. On having confirmation that in fact the accused was a Protestant his Lordship proceeded to direct the jury to acquit him. Am I or my co-religionists to assume from this that if the accused man had been a Catholic then his Lordship would have allowed the case to go to the jury with all the attendant risks?'

What worried the Campaign most was that when the letter was drawn to the attention of Lord Hailsham, he expressed the view that 'little credence was to be attached to anonymous letters of this kind'. When the Lord Chancellor of England had such a poor insight into how Catholic lawyers are situated in Northern Ireland we knew that we had still a lot of work to do.

Early in 1964, after the Campaign had collected and published a large amount of information on religious discrimination, we decided that legal action should be taken against an urban district council in the specific matter of religious discrimination in allocating houses. An eminent legal authority was engaged and he informed members of the Campaign that the Government of Ireland Act offered no adequate method of securing redress against discrimination. The Unionist party, in power since 1922, was careful not to pass any law contravening the 1920 Act, nor did they need to do so. The Unionists simply used their political majority to do as they wished, and in areas like Derry where they lacked a majority, they gerrymandered.

At a public lecture in the Queen's University, Belfast in February 1965, Jim McCartney LL.B. of the Faculty of Law, outlined some relevant sections of the Act under which Roman Catholics could seek redress against discrimination. Later in the year this theme was further elaborated in another public lecture given by Mr H.G. Calvert LL.M. also of

Queen's University Law Faculty, entitled 'Northern Ireland, religious discrimination and legal restraint'. In it he too indicated a method whereby discrimination against Catholics could be opposed.

Mr Calvert also made the point that the Legal Aid Scheme which came into operation in Northern Ireland in November 1965, seventeen years after it was instituted in the rest of the United Kingdom, should be of enormous advantage to the underprivileged working-class Catholics, who had suffered a great deal.

The Campaign consulted a solicitor in November 1965, and instructed him, on behalf of a Catholic worker, to commence proceedings against Dungannon Urban District Council for discrimination in the matter of council housing allocation. This man was born and lived all his life in Dungannon, but had been lately forced to live outside the town boundary to secure a house. He was a married man with children. He was at that time living in a damp, rat-infested house. He was on the Council's waiting list for eight years, and had been proposed for a house by Dungannon opposition councillors no less that sixteen times between July 1964 and August 1966 without success. During that time the Council had allocated houses to young newly-wed Protestants coming from as far as forty miles away and to Protestants who already occupied excellent council houses. Some of these people were not even on the council's housing waiting list.

Surely if there was protection under the Government of Ireland Act it could be invoked here. If Legal Aid existed, surely this man should be able to avail of it. When a solicitor lodged the Legal Aid application form with the Law Society of Northern Ireland its secretary wrote to him asking under what heading the Legal Aid was being sought, whether it was 'action for declaration or application for order of mandamus, prohibition or certiorari'. Rather than prejudice the application by submitting it in the wrong way, our solicitor advised us that it would be safer to consult Senior Counsel about the method being used. This cost money which was paid out of the Campaign funds.

Senior Counsel advised us that technicalities in law might make it impossible for the litigant to take direct action against Dungannon Urban Council, and it would be better if the action were brought by the ratepayer in the Council area. Tony Sheridan, a working man, a ratepayer and a worthy supporter of the squatters and civil rights generally, aggrieved at the misuse of council powers in the allocation of houses, offered to be the plaintiff and Legal Aid was applied for on his behalf.

The services of Junior Counsel were required to prepare and submit an amended Legal Aid application form. Expenses were mounting. The Campaign was notified that Legal Aid had been refused, the refusal saying, 'the proceedings to which the application related are not proceedings for which Legal Aid can be given'. There was no further information about the reason for its rejection.

Advice of Counsel was again sought and an appeal made against the refusal, the case being argued before the Legal Aid Committee by Junior Counsel on 23 September 1966. The Committee reserved its decision and not until 2 November did it announce the rejection of the appeal because the applicant 'had not shown reasonable grounds for taking or being party to proceedings'. Such rejection of Legal Aid appeared to be contrary to the spirit and purpose of the Legal Aid scheme.

Our legal advisers informed us that for working people to finance litigation themselves, up as far as the House of Lords, where their opponents would undoubtedly force it if they lost the case in a lower court, could cost £20,000. Therefore denials of Legal Aid amounts to denial of access to the courts. This effectively prevents most Northern Ireland citizens from taking Sir Alec Douglas-Home's advice (of which I have already written) or indeed from taking the same advice given by many Northern Ireland Government ministers, the latest being that of the Attorney General of the time, Mr E.W. Jones, QC, when he spoke in Derry on 29 October 1966— namely, to seek legal redress against religious discrimination.

The Campaign wrote to Mr Harold Wilson informing him of all these details, and quoting the saying 'Delay of justice is injustice' without success. We even went so far as to write to the Home Secretary, Mr R. Jenkins, asking him if he would allow money for the case from Westminster-controlled funds. The reply, signed for him by Mr J.A. Chilcot, said 'The provision of Legal Aid in Northern Ireland is, I am afraid, a matter solely for the Northern Ireland authorities. United

Kingdom funds could not be used to finance legal proceedings in Northern Ireland, and I fear there would not therefore be much purpose in approaching the Prime Minister to ask for a direct grant.'

The outcome of all this effort was demonstrated to me in the most forcible way possible, the morning after the failure of our efforts to obtain social justice for the homeless in Northern Ireland. Two separate, unconnected, middle-aged farmers in my morning surgery said virtually the same thing to me. 'You have done your best to work things legally about discrimination and you have failed, there is nothing for it now, doctor, but the gun!'

British Labour, and the Tories before them, dallied too long, matters were now out of control. That this has been well proven since that day cannot be denied.

It may seem that I show prejudice against Labour, but consider the facts. Mr Harold Wilson made certain promises about discrimination to the Campaign for Social Justice in July and September 1964 before the election of that year (see *The Plain Truth* in the Appendix). On the strength of those promises we worked very hard to mobilise the Irish in Britain to vote Labour. We had hundreds of sheets printed detailing Mr Wilson's promises. In the big cities in England where there was a large Irish population it was interesting to see on television the placards in the halls where election meetings were being held calling for the Irish to vote for their local Labour candidate. It is more than likely that the Irish vote put Mr Harold Wilson into number ten Downing Street.

What is regarded as the definitive book written about that election was *The making of the Prime Minister* by Anthony Howard and Richard West. Read on page 225, 'Six hours later he was in Downing Street. The actual victory was as close as the dreaded defeat his slide-rule had forecast. If 900 people scattered through eight key constituencies had voted Tory instead of Labour—or indeed had they simply abstained—it would have been Home's right to continue in office. The last day of Wilson's long rise to power passed in a nightmare of alternate hope and terror.'

In the early days of our activities I was talking to the elderly Nationalist Stormont MP, Joe Stewart, and telling him about our efforts to persuade the Irish in Britain to vote for Labour

49

because of Mr Wilson's promises. 'You are wasting your time, Conn,' he said, 'The Labour crowd never gave us anything. Anything we did get we got from the Tories.'

After we had licked our wounds in the Legal Aid struggle we looked about to see what we could do next to help. Our press release of 8.00 p.m. on Saturday 20 July 1968 indicated our intention.

> We are in a position to inform the press that the Campaign for Social Justice in Northern Ireland, with the help of other groups of individuals, is now prepared to assist in the presentation of complaints to the Court of Human Rights at Strasbourg. The first few cases have already been lodged with the Strasbourg Authorities.
>
> Complaints will cover a wide area of Northern Ireland Affairs and are being filed under the following: (1) The Special Powers Act, (2) Voting Injustices, (3) Discrimination in Employment, (4) Discrimination in Housing.
>
> All complaints are of course being filed against the British Government, which has supreme authority over the subordinate Belfast Parliament. A noted American attorney and an eminent solicitor from Belfast have been engaged by the litigants to present the cases. Present indications are that the British Government will strain every nerve to block the appeals to Strasbourg, and progress may be slow, but the Campaign is assured that, if enough evidence is forthcoming, court hearings will be forced. The Campaign for Social Justice wishes to emphasise that individuals with genuine grievances now have an opportunity to come forward, and eventually to have their complaints investigated by the highest court in Western Europe. It is hoped that Unionists who reacted so strongly in the past to attempts to obtain equal rights for all in Northern Ireland by force, will now applaud this constitutional endeavour.

We decided, although we had received by now great help from the Ulster lawyers, to try this time with an American, James C. Heaney of Buffalo, USA. It was agreed that he would be helped by Northern Ireland solicitors behind the scenes, always provided that their names were not made public.

The procedure was that a sub-committee of the Commission

would review the complaints lodged and if satisfied that they came within jurisdiction, the commission would ask the defending country to file an answer. The Northern Ireland Civil Rights Association supported us. The Commission gave the British Government two months to answer the charges.

Our first witness was another Dungannon stalwart, Matthew McKenna, who was soon to realise what he was up against when the anonymous threats began to arrive.

Collections to support Mr Heaney were made in the USA by the organisation of which he was the president, the American Congress for Irish Freedom. Unfortunately their resources and ours were not enough to transport witnesses to Strasbourg and in the end the attempt had to be abandoned— but not before valuable publicity had been gained and more people made aware that the Catholic minority in Northern Ireland had serious problems.

The Mater Hospital, Belfast

Since this hospital was established in 1883 it has always been an institution in the Catholic life of the province. Nursing was done mainly by Convent of Mercy Sisters, and the hospital had all the appurtenances of a Catholic establishment, including a chapel. It has always been the principal medical centre for the North side of Belfast. It is a training centre both for doctors attached to Queen's University and for nurses and is now the only wholly Catholic training centre in the United Kingdom. The hospital is in fact essentially part of the Ministry of Healing of the Church, and thus could never be placed under wholly secular control.

The fact that the Mater Hospital is situated near the Protestant stronghold of Shankill, whilst the leading National Health hospital, the Royal Victoria (Protestant in medical staffing and outlook) is in the Catholic Falls Road area, must surely have contributed to better community relations in all Belfast. It is well known that there are many dyed-in-the-wool working-class Protestants from Shankill who have shown intense loyalty to the Mater.

Trouble was anticipated when Britain brought in a comprehensive new Health Act in 1948. Mr William Grant, the Minister of Health at the time, with typical Ulster Unionist Party finesse, declared, concerning the Mater, '100% in or

100% out'. This was not justified because when the Health Act was going through the Westminster parliament a promise was given by the Home Secretary, Mr Chuter Ede, that the subordinate Stormont parliament would introduce some sort of safeguarding clause in the Northern Ireland Act, as was done in the English and Scottish Acts. This was in order to give consideration to the previous religious character of the hospitals concerned (*Hansard* Vol. 439 No. 130). The Northern Ireland Act does not include any such clause, and when one was proposed in Stormont it was rejected (*Hansard* Vol. 65 No. 18).

The Campaign for Social Justice in Northern Ireland had an extra interest in the injustice to the Mater since two of our Committee members, Peter Gormley and Conor Gilligan, were on the staff of the hospital. Thus, in May 1965 we prepared a six-page memorandum which was given to the Campaign for Democracy in Ulster; some of the points made were:

> The Mater surgeons and physicians work at a great financial disadvantage compared with their colleagues in the Health Service. A consultant working maximum part-time sessions receives £2,000, whereas his colleague doing the same number of sessions in the National Health Service receives almost twice this amount, plus the chance of a 'merit award'.
>
> Their sources of income are restricted to domiciliary consultations, what they can earn in private practice, and what the Mater Hospital Board can afford to pay them.
>
> With the exception of one temporary part-time appointment those doctors had not been allowed to serve on the staff of other state hospitals, though several had applied for consultant posts several times. The most extreme example of this was when a Mater Hospital physician, in his early thirties and with his MD and MRCP (London) degrees applied for a job in a small provincial hospital—he was not appointed. The successful candidate was a doctor whom the Mater man had just finished coaching for a postgraduate degree in Queen's University, Belfast.
>
> Since the National Health Service began, the Mater

Hospital has spent over one and a quarter million pounds. The strain of collecting this money has been another burden on the Catholic community. Many attempts have been made inside and outside Parliament to reduce this injustice. The Northern Ireland Labour Party has frequently called for state aid, as have the trade unions, the Liberal Party and the Nationalist Party.

As in so many other situations, the solution to the problem, as well as the responsibility for allowing it to develop, appears to us to lie unequivocally with the Westminster Government. Two hundred and thirty-two hospitals in England and Scotland, which, like the Mater, opted out of the National Health Service, receive payments by contractual arrangement with the Regional Hospital Boards. In some cases this means complete payment of maintenance, salaries, heating, cleaning, medical and other provisions. In other cases the local board pays a fixed sum per patient per week. Going on 1952 figures, three instances of payment for the year are quoted. In Middlesex a 174-bed hospital received £52,100. The Mater has 190 beds. In two cases, again using 1952 figures, voluntary hospitals were receiving £11 per week per patient. In all cases the hospital authorities had retained ownership and control.

These arrangements were possible because of Section 61 in the English Act and Section 60 in the Scottish Act. There was another out-of-step provision in the Northern Act. In Britain the teaching hospitals, which the Mater has always been, where doctors and nurses undergo training, were treated differently from the main body of hospitals, because teaching hospitals are more expensive to run and must maintain the highest standards in regard to new equipment and methods. They came directly under the wing of the Ministry of Health in England and Wales, rather than under the regional hospital boards. In this kind of situation it is necessary that consultant doctors, in the Mater as well qualified as their colleagues in the National Health Service, should be fully paid and provision for their retirement be secured. General hospital standards should be high with modernisation of equipment. Here again the

Mater lost out in spite of its long record of service to all religious denominations and its heroic work during the air raids in the last war.

Since the enabling Act to introduce the National Health Service to Northern Ireland went on the Statute Book it is understandable, as the years went by, that the local Catholic bishop should have a healthy suspicion about government intentions, considering how Catholics were faring in other fields. At intervals various public figures tried to prick Protestant consciences, by keeping the problem before the public. In November 1963, the Vicar General, Monsignor Mullally, in a speech at the Hospital prize giving, pointed out that 400 patients had been treated in the wards and over 53,000 as out-patients. Not a penny was received from the state. He also detailed the successes of the nursing staff in the recent examinations.

In mid 1964 negotiations were started between Bishop William Philbin and his Board, and the Minister of Health, Mr William Morgan. A Private Member's Bill was introduced in Stormont at about the same time, apparently with the intention of helping things along. Many confidential meetings were held by the parties but by April 1965 an impasse had been reached. Dr Philbin, after Mr Morgan had made the discussions public without previous consultation with him, issued a statement on 29 April 1965 complaining about this breach of faith and reversal of attitude. Subsequently two meetings with the Minister were called off by him. The negotiations had ended in failure. The whole transactions are well covered by the *Irish News* of the time.

In the 1965 Queen's speech for the opening of Parliament a new deal was promised for the Mater. By 1967 the proposals were announced. Firstly the statutory bar which ruled out any negotiations with exempted hospitals was to be removed, and secondly guarantees about maintenance of the hospitals' religious character were to be inserted. These proposals only brought the law into line with Britain, and reversed the arrangements brought in by Mr William Grant, Minister of Health at the time of the new Health Act. On 1 January 1972, and only then, did the Mater become part of the National Health Service. The doctors received no back pay for the years they had been outside the scheme. It was arranged that the Board of Management should pay all doctors and nurses back superannuation contributions. They at least could then look forward to the same pensions enjoyed by their colleagues who had been in the Service from the beginning.

As time went on, membership of the Committee of the Campaign for Social Justice changed somewhat. We welcomed James McCartney, LL B, of Queen's University, Belfast whom we regarded as a considerable acquisition to our ranks. The late Jack McAnerney of Belfast also joined us. He was an extremely hard worker and an important member of the Northern Ireland Civil Rights Association. Finally, Michael McLaughlin, PT, of Dungannon was added. I regard him as the best back-room boy the minority community had working for it. He was responsible for the population analysis contained in *The Plain Truth*.

Leo Sullivan, Tom McLaughlin and Maurice Byrne left us. Sadly, we did not see eye to eye with Olive Scott on an organisational matter. She thought that we should make our Campaign public and widen the membership. The majority did not agree. For my part, the effort of arguing every point with a hall-full of people would have been frustrating. At that time public meetings were becoming more and more noisy and quarrelsome. Real democracy would have been too slow for our pressing problems.

3.
UP OFF THEIR KNEES

THE SPIRIT of resistance of the Dungannon Homeless Citizens League, of the newly elected councillors of the town, of the Campaign for Social Justice and later of the Northern Ireland Civil Rights Association, gave new heart to the minority community. The first success was undoubtedly when Lough Neagh Fishermen's Co-Operative Society gained control of the Toome Eel Fishery. This valuable resource had been owned by London eel merchants who required local men to obtain permits to fish the Lough. Many boats operated illegally. The conflict between water bailiffs and the fishermen had been going on for nearly three hundred years.

Mainly through the efforts of a Dungannon solicitor, Paddy Duffy, a Co-Operative was formed in midsummer 1965. It obtained a twenty per cent stake in the Toome Eel Fishery. In 1971 the 300 fishermen were in the last stages of a negotiation to buy the syndicate outright when the Government stepped in and, with enabling legislation virtually in place, was about to take over the remaining eighty per cent of the shares. Father Oliver Kennedy, a local curate, who had been playing a major role in the affair, aided by Paddy Duffy, took a strong line with the Government who, rightly estimating that if they tried to railroad the fishermen they would have a stiff fight on their hands, withdrew their bid. On 15 December 1971 the fishermen become the sole owners of the eel fishery. Since then it has grown from strength to strength.

Searching around for a project to give employment to the many Dungannon jobless, a local curate, Father Austin Eustace, hit on the idea of a cut glass factory. After months of research he was in a position to ask people to invest in his idea. This they did with exceptional generosity, money coming in from rich and relatively poor. Before long Tyrone Crystal was in operation, ambitiously working all the procedures from the original 'gather' of molten glass to the lead crystal wine glasses, decanters, vases, bowls and other novelty items.

Unfortunately Father Eustace was trained to preach the Gospel and not to run a modern factory. The inevitable happened. The financial position deteriorated to over a million pounds of debt. At this stage the British authorities, through the Ulster Office, took a hand, and promised that they would pay the bills provided an efficient management was in charge. Closure was thus prevented when Edendork Co-Operative took over. The managing director of this concern was a dynamic young man, Pat Killen, who had put the parent company on its feet. Supported by a progressive Board of Directors, his almost unlimited energy was matched by his co-director and personnel manager, Patsy McCooey's deep understanding of what made Dungannon tick. The result has been that Tyrone Crystal is now a factory with an almost world-wide market. The workers are now well paid and the investors are receiving dividends.

Quietly and almost unnoticed, a third concern was forging ahead. Named Powescreen, its first activity was the fabrication of elevators and sand screening equipment. However, this multi-million pound company, employing a large workforce, now has interests in the United States and also engages in real estate deals.

These are Tyrone successes but all over Northern Ireland nationalist men and women were moving upwards in Government offices such as Departments of Environment, Economic Development and the Health and Social Services. Older supporters of the civil rights movement have noted that these thrusting younger people are slow to admit that their progress was only made possible by the exertions of the movement. Talent in the old days before Britain took over from Stormont was seldom rewarded in the minority community.

The injustices in local authority housing had long been generating anger in Northern Ireland and here again Dungannon led the field. Father Eamonn Casey, founder of the Catholic Housing Aid Society in England, visited us. For the first time we became aware of Housing Associations, which were common in England. There they receive government approval and support, local authorities sometimes vesting land on their behalf. Dungannon and District Housing Association was formed in 1963 when nine business and professional men from the area got together. They included in their number an architect, a solicitor, a builder and an accountant. The organisation joined the British National Federation of Housing Associations. Four pieces of ground were purchased in Dungannon and Coalisland. We expected obstruction from the Urban Council and it was not long before it surfaced. At Cunningham's Lane the plan for 100 houses was rejected on a question of density. At appeal, at which density was fixed, neither the Council's architect nor their engineer made any mention of a difficulty about sewage disposal, yet when the house plans were again submitted with the amended density they were rejected because of alleged sewage problems. After a great deal of pressure and delay, permission was granted for thirty-six houses on this site. This small number was all that was allowed on the seventeen acres which the Association had purchased. The fact that these houses were not opened till December 1970 is some indication of the obstruction which had to be overcome. Meanwhile two pieces of ground in the Dungannon area were obtained in the rural area. Running true to form, the Tyrone County Council refused the planning application and was so obstructive that these sites had to be abandoned. Sixteen houses were planned for Coalisland and these went ahead. But the show piece of the early efforts, involving self help, was undoubtedly the Cunningham's Lane houses, named the Gortnasaor estate. Building began in March 1969. Each of the thirty-six lucky residents, several of whom belonged to the Homeless Citizens League and had taken part in the squatting operation, worked fifteen hours a week to reduce the costs. Each home had three bedrooms, a garage, central heating, and cost about half the usual market price. In ten years time all loans were to be repaid and the residents would own their homes. The opening was performed with a great flourish by Cardinal Conway who referred favourably to the £70,000 in loans granted by the Ministry of Development, loans which I am quite sure would not have been available in 1963 when we started. Later, houses were built at three other sites in rural Tyrone. The

Housing Association is still in being and active, and the idea has now been taken up all over the North. There is an interesting postscript to the whole affair. The members of the Housing Association have watched with enormous satisfaction how very many of the original builders of Gortnasaor, who had slaved so hard in their off-time to build the houses, have now sold them and gone up-market, several to luxury homes. The desire of Peter Gormley, Brian Gregory and the others 'to get the people up off their knees' has been well justified, although there is still a considerable way to go.

4.
PARTY POLITICS

ONE OF Patricia's most treasured possessions is a tattered piece of duplicating paper headed 'Maghery Convention' summoning interested members of the minority community to a meeting which, when it occurred on 19 April 1964, turned out to be one of the most exhilarating experiences I had ever known. It happened like this.

When the 1959 British general election was over, there was considerable resentment amongst the Ulster Catholics of all shades of opinion. There existed at that time the Nationalist Party, which held nine out of the fifty-two seats at Stormont, mostly in country areas. They did not compete with the Republicans for the Westminster seats, the reason being that a custom had developed that Nationalists did not contest these; this was so that they would have a free run for their bread-and-butter seats at Stormont, unopposed by the Republicans. In the 1959 Westminster Election Sinn Féin polled about 60,000 votes out of an electorate of nearly 900,000. This was because the people could not be bothered to vote for persons who would not attend Westminster, and for men who were promoting a violent solution to the Irish problem. As well as that, some Sinn Féin candidates were in gaol and there was very restricted help at the polls, and little funds. In the city of Belfast there were no Nationalist representatives. The men there were Harry Diamond—Socialist Republican, Gerry Fitt—Labour, and Frank Hanna—Independent Labour.

The Nationalists were entirely without drive, content to obtain minor favours for constituents from the various Unionist Governments, each running their local council areas, employing 'yes men'. There was one group of people associated with the MPs for whom those who knew them had enormous respect, the Registration Agents. These were the dedicated men who kept the voting registers. They attended what were called the 'Revision Sessions' where the well organised and paid Unionist officials tried their best to deny non-Unionists the opportunity to vote by querying their right to be on the register. People frequently had to present themselves in person to satisfy the authorities and there was much bickering and argument to secure voting rights.

There was a strong feeling in nationalist circles that unless action was taken quickly to produce some sort of an organisation to articulate the philosophy of Nationalism, the urge towards Irish unity might peter out. As usual the Irish were split into Nationalists and Republicans, and against the one Unionist Party, as it then was, the chance of seats at Westminster was nil. The Nationalists in Stormont secured seats by putting up candidates in underprivileged areas or in areas where there were virtually no Unionists living. At Stormont elections Republicans helped Nationalist candidates and for Westminster the opposite occurred.

Because the Nationalists had no organisation, people had little idea what they were thinking and were not in a position to influence them. The Nationalists disliked the Belfast anti-Unionist politicans for their leftward leanings. Even among the three Belfastmen there was little co-operation. There were ratepayers associations here and there, virtually ignored by the politicans. In Newry and Warrenpoint there were Irish Labour groups but they had no access to Stormont. Charlie Stewart, QC, was an MP elected by the Queen's University graduates, but he went his own way, a very decent man but he had, I believe, no rapport with the other MPs. Young people, of course, regarded the whole matter as a farce!

The Catholic Church was sympathetic to Nationalists because they were conservative and biddable. Very often when Nationalists held a meeting it was run by the local parish priest who dominated most important gatherings such as the selection of candidates for election. Many people, including Patricia and I, regarded this as an unhealthy situation.

I have always felt that the reason the Catholic Church supported and even promoted the Nationalist Party was because Naitonalists were happy with very small concessions from the Unionists, and were never likely to have the fire in their bellies to cause serious Unionist upset. One of the

Catholic Church's main concerns in Northern Ireland was the welfare of the Catholic schools. These enjoyed a subsidy of sixty-five per cent of the cost of the buildings, and the Government paid teachers' salaries and sundry expenses like heating and lighting. A Catholic uprising might jeopordise all this.

In the early days of our Campaign we were visited in Dungannon by a mainly middle-aged group of English Catholic laymen and women, who, of course, discussed social justice, but before they left they asked us in a very compelling way to visit the newly appointed Cardinal Conway and, 'before he was smothered in the sycophantic cotton wool of Irish clerical life' to speak to him about the world as we saw it. We thought this would be a good idea since it would allow us to express our reservations about the direct involvement of the Catholic Church in Nationalist politics. To Dr Conway's credit he appeared to move in this direction. We do not claim that we were the only people who approached him about it. When we were with the Cardinal, who was most cordial, we talked about many other matters not concerned with this book. I did tell him that I thought it a social injustice that Protestants in the Republic of Ireland could not have contraception or divorce if they wanted them. This did not go down well!

About this time an important article written by a schoolteacher Michael McKeown, appeared in the magazine *Hibernia*. He called for a properly organised Nationalist Party. At the same time a new group, sponsored by James Scott, a professor of dentistry in Queen's University, and by his wife Olive, one of our Campaign members, was taking shape. It was named 'National Unity'. It was unashamedly antipartition and middle class but full of ideas. National Unity based its appeal, firstly on the need to make re-unification conditional on consent, and secondly, on the need for a united opposition. The notion of the consent of the majority was a recognition that not only Protestants but a substantial number of Catholics were apathetic to the ideal of Irish unity. Any 'New Nationalism' in the province would therefore have to spring from the integration of the two politico-religious traditions and not from the domination of one by the other. This nationalism rejected violence as a means. The hardworking group gave lectures and held debates. They produced a well-written magazine, *The New Nation*. The National Unity group worked with all anti-partitionist candidates and succeeded in preventing a split in the 1962 Stormont election in the mid-Tyrone constituency, thereby regaining the seat. They continued to press the Nationalist politicians to organise a proper political party and met them several times at Stormont. I must confess I regarded it as naiveté on their part to expect to change the cosy setup. As someone suggested, they would have been given the usual answer, 'Go home and learn Irish and leave the rest to us and the rising Catholic birth rate.'

But nemesis was on the way. There was a television debate between James O'Reilly, MP for Mourne, and the late Mr Brian Faulkner. It was chaired by a slick Englishman called Kenneth Harris, who seemed to me bewildered by what he heard. James O'Reilly was out of his depth. The subject was discrimination and the shrewd Mr Faulkner walked rings around O'Reilly on a subject where Faulkner would not have had a leg to stand on had he been faced by a competent adversary. Like everyone else who saw the programme, we squirmed in our seats. A few days later we were overjoyed to receive in the post a summons to the Maghery Convention. The invitation had come, of course, from National Unity.

The finding of a venue proved difficult for the organisers. In Northern Ireland the Unionists had, and still have, almost complete control over town halls and public buildings generally. The Catholic Parochial Hall in Portadown was secured, then permission was withdrawn. Eventually Maghery Hotel made their ballroom available. Great credit and thanks is due to the Mackle family for providing this service at such a vital time. Sadly, the hotel was later blown up and burned, although this had probably nothing to do with the Maghery gathering.

Although at this time meetings were still well conducted with none of the ill-mannered upsets we had to put up with later, there were great tensions in the air and it required a very efficient chairman to handle the 250 pent-up members of the assembly. We had this in Bill McMullan, a teacher from Ardglass.

People attended from every corner of the North, and most of

the Nationalist MPs and senators were present. Sinn Féin was not. Another teacher, Gerry Quigley, opened a very rousing speech with the sentence, 'I come here out of frustration.'

After four hours of serious and heated debate it was very clear that if the politicians would not co-operate by setting up a proper political machine, then the others present would do it themselves. Almost the only people who supported the politicians in their resistance were some of the Derry contingent as well as Fermanagh and South Down attenders. This did not surprise Patricia and me after our visit to Derry.

The motion, proposed by Michael McKeown and seconded by John Mee was put to the meeting 'that this assembly of persons, convinced of the need for a National Political Front to stimulate the growth of Nationalist constituency organisations, to facilitate Nationalist candidates being selected and to secure adequate representation in all public bodies, decides in conjunction with other Nationalist parliamentary representatives and other MPs who support the National Ideal, to take immediate steps to create the democratic machinery of a normal political party'. This resolution was carried almost unanimously. It was further decided to set up a Provisional Council composed of all existing senators and MPs who supported the national ideal, together with one delegate from each of the Northern Ireland constituencies, with powers of co-option up to a maximum of six. I was chosen for Fermanagh-South Tyrone and Tom McLaughlin for Armagh. An invitation was then made to all existing Nationalist organisations to subscribe to the resolution. A secretary, Miss Maura McFadden, was appointed.

An over-optimistic instruction was given by the meeting that the National Political Front would set about devising a policy on housing, social justice, employment, education, agriculture and relations with the rest of Ireland. I doubted if we would ever get that far.

The *New Nation* supported the proposed policies:

> The functions of a small Nationalist Party at Stormont and Westminster must be to ensure that no artificial impediments be permitted to interfere with the national economic and social trends which are forcing the two parts of Ireland closer together. What this means is that the

Nationalists will have to be in a position to answer every Unionist objection to better North-South relations with logic and common sense, but will mean much more than a revitalisation of activity in the constituencies and in Parliament. It will link the Nationalist parliamentary party with the people. It will make it possible for younger and more active nationalists to play a part in politics.

Despite some early objections, it was obvious that the overwhelming majority of those in attendance were in favour of the new movement. Cahir Healy, Joe Connellan and Patrick Gormley supported the plan. Indeed Mr Gormley had previously been pushing these kinds of ideas. He had even been advocating a headquarters in a specific location, also suggesting what was a very daring, even inflammatory idea, a radical left-of-centre party. Eddie McAteer attempted to discredit the motives of the assembly and his image suffered a setback in so far as his claims to leadership of the party were concerned.

Meetings of the Committee of the Provisional Council were held at intervals in the International Hotel, Belfast. They achieved very little. The Nationalist politicians were on the defensive. They contributed nothing. Eddie McAteer and Senator Lennon sat huddled together, Lennon priming his colleagues when controversial matters occurred. I thought that Gerry Quigley at times swung too far towards the Nationalist position, but this is perhaps because of my civil rights black or white instincts. It was this same sort of feeling of right or wrong which would have made both Patricia and me unsuitable for the compromises required for party politics. Thus we never joined any of them. In Gerry Quigley's case he may have been trying to string the Nationalists along and thereby achieve something. Gerry Fitt was strangely quiet. I think he felt overwhelmed with all the green Tory brainpower, as he would see it. In the end the exercise gradually tailed off but leaving enough zest behind to make sure that things would never be the same again.

Because of the Natonalists' practice not to contest seats unless they could be sure of winning, the method by which their candidates were elected was greatly open to question. Since there was no formal party membership, a 'Convention' was called when the need arose. There was a degree of selective invitation to these affairs. Usually the Registration Agents and the district councillors attended. The Registration Agents had some independence, although, because of the nature of their work, they were usually handpicked by the MPs and not chosen by the people.

After Patricia was elected to Dungannon Council as part of the new-broom policy existing there, she was invited to a Convention in Enniskillen. In fact the Convention was only to decide that the Nationalists were not going to oppose Sinn Féin. She returned to me that evening in a towering rage and horror-stricken that matters had sunk to so low a level. To begin with, the meeting was held midweek, and in the morning, when ordinary working people could not possibly have attended. Most delegates there were old. When a vote was taken, the only two to vote against leaving the field free to the Republicans were the two Dungannon councillors, Jim Corrigan and Patricia.

The new wave obviously had a long, long way to go. Meanwhile, presumably to recover some of their prestige, the Nationalists announced a thirty-nine point 'New Look' party statement 'a policy of progressive Nationalism concerned not only with the present and past but the future'. This was issued on 20 November 1964. At a press conference, presided over by Eddie McAteer, he declared that the Nationalists were going to examine all their sacred cows such as refusing to be the official opposition at Stormont. He talked about 'a new ferment of thinking'. He denied that the National Political Front had any part in the project.

The Nationalists for the first time admitted that partition could end only when the majority wished it. Force, which had been successful in the past, was now excluded as a means. The only way that partition could be ended was by welding existing Nationalists into an effective political fighting machine. This method would win over numbers of moderate Protestants who believed that a United Ireland was in their own interests. Catholics could abandon their old bitter feelings so that the 'two communities in the Six Counties could unite' (to suggest that Unionists unite after calling the state the 'Six Counties' was a poor first step, since the Unionists heartily disliked the term). The Nationalists also proposed that they should start to help in the running of Northern Ireland. They were prepared to abandon the notion of a Gaelic Catholic United Ireland and mentioned the possibility of a federal solution. These proposals obviously did not fire the people's imagination, since the party, if anything, continued to regress. And there was absolutely no chance that Sinn Féin, whose members always disliked the Nationalists intensely, would fall in with them.

Yet another attempt to form an opposition with Nationalist views was made in the Belfast area. Called the National Democratic Party, its secretary was one of our Campaign members, Séan McGivern. In their preliminary report they spoke of 'the drive for the achievement of unity receiving a setback by the failure of the National Political Front'. The position appeared to have been restored when the Nationalist Party publicly accepted the principle of democratic organisation and invited other members of Parliament to join them in the formation of a united party. The National Democratic Party was launched to contribute towards the fulfilment of this need by creating a political organisation in the Belfast area. The decision to establish the party had the approval of the leader of the Nationalist Party and the inaugural meeting on 7 February gave the Area Council a remit to effect the formal integration of both organisations. After consultation with Mr McAteer, a draft constitution was adopted by the Area Council on 14 March. Then on 6 April Mr McAteer informed the chairman of the Area Council that the Nationalist parliamentary party at its meeting on 6 April had decided not to proceed with the merger, the draft constitution having received little support from the meeting. The Area Council asked for a meeting with the Nationalist Party and when this took place only Austin Currie MP turned up, saying that he was there in a personal capacity only.

Later in 1965, a special conference was convened to reaffirm the twin aims of the party as being the creation of a united as well as an organised Nationalist political party. A resolution was passed re-naming the party the 'National Democratic Party'. It set out to organise the ordinary political machinery. Between 1965 and 1970 six conferences were held and these provided an important focal point for the formation of policy. The conference also elected two governing bodies, the central

67

council and the executive. The National Democratic Party did not organise in the areas where the Nationalist Party was already prominent, the party being generally restricted to Belfast. There were eventually ten local associations including one in Queen's University. The relatively small membership and middle-class predominance with a vaguely socialist outlook ensured a high level of general cohesion, which at least was an advance on the Nationalists. The party fought two Stormont elections in 1965 and 1969. Only one candidate was successful, being returned unopposed in 1965. It had more successes at a local level. Unfortunately, with no worthwhile parliamentary representation, it gradually faded away.

To sum up, the National Democratic Party, National Unity and the National Party were three groups starting more or less from scratch, all generating waves but at the same time floundering. Nevertheless, keen, intelligent and much better educated people were flexing disused muscles and orientating themselves for what they knew was the struggle ahead.

Three milestones were still to be passed, namely, three Conventions to select Westminster candidates. Then and only then was the minority ready for the formation of the Social Democratic and Labour Party, the SDLP.

The Fermanagh-South Tyrone Election, 1966
The electors of the constituency were thoroughly sick of split votes and 'abstention'. Leading the disaffection were the Registration Agents who had been working especially hard to have the voting registers brought up-to-date. Patricia, after long talks with these men, for whom she had enormous respect, indeed affection, hit on the idea of a 'Unity Convention' to select one candidate. After a few preliminary meetings a Continuity Committee was formed. Immediately after this the Registration Agents set to work booking halls and arranging publicity.

There can be no doubt that the new move was welcomed by almost everyone, including the small Liberal and Labour segments, but not by the Republicans who seemed, at first, unable to handle the situation. The Nationalists also feared the new broom.

Meetings were held in Enniskillen, Derrygonnelly, Garrison, Dungannon, Irvinestown, Fivemiletown, Augher, Coo-

68

neen, Roslea and Fintona. It was very difficult to find venues for these gatherings. Hibernian halls were our only sources in this Unionist-dominated countryside. Heating and other facilities were frequently very primitive, but this was counteracted by the enthusiasm of the people. I have rarely encountered such a warm welcome as the group of Dungannon supporters received when they arrived at these out-of-the-way places. The praise heaped on Patricia and her fellow urban councillors, especially by the older men and women, who had rarely experienced a political public meeting before, was most gratifying. Anyone interested in becoming the Westminster MP was given the opportunity of presenting his point of view, which was listened to with rapt attention. The only discordant note was struck when once, during Patricia's speech of introduction, Mr Ruari O'Bradaigh and his followers tramped noisily into the hall. This was an exception. Usually Republicans were content to explain their position with some heat. They were politely listened to.

This is a typical example of how the events were run. The platform party consisted of Austin Currie, the Rev. Albert McElroy, Desmond Wright, J.J. Donnelly, James Lynch, Jack Hassard and Patricia. On that particular occasion Paddy Duffy was in the chair. Only Desmond Wright, J.J. Donnelly and James Lynch said they were prepared to stand, if chosen. Patricia started the ball rolling by explaining the method whereby meetings in various places would choose delegates to attend a Selection Convention in Enniskillen. Thirty-five such meetings were held. The Republicans, meanwhile, went ahead with their own Convention and chose as their candidate Mr O'Bradaigh.

The Unity Convention, when it took place, was well run with appropriate Standing Orders. The Chairman was Gerry Magee. Republicans attended and took a full part in the proceedings. All the Nationalist MPs and senators were also invited, and were present, except Austin Currie who had a speaking engagement in Birmingham. The first vote taken was whether to contest the election or not. The result, to contest 131, not to contest 83. As well as Messrs Wright, Lynch and Donnelly, D. O'Rourke had submitted himself for selection as a candidate. Voting took place and Desmond Wright was chosen. He was a Protestant, an old boy of

Dungannon Royal School, who had previously been interned for his Republican views. By profession he was a photographer. There were strong protests from the floor, by Republicans. The meeting then adjourned. Whilst we were relaxing, we noticed that Desmond Wright had been called into an adjoining room by a group of men. After an interval he reappeared, white and shaking. He announced to the Convention that he was withdrawing. At this stage the Republicans left. One of their number, presumably carried away by the rhetoric of the Unity speakers, remained. His colleagues opened the window, under which he was sitting, from the outside, seized him and dragged him out.

The other candidates were asked if they were prepared to stand and all agreed. Another vote was taken. It was won by Councillor J.J. Donnelly of Enniskillen. The meeting was over, we had a Unity candidate, a man of unlimited courage and determination. The hard slog of canvassing for him began. The election meetings were well attended but, needless to say, the Republicans gave some trouble. Maurice Byrne and Plunkett O'Donnell were stoned. We noticed that after meetings were over in the various Fermanagh districts, we were shadowed home by a white motor vehicle. Who it was we never knew, but we could guess.

The Nationalist politicians, including Austin Currie, took no part in the canvassing or helped in any way with the voting procedures, indeed some of the older ones worked against Jim Donnelly who courageously bore insults and abuse from his opponents. During the election campaign the Fermanagh branch of the Northern Ireland Labour Party made a sour and divisive intervention by issuing a statement saying that they had no part in the combined effort.

A noteworthy helper was Plunkett O'Donnell, a building contractor from Dungannon, who was entirely convinced that we were making the correct approach to the election, and that 'abstention' was no longer an acceptable protest. This was important because Plunkett was a Republican who had been interned in the 1956 era. Even when the relatively small amount of republican violence (which, of course, was still too much) had ended, Plunkett, like another Republican, Art McCaughey, was kept in prison because he would not sign some ridiculous document guaranteeing his good conduct and respect for Unionist hegemony. People like these two men were, and still are, as I see it, in the real republican tradition of 1916. Their approach cannot be compared with that of the present mode with its wholesale murders, extortion and Marxist concepts. If republicianism, in the heady days of the 1966 Unity Convention, could have followed the lead of people like Plunkett how different things would have been today!

The result of the election held on 31 March 1966 was Marquis of Hamilton (Unionist) 29,352 votes, J.J. Donnelly (Unity) 14,645, Ruari O'Bradaigh 10,370. 9,536 people did not vote. Presumably they were mainly Nationalists who wanted to show their disillusionment.

One of my favourite themes, when I attended Unity meetings, was that the person who received the lesser number of votes cast was the one who had split the Nationalist vote. Here the responsibility surely lay fairly and squarely with the Republicans.

The Mid-Ulster By-Election 1969

The events I am about to describe occurred nearly twenty years ago, yet they are as vivid in my mind, and I am sure in the minds of the thousands of Mid-Ulster people, as if they happened last year.

For weeks the *Irish News* had been alternately scolding and coaxing its readers to do something about the multiplicity of potential candidates already in the field. Patricia was approached by various people, including Bernadette Devlin, to hear if she had any suggestions. The prospect was bleak. The constituency is the largest in Northern Ireland, is part mountainous, desperately underprivileged and very republican.

Patricia inserted an advertisement calling a meeting in Carrickmore to discuss the election. The result was much more than she had hoped for. On a snowy night almost 800 people from all over the constituency attended, probably the most representative gathering ever held in the area. We knew at once that the wish was for one candidate. With our hearts in our mouths, because we realised that we were dealing with an emotional, nationalistic and sensitive people, the meeting was called to order by Dr Charlie Sullivan, Strabane. Patricia was elected chairman.

At this stage what worried the audience was the fact that the Republicans had already selected the abstentionist Kevin Agnew, a wealthy Maghera solicitor, as their candidate. There had been talk that they might withdraw him if Bernadette Devlin were to stand. These were only vague rumours.

I explained how the Unity Convention in the Fermanagh South Tyrone election was operated. It was decided to follow the same method. A Steering Committee was chosen and meetings were to be arranged at the main centres in the constituency, Maghera, Magherafelt, Cookstown, Omagh and Strabane.

In Bernadette Devlin's book *The Price of my Soul* there are several inexactitudes. She says that 'the first meeting [of the Unity movement] was hilarious and disgusting and scandalous'. Absolute nonsense. It was responsible, intense and very serious. The platform party was made up of Kennedy Scott, Free Ireland Party, from Dublin; Austin Currie, MP; Seamus Lavery, Lurgan; Lawrence Loughran, Cookstown; Phelim O'Neill, Joe Cunningham, Patsy McDonald and Michael Cunningham all of Omagh; and Bernadette. Kevin Agnew spoke from the floor. In the beginning there was no Constituency Committee in Maghera. The meeting there was stormy but everyone had their say. The violent intensity of the Republican speakers left us gasping.

Kevin Agnew attended most of the meetings. As we tried to hold the whole project together it was necessary to be most careful not to offend him or his associates. I remember, as if it was yesterday, how Paddy Duffy, the chairman, playing a straight bat at the Magherafelt meeting, refused to be flustered when Kevin declared that he would prefer to see grass growing on the streets of Cookstown than have the British forces there. In Cookstown itself a woman member of the audience told the meeting that she was perturbed by a statement of Kevin Agnew's that he did not want to see factories in Mid-Ulster if the Union Jack was flying over them. Paddy Duggan, one of the convenors of the series of meetings, said that, whilst he did not agree with the abstentionist policy, he would support Mr Agnew. I kept thinking that these confused thoughts and cross-purposes were a by-product of an underprivileged community having been pushed into these remote mountainous areas by the British, the Unionists keeping them there. The negro civil rights leader, Bayard Ruskin's aphorism summed it all up when he said 'People who feel a part of the structure do not attack it.'

Bernadette's performance at the meetings was sheer magic. The word charisma might have been coined for her. We knew that in the end Republican resistance would be broken down and so it was. At the Unity Convention at Carrickmore, presided over by P.J. Rafferty, the 225 delegates, many of them Republicans, heard him read out a letter from Kevin Agnew. In it he stated that 'in view of the disunity which has been created in Mid-Ulster in recent weeks by the activities of some people from within and outside the constituency, who are intent on nominating a candidate to oppose me—thereby splitting the anti-Unionist vote—with the authority and consent of the Republican movement and the Mid-Ulster Election Committee, I have decided to withdraw from the contest'. Then Austin Currie withdrew, receiving three standing ovations for his action. There were very many tributes to Kevin Agnew. Patricia and I took no further part in the election because this was not our own constituency. Louden Seth, a PD associate of Bernadette's, was appointed her agent. Local committees were formed. One of the most active was that organised by Mrs Betty Noone of Maghera.

Needless to say, Bernadette had some trouble at election meetings from Paisleyite mobs. Indeed, one in Moneymore had to be abandoned, but, true to her fearless nature, she was back the next night when, well protected by police, she successfully addressed the gathering. There was support, in her final meeting at Carrickmore, from Gerry Fitt, John Hume, Ivan Cooper, Austin Currie, Tom Gormley—all MPs, a TD from the Republic of Ireland, the Derry Citizens Action Committee and the People's Democracy.

On 14 April 1969, the Campaign for Social Justice wrote to Mr Harold Wilson thus:

We are having a Westminster Election on next Thursday, as you are aware. People who must surely be associated

73

with you, because they are carrying your flag, are attacking and ill-treating the little girl of twenty-one years, our Unity candidate, Miss Bernadette Devlin. The enclosed cuttings describe how those contemptible bullies are acting—whether they support the polished O'Neill, or the extreme Craig makes no difference—and it is happening almost every evening. Because you have done nothing that we can see to prevent it, we expect the usual intimidation of Roman Catholic voters in Protestant areas, some will be afraid to go and vote, more courageous ones will have to push their way through menacing Unionist lackeys in the corridors of the voting rooms. Personation officers will be stoned as they leave the Polling Stations. No doubt, too, there will be spurious Unionist votes deposited in the ballot boxes before the voting starts. You and your Speaker's Conference on Electoral Law are well aware of these and other abuses, because we have already told you.

And of course Bernadette won the election held on 17 April 1969, won it decisively, beating Mrs Forrest by 33,648 to 29,437 in a record 91.78 per cent poll. In Carrickmore there was said to be a 97 per cent poll, in Gortin 98, in Pomeroy 95.

The Fermanagh-South Tyrone Election 1970
When this election was called the group which worked in 1966 went into action again. It was not nearly as easy this time. There were a great many more self-assured people, there was greater diversity of thought and the standard of behaviour at meetings had gone down.

As before, the same plan was adopted. The two contenders for the seat were Austin Currie and Frank McManus. The latter was a secondary teacher in St Michael's College, Enniskillen and Chairman of the Fermanagh Civil Rights Association.

The pre-Convention meetings were fewer in number. The Chairman had a very difficult job keeping some sort of order. At one meeting a Nationalist group suggested with rancour that there was a move afoot to launch 'the Social Justice Party'. We immediately denied this ridiculous suggestion.

At the Unity Convention Frank McManus was sucessful. This time, possibly because he was republican in his views, there was no other Nationalist candidate. He made it clear that he was a Republican but was an 'attender'. Whilst he agreed that the final solution of the Irish problem was reunification, force would never solve the problem. 'Physical force would only exacerbate the fears of the Protestant majority'. He declared that he would support the British Labour party at Westminster (*Irish Times* 22.6.70). There was general satisfaction with his approach.

The election meetings were, at times, stormy. In Fivemiletown Protestant extremists, furious that at last they were to have active opposition, kept up a barrage of shouts of 'We want Paisley.' Stones, bottles and eggs were thrown at the platform party. Austin Currie, who was present in a supporting role, received a headwound from a bottle, Frank McManus was struck on the face by a stone. Windows in the centre of the town were broken and McManus's car was damaged. The police intervened but were hopelessly outnumbered. After the meeting the candidate had to make a detour to avoid an ambush by a crowd of about two hundred persons. Earlier that evening the speakers were heckled in Augher and Clogher. In Dungannon's Market Square there were about 600 supporters present and 200 opponents. The Paisleyites heckled, jeered and threw stones, pennies and pieces of glass. Windows were broken in Market Square and Church Street. The police had to separate the opposing crowds; several people were arrested.

The result of the election held on 19 June 1970 was a splendid win for Frank McManus who polled 32,832 votes against the Marquis of Hamilton's 31,390. Unfortunately, Mr McManus, after election, did not conform to the make-up of a Unity candidate who was put into the position not only by Republicans but by various shades of Nationalist, as well as some Liberal and Northern Ireland Labour party voters.

It was the time of the Border Plebiscite. Mr McManus expressed himself as totally against participation in it, but some people felt that because the Plebiscite had a chance of removing the Border issue from day-to-day politics, it was a good thing. Abstention from the Poll might be interpreted as a shamefaced admission by the minority that they wanted to remain in the United Kingdom. Without consultation with his constituents, Mr McManus took a prominent part in the formation of Dáil Uladh by joining the Comhairle. He voted at Westminster against the suspension of Stormont. Again, without consultation, he became Chairman of Northern Resistance, a splinter group from NICRA. Eventually, without advice from those who put him in, he withdrew from Westminster.

All these activities suggested that the ideal of a Unity candidate was no longer attainable. The only method for the future seemed to be to go forward resolutely against all comers, and sink or swim thereby.

The Social Democratic and Labour Party

One evening in the early days of the Campaign, Patricia came home from her Credit Union meeting in what was for her, considering the times that were in it, an enthusiastic frame of mind. 'I have just met someone who has great drive and intelligence. He is the first person I have come across who has the sort of leadership quality we so badly need.' This man, who came down from Derry as a guest speaker to further the aims of the emerging Credit Union movement, was called John Hume.

In those days there was the desire, indeed anxiety, that the awakening of minority political life should be encouraged. The problem at this stage was Gerry Fitt. Gerry had been working hard in Stormont for years, and was an experienced performer whom I am sure the Unionists detested (if the way they kicked, punched, and abused him at election times as he approached polling stations or went in to the count was anything to go by). We were delighted when in April 1966 he was elected to Westminster.

We immediately began to ply him with our facts and figures. He used these to great effect, and what is more, unlike many other MPs at Stormont, he complied with our requests and played his hand as we thought it should be played. There was an odd grumble from some of our English supporters that he was too left wing: 'Get Gerry to be a bit less friendly with the left wingers of the Labour Party, tell him to concentrate more on the Right.' Gerry was operating as best he could. The left wing politicians were the ones with whom he had most in common—and they were interested, which is more than could be said of the Catholic Westminster MPs, mainly Tory, whom we, and I suppose he, had approached.

I wrote to Gerry. I am now looking at the carbon of the scribbled plea I made to him, telling of 'a meeting about to take place of Paddy Duffy, Hume and Currie and perhaps Bernadette Devlin to get a party off the ground'. I told him I thought he could not afford not to participate. I was well aware that, to a great degree, Gerry was a loner, but if the gap between the city and country in Northern Ireland was to be bridged, Gerry had to be included in the new party. Sometimes I feel I pushed him into something to which he was not really suited, and I felt very unhappy when he left the party. But then, he did an enormous amount of good by taking the lead he did and in his work for the party he found a great deal to interest him, and now is a Lord of the Realm (an end point that perhaps some may not approve of!).

It is hard indeed to understand his going. They tell me that towards the end he was a poor attender, even at important party meetings. Once Paddy Devlin resigned he was, in my eyes at least, the only genuine working man's representative remaining. Perhaps the middle-class ambience of the party gatherings was too much for him. I know he resented the SDLP contacts with what he regarded as the high tory politicians down South.

Gerry served the minority of Belfast, indeed all of Northern Ireland, well, and I for one regarded it as a serious reflection on our race when mobs attacked his house, virtually destroyed it, and terrorised his wife and family. Once he had to repel invaders on the stairway of his home with a loaded revolver. Eventually he was driven out of Northern Ireland, mainly because of his intense hatred of violence. This he condemned in a way that did not please everybody. All this must inevitably have soured him.

The New Social Democratic and Labour Party started up with a great flourish on 21 August 1970. In their opening announcement, contained in a large advertisement in the Northern papers, they declared that they would be a left of centre party, and they included in their policy preamble every aim one could wish for in a democratic party. One of their goals was stated thus: 'To promote co-operation, friendship and understanding between North and South, with a view to the eventual reunification of Ireland through the consent of the majority of the people of North and South'. There was no suggestion of extremism in any of their statements at their opening press conference. They hoped that Protestants would join them.

At the conference table were Ivan Cooper, MP, Austin Currie, MP, Paddy Devlin, MP, Gerry Fitt, MP, John Hume, MP, and Senator Paddy Wilson (later the victim of a sectarian killing). Paddy O'Hanlon, MP, was also a founder member. The new party appeared to work well together and gathered in new members in large or small numbers depending on the drive and dedication of the local MP and his close associates. One fact I found gratifying was that now for the first time, there was the same party representing the minority in operation in the country areas as in the cities. Two hard working and articulate medical practitioners Joe Hendron and Alastair McDonnell, as well as Brian Feeney, were leading members in Belfast.

It is very difficult for an Irishman to approve of all that a political party says or does. I am no exception. When the Campaign for Social Justice was wound up, in our final statement we said: 'From now on, the work of making the White Paper a reality, and of safeguarding the rights of all the citizens in the pluralistic society of the future, will be in the hands of the politicians elected to the Assembly by the people of Northern Ireland.' In other words we expected that our grindingly hard work of publicity and exposure of injustices would be carried on by the SDLP. I could see little sign of this. Most energy seemed to be going into trying to strengthen the North-South position. There were those helicopter flights to see the Dublin politicians, and a great deal of anti-partitionist talk. Executive meetings of the new party were held in Bunbeg, deep in the Donegal Gaeltacht, when they should have been in Banbridge or some other Northern Irish town. A Protestant I knew, and one who would have been a real acquisition, was thinking of joining the party, but at this stage he told me that he had changed his mind. I did not ask him why, because we in the Campaign stressed our non-party stance, and I always avoided party political discussions.

Indeed, profanely perhaps, I found myself saying 'These are merely the old Nationalists with a crease in their trousers.' If the underdog Catholics were to gain their rightful place in

Ulster there could not be the slightest postponement in the pressure for the fulfilment of the reform process. Nevertheless the membership, virtually all Catholic, was growing. Their best leaders had been civil rights pioneers. John Hume himself (the details of his life story can be read in the book by Barry White) became a member of the European Parliament, and travelled the western world promoting the SDLP cause.

There was Austin Currie, probably the least rewarded of all the leaders, who after his Caledon squatting episode, and his initiative in helping to promote the first Northern Ireland Civil Rights march was now known and admired as much in the Republic as in the North. For his dedication Austin was rewarded by having his home attacked over thirty times, often with bombs. His wife Anita was outrageously beaten up by Protestant extremists. Her subsequent superb television appearance with her poor battered face was a milestone in the whole civil rights struggle. Austin's estate agency premises in Irish Street, Dungannon was repeatedly wrecked, probably by the Republicans because he intervened against them in Westminster elections. Ivan Cooper was very active in the civil rights movement, and later in the SDLP. What distinguishes him from his colleagues is that he is a Protestant. Lately he seems to have lost a great deal of his interest in politics.

A somewhat later acquisition to the party was Seamus Mallon. Later he, as well as another experienced local Councillor, Eddie McGrady, became competent Westminster Members of Parliament.

The party's outstanding woman member, Mrs Bríd Rodgers, was in the past its chairperson, then its secretary. An early civil righter, she was a valued helper of the Campaign for Social Justice, collecting statistics concerning the Lurgan area. This was an activity in which she received virtually no help from the middle-class residents of the town. She was a member of the NICRA executive and a senator in Dr Garret Fitzgerald's Coalition. She is one of the SDLP's best television performers and as a local representative for the Craigavon-Portadown area has often had her hands full with local problems.

Although there are some women members, the SDLP is not

the best party to belong to if you are a woman, the educational system in the North being such that all leading SDLP politicians were taught first at a single-sex primary school, then by priests or Christian Brothers, some till they were twenty-one years old. This does not tend to produce ardent feminists. One can detect in them at times an episcopal approach to affairs.

There are now many well educated Catholic women about, far from satisfied by an approach to life confined to *kinder küche kleider*. Women's discreet and measured judgments should play a good part in Irish decision making. Indeed there are some who say that, had Irish affairs been handled by women for the last three or four hundred years, we would not be in the mess, both North and South, in which we now find ourselves.

Nevertheless the minority can count itself lucky in having a properly organised political party to speak for it. In spite of no proper remuneration the SDLP members have struggled on. We will always be greatly in their debt. They have resolutely refused to enter Stormont politics until they have a firm promise of shared power. With this I totally agree. The Alliance party has generally supported this point of view, but at times has vacillated when the bribe of progress to devolution has been offered. This is weakness. Considering the people the opposition parties will have to deal with in the future, only cast-iron guarantees would be adequate.

The Liberal Party

In the early days of our Campaign the Liberal Party was a relatively small group of mainly middle-class people. Its chairman was the Rev. Albert McElroy MA, of Newtownards, a minister of the Non-Subscribing Presbyterian Church. He had unlimited courage and an astringent utterance. He was also a prolific letter writer, never afraid to slate the Unionist Government. In those early days there were few who dared to do this. A favourite axiom of his was: 'Running an opposition party in Northern Ireland is like running an underground movement in an occupied country.' Always prepared to express himself pungently, he described one of our Campaign Newsletters as 'one-sided, partisan and non-objective'—perhaps! He ended his letter to Patricia 'Kindest regards' and I knew he meant it.

One felt that Northern Ireland Liberals trod the middle way so well that they trod themselves out of existence. But not before the sole Liberal in the Stormont Parliament, Miss Sheila Murnaghan, the member for Queen's University, had presented her Human Rights Bill (Northern Ireland) five times during 1967–68 and had it rejected five times by the unfeeling Unionists. Miss Murnaghan framed her Bill taking into account the most modern ideas on community relations in Britain and the USA. The Bill had twenty-four clauses and was a masterpiece of drafting and a headline for moderation in Northern Ireland. As she herself observed 'the Unionists did not trouble to consider it, merely voting it out'. For example, on the fourth time it was presented it was rejected by twenty-two votes to eight.

To offer a commentary on the work of the Liberal Party in Northern Ireland is mainly to list a series of vicissitudes. The Secretary of the Ulster Liberal Association for five years was a Miss Islay Donaldson. She recounted her trials in a long article in the *Irish Times*. Because of her activity in the party the Unionists treated her very badly, the Paisleyites worse. In the end she left Northern Ireland sorrowing 'to leave kindly and hardworking people' and saying that 'without the Orange Order Northern Ireland would be a good and pleasant place to live in'. Another Liberal notable, Stanley Wynne, reported that the Chairman of the Young Liberals in Northern Ireland was approached by 'a person of high position in another party' and intimidated out of office. By 1964 Rev. Albert McElroy still found it necessary to criticise the Unionist Party with recently appointed Capt. O'Neill at its head. 'The new look Unionist Party is a pure myth. The spirit is still "Kick the Pope and Boyne Water".'

In October 1964, four Liberal candidates contested the imperial election. All four lost their deposits. In Fermanagh-South Tyrone the candidate was Giles Fitzherbert. He and his wife, the daughter of Evelyn Waugh, who was expecting a baby at the time, were attacked by mobs, once having their car damaged. The constituency has never had a reputation for liberalism or Liberalism so he had to be content with 6,006 votes against the Unionist Marquis of Hamilton's 30,010. In November 1965, Claude Wilton, Liberal candidate for a seat in the Stormont parliament, was prevented from holding his meetings in Derry by the Young Unionists. Also, the Unionist, Rev. John Brown, President of the North Ward Unionist Association and an official of the B-Specials, admitted that he had removed Liberal posters in the Waterside of Derry 'in the interest of road safety'. In Derrygonnelly, Co. Fermanagh, Rev. McElroy was met by a fusillade of eggs when he was speaking as the Liberal candidate for Fermanagh-South Tyrone. The party appealed unsuccessfully to Westminster against voting irregularities which were widespread in Northern Ireland.

At the Liberal Assembly in Blackpool in 1967 and again at their Assembly in 1968, there were continued appeals by Northern Ireland delegates for electoral reform and civil rights, with little or no effect.

The Northern Ireland Labour Party

No one has ever suggested to me that there were any skeletons in the Labour Party cupboard. Like the Alliance Party its organisation operates in a way which befits a western democratic political party. It is non-sectarian and has always had both Protestant and Catholic members. Only when a few bigoted members secured control of a local constituency area did Northern Ireland Labour present an intolerant image. In its later years, organisation was good in the hands of Sam Napier who wanted to widen the scope of the party by extending it outside Belfast. When the Nationalists became the official opposition at Stormont in early 1965, the four NILP MPs attacked the decision. Sam Napier thought this ill-advised and antagonisms became so strong that he eventually left the party.

Like the Alliance Party, Labour has never experienced the ultimate test of power. Because both parties have continuously to cope with the fact that they support the partition of Ireland, their scope is restricted. Opinions which please one section displease the other. Simplistically one might describe the Labour Party as a working-class party, while the Alliance is middle class.

Labour's maximum success in the Stormont parliament was eight seats, seven of which were in Belfast. When our Campaign was launched they held four seats, two of which were lost in the 1965 election. Paisleyite anti-ecumenism and even the absurd Belfast dispute about whether the swings in children's playgrounds should be used on Sundays caused strife amongst the members and reduced their numbers.

It was then that the rift between Sam Napier and some of his associates in the party began. The outcome of the dispute was that, in November 1964, Belfast Corporation, with some Labour support, decided to lock up the swings on Sundays.

In February 1964, William Blease, Vivian Simpson, MP, and Jack Hassard were calling for a points system in housing allocation, for the end of religious discrimination and for a united community. In March of that year in an article in the *Guardian* Charles Brett, the Chairman of the party, pleaded for an enquiry into allegations of religious discrimination. He supplied figures to support his case.

The Annual Conference in April 1965 gave some indication of the varying approaches of Catholics and Protestants in the party. Members pointed out that the twelve Ulster Unionists elected to Westminster the previous October 'were elected on a basis of sectarianism'. Yet the Executive opposed a recommendation from the floor that an enquiry into religious discrimination in Northern Ireland be set up. This was nevertheless passed. The party also approved an appeal to Mr Harold Wilson to include Northern Ireland in the forthcoming Westminster Act to oppose racial discrimination. At the meeting some members complained that the NILP was supporting the Unionists. In that month the Executive sent forward their memorandum to the Speakers Conference on Electoral Law. Among other suggestions it proposed revision of the constitution of the Senate and the abolition of business and company votes. It also called for revision of local government boundaries which it claimed were frequently gerrymandered.

In 1967 the party found itself under attack for considering the possibility of an all-Ireland Council of Labour, and it subsequently asserted itself in supporting Capt. O'Neill in his sacking of Mr Harry West, MP. Getting together with the Irish Congress of Trade Unions in that year, the Party submitted a joint memorandum to Capt. O'Neill telling him that the violence was due to the obdurate Unionist Party.

July has always been a month when Protestants and Catholics are most disunited. Thus in 1968 the NILP would not suppport the Nationalist opposition in Stormont in their attempt to have the British Race Relations Bill extended to cover religious discrimination and to apply to Northern Ireland, giving as the reason the fact that Gerry Fitt, MP, had threatened to withdraw support from Mr Wilson's administration if his claims for the Northern Ireland minority were not met.

In August 1971, the Northern Ireland Labour Party announced proposals for a 'Community Government'. This was to be a two-year period of social reconstruction during which Mr Faulkner would lead a coalition administration in which Catholics and Protestants would be represented, using proportional representation to choose members. This excellent initiative unfortunately was not taken up until, when the Tories returned to power, something akin was organised as the Power Sharing Executive. The Dungannon area had an outstanding Labour representative in Jack Hassard. Jack is a Protestant and unlike many pretentious and troublemaking Unionists, was a combatant in World War 2, where he distinguished himself in the Dunkirk evacuation. He opposed every discriminatory act by the Dungannon Urban Council of which he was a member. In December 1965 he contested the South Tyrone seat at Stormont and received 4,862 votes against Mr John Taylor's 8,935. His representatives at polling stations were attacked, the dead were voted for, Presiding Officers co-operated with the Unionists, some even abusing people who were likely to vote for Jack Hassard. He was stoned by Unionist supporters. At the end of 1968 he announced his retirement from politics because of murder threats against him and abuse of his wife and family. The final outrage was when his car window was broken by a mobster wielding an axe, his family being in the car at the time.

This lion-hearted man had the ability to draw support from every section of the Catholic community. On one occasion he topped the poll in the Catholic ghetto ward for the local Council election. It is interesting to note that in retirement he has maintained his good humour and a normal mental approach to life. There have been many cases of courageous Protestants who, in the end, have faded from the scene, their resistance sapped by the almost unbearable pressures from their co-religionists.

The People's Democracy

In the early days of the civil rights agitation Queen's University was shockingly apathetic to the longstanding injustices in Northern Ireland, but on 9 October 1968, the students were so aroused as to organise a march to City Hall, Belfast. They were obstructed in Shaftesbury Square by hardline Paisleyite elements who were holding a counter-demonstration. The police re-routed them and in Linenhall Street a sit-down demonstration took place. Shortly afterwards the most militant activists, amongst whom were Michael Farrell, Eamonn McCann, Cyril Toman, Kevin Boyle, Bernadette Devlin, Louden Seth and John Murphy, got together and named themselves the 'People's Democracy'. It was noteworthy that, associated with the authentic student cadre, there were strongly left-wing and revolutionary elements having ideological links with the international 'new left'. PD rhetoric was militant and anti-sectarian. 'Creed out, class war in' was one of their slogans.

At a later date two further marches were prevented from going through Shaftesbury Square by counter-demonstrators led by the Rev. Ian Paisley and Major Ronald Bunting. The marches had to be re-routed by the police, and after this they were abandoned and teach-ins held instead. There has always been antagonism against police methods allowing counter-demonstrations to upset properly notified marches. No reputable government would have allowed this ploy to develop.

The PDs were offered the services of the Northern Ireland branch of the Society of Labour Lawyers by Vincent Hanna, a local solicitor. Because these lawyers had close ties with the Wilson Government this was an important breakthrough for them. About twenty-five members of the teaching staff of Queen's University helped the PDs in their work. Extreme Protestants agitated to have all grants of those PD members who were studying at the university stopped.

In a letter written by Kevin Boyle, a law lecturer at Queen's University, to the Taoiseach, they took strong objection to attempts being made in the Republic to link Partition and civil rights in Northern Ireland. They also objected to the Republic's stand on contraception and divorce and to the 'special position of the Catholic Church'. The PD always felt threatened by the Young Socialist Alliance who were frequently troublesome and violent at marches and demonstrations.

The organisation issued a news sheet, the *P.D. Voice*, but their main production was a two-page publication which they termed their 'newspaper'. In both they were declamatory about all the abuses which our Campaign was publicising but combined with this was a good deal of vulgar personal abuse of the Unionist leaders including the 'lousy lawyers at Stormont' and various individual policemen. There was an attempt to woo disadvantaged working-class Protestants. The following groups merited PD disapproval; 'Civil Rights people who had a bit of property and a stake in the country'; Fianna Fail including its 'businessman's club'; its 'hacks from Dungannon'; Charles Haughey and Jack Lynch; Also, Aidan (count the Catholics) Corrigan, Neil Blaney (the Free State's answer to Enoch Powell), the Archbishop of Dublin, Gerry Lennon and Eddie McAteer and the Nationalist Party generally (the lime green Tories), the Ancient Order of Hibernians and McCluskey and his Dungannon group.

Burntollet
On 1 January 1969, just when Capt. O'Neill thought he had won a respite from civil rights agitation, the PD set out on their march from Belfast to Derry. Obviously this was likely to be a hazardous undertaking. There were about forty people leaving Belfast. From the first they were harassed by an extremist Protestant, Major Ronald Bunting. He was an associate of the Rev. Ian Paisley. There was a muster of about seventy of his organisation, the Loyal Citizens of Ulster. These people preceded the march when it set off, and continued to abuse the marchers with obscenities.

At the main bridge in the town of Antrim there was a large crowd, led by Bunting, obstructing the way forward. For hours the police refused to clear a passage, during which time the marchers were abused verbally and some were punched. In the end they were transported by police tender to the night stop, a community hall at Whitehall.

As the march proceeded, the Minister of Labour, as he then was, Major Chichester-Clark, and his brother Robin, a Westminster MP, appeared, noted the police inaction against the counter-demonstrators and retired without ordering the removal of the Paisleyites.

The next night was spent in Maghera where the Protestant guerilla parties, now out of control, smashed shops and houses in the town. After further delays the marchers set out for Dungiven. By now their numbers had increased to several hundred. Then on to Claudy.

At that stage the Rev. Ian Paisley and Major Bunting held a 'religious service' in Derry in order to mobilise Protestants there. This ended in a riot in which Bunting's car was burned by incensed Catholics.

Meanwhile the Unionists near Claudy were preparing for what was to be one of the most horrific events in British Ulster.

As the marchers approached Burntollet bridge the police warned them that they could not guarantee their safety. Then the Protestants attacked. There were about 300 of them, wearing armbands to distinguish them from Catholics. Rocks, previously positioned in heaps, undisturbed by police, were thrown at the marchers who were then attacked with nail-studded clubs. As the members of the procession, completely disorganised, tried to escape they were kicked and punched, some into unconsciousness. Many were young women and even girls. They were attacked indiscriminately with bottles, iron bars, and staves. Some girl marchers were thrown into the river. By now they were a shambles of weeping women and blood-stained men, and still being abused by Protestants. The fact that there were some marchers lying unconscious on the roadway did not seem to influence their tormentors.

The police were completely indifferent to everything that passed, some chatting amiably with the Protestants. There was no police attempt to arrest the attackers, amongst whom were some B-Specials.

Eventually the marchers arrived in Derry where they were again attacked by Protestants. They were defended by Derry Catholics. Here the police ran amok, batoning Catholics on sight.

Fortunately, television and press were in attendance from the beginning of the march, so that the events can never be denied. This scrappy summary is completely inadequate. The full record should be read in *Burntollet* (LRS Publishers) or the

87

Irish News of the dates given. Following on Burntollet only a few people were charged with minor offences in spite of the fact that over eighty people were identified from press photographs and television film footage. These people were pardoned in a General Amnesty ordered by Major Chichester-Clark when he became Prime Minister.

As the students returned after the Christmas holidays in 1969 the PD was divided on whether to allow Capt. O'Neill some leeway to fulfil his promises of reform or to continue to march and agitate. Some students were still in hospital as a sequel to Burntollet and others still had bandaged heads after the vicious attacks by Paisleyites with stones and bottles and bricks. There was a feeling among the students of disgust and despair. The more conservative Queen's University students greatly resented Capt. O'Neill's description of them as 'Republicans, anarchists, revolutionary socialists and hooligans'. They took great exception to the statement of Capt. William Long, then the Minister of Home Affairs, that he found a two-hour meeting with Mr Paisley and Mr Bunting to discuss Burntollet 'congenial'.

In February 1969 Captain O'Neill called a Stormont election. The People's Democracy fought eight seats. Bernadette Devlin opposed Major Chichester-Clark in South Derry, Eamonn McCann opposed Eddie McAteer in the Foyle division of Derry, Michael Farrell opposed Captain O'Neill in Bannside. They did badly, obtaining mostly Catholic votes in what were Protestant strongholds. In many areas the candidates had a very rough ride. In Enniskillen Bowes Egan, one of their candidates, was attacked by the crowd. Bernadette Devlin was attacked in both Moneymore and Tobermore. The PD speakers were set upon in Brookeborough. In mid-Armagh Cyril Toman described how at six polling stations his workers were obstructed and attacked.

In spite of the election rout the People's Democracy would not throw in the towel. At a meeting in Lurgan one of their number, a daughter of Paddy Devlin, was knocked unconscious by a blow of a blackthorn walking-stick wielded by a District Inspector of the RUC. They held a protest sit-in in Armagh Council offices on behalf of fourteen pensioners living in atrocious houses at Mill Row, Armagh.

In late July 1969 there was a demonstration in Enniskillen.

Violence ocurred and thirty-seven members of the party were arrested. This produced a picket at Crumlin Road, Belfast prison led by Bernadette Devlin.

Events like their 'mock trial' of Fermanagh Council in Enniskillen town hall (Judge Michael Farrell) were calculated to infuriate local Unionists, and, indeed, did so. They held a conference in Coalisland on 1 March 1970 in which the speakers, John McGuffin and Cyril Toman claimed that their membership stood at 550. They then formed branches at Portglenone and Ardboe.

Needless to say the PD never grew into a large political party in Northern Ireland. There was, however, no denying their madcap courage, and by drawing political blood they helped to keep matters fluid. They played an increasing but far from cohesive part in the later stages of the Northern Ireland Civil Rights Association.

When young militants fail to mature by the time they reach middle age, they can appear rather pathetic. This perhaps could be applied today to some people who were members of the PD.

The Alliance Party

In April 1970 there appeared on television a group of tense, almost distraught men whom we had never seen before. They were taking what was for them a very risky step, the outcome of which could not be even guessed at. They were setting themselves up as a new political party, challenging the Unionist monolith at a time when to do so was at the very least a hazardous procedure.

They projected integrity and still do, although, like Labour, they have continually to cope with the ancient problem of their attitude to the 'border' and the side issues that this problem throws up. They unequivocally favour the British connection.

When the Alliance Party is mentioned one thinks of Oliver (now Sir Oliver) Napier, Robert Cooper (now head of the Fair Employment Agency) and David Cooke (once the Lord Mayor of Belfast) as well as John Cushnahan, Robin Glendenning, Séan Neeson and Seamus Close.

The party claims equal support from Protestants and Catholics. In the beginning their support came mainly from the defunct Liberal Party, defectors from Labour, and O'Neill Unionists after O'Neill stepped down from the Premiership. Their approach also appealed to some young Catholic bureaucrats and technocrats and their wives who had progressed up the ladder since Britain had intervened in the job allocation procedures.

In their effort to participate in the normal running of Northern Ireland, they attended William Whitelaw's Conference at Darlington in March 1971, their aim being to set up a devolved government. They were joined in this abortive effort by the Official Unionists and Northern Ireland Labour, but not by the SDLP or the Democratic Unionists.

Ploughing the furrow that they do, they frequently raise nationalist hackles. The Derry branch of the party complained that Mr McAteer introduced the 'border' issue at times of tension in the local community; this they described as 'political showmanship which widens the chasm between the factions for the sake of a cheap headline'.

Endeavouring to promote community harmony, Basil Glass reminded his fellow Protestants that 'for every Catholic who marches at Easter more than a hundred of his co-religionists will be staying at home in silent protest against the terrorists.'.

Robin Glendenning attacked an inflammatory statement by his co-religionist, the Protestant Dean of Clogher, that 'Protestants will die rather than submit. The people will take the authority and find the means themselves [if the Government refuses to act]'. Robert Cooper condemned the Nationalist civil disobedience campaign, but went on to declare that 'Alliance was pledged to defeat the Unionist Party'. The central executive of the party stated that the withdrawal of the opposition from Stormont was wholly irresponsible.

Expressing such strong opinions on such contentious issues inevitably reduces their mass appeal to Catholics, and it is interesting to note that both political extremes in Northern Ireland rarely attack them either by words or physically.

The Unionist 'Moderates'
Not all Unionists belonged to the 'not an inch' brigade but most did. However, there were honourable exceptions who joined a large number of Protestant clergymen led by Rev. Eric Gallagher in advocating reforms. In what most National-

ists regarded as his milk and water way, Captain O'Neill, too, was a reformer. There must have been few who doubted that he was a well-meaning man. He faced an impossible task in trying to reform the Unionist party, dominated as it was, and still is, by the Orange Order. Resistance to his attempts came to a head at the time of the Stormont election in February 1969. The Fermanagh Unionist Association expelled the Duke of Westminster, the Earl of Erne, Rev. T.H. Stewart and Mr H.S. Porter for supporting pro-O'Neill candidates.

Here are some examples of temperate sentiments expressed by Unionists:

On 7 July 1965, Sir George Clarke, Grand Master of the Orange Order, was a Stormont Senate critic of the choice of Craigavon as the new city's name. 'There are many beautiful Irish names in the area.' Mr Victor Cooke, another Unionist member, said that he 'never had any great enthusiasm for the placing of the New City and he had no great enthusiasm for the name Craigavon'.

Dr Robert Nixon, MP, on 17 October 1966, called for one man one vote in local government elections.

Mr Nat. Minford, MP, stated at Stormont on 3 November 1966 that in his opinion 'it was wrong for a city like Derry, where two thirds of the population was Catholic, that Protestants should control the City'.

Mr Phelim O'Neill, the Unionist member for North Antrim at Stormont, was expelled from the Orange Order in June 1968. On the same day it also expelled Colonel Henry Cramsie who, with Mr O'Neill, had attended a Catholic church service two years before. When the one man—one vote controversy was at its height there were only three Unionists who spoke up clearly in its favour, Miss Bessie Maconachie, Phelim O'Neill and Robert Simpson. Mr Walter Scott, MP, favoured progress but at a slow rate.

The Clifton Young Unionists, Belfast, in November 1968, declared that the reforms 'were too little, too late. The blame must rest fairly and squarely on the shoulders of those members of the Unionist Party who were not only not interested in finding solutions to our problems but for many years have denied that there was a problem.'

In September 1969 Mr Phelim O'Neill, then Minister of Agriculture at Stormont, was on the same theme as the Clifton

Young Unionists, that the basic trouble with the Unionist Party was that they had always done too little, too late. After the war, he said, change should have begun. 'The plain hard fact is that there were elements in the Unionist Party who always resisted change at every turn. I say quite frankly that basically is the fundamental reason why we find ourselves in our present difficulties today.'

Sir Robert Porter, QC, ex-Minister of Home Affairs, was equivocal about the Orange Order in June 1971 when he said 'I cannot in conscience associate myself with their attitude [about defiance of the ban on a march in the Catholic town of Dungiven]'.

Dick Ferguson, a former Unionist MP, who resigned from the Orange Order and shortly afterwards from his Stormont seat, said in March 1972, 'Given the right overtures from the South, increasing numbers of Northern Ireland Protestants would come to accept the idea of a "new" Ireland.'

George Forrest, Westminster Unionist MP, was dragged from a political platform and beaten into unconsciousness by a group of Orangemen in July 1967. His crime was support for Capt. O'Neill's inadequate reforms.

Again in July 1967 the Unionist Party whip was withdrawn from the newly-elected Mayor of Enniskillen, Alderman Richard Burton and Jack McAuley of Larne because they attended a Catholic wedding service.

There may have been other moderate Unionists saying moderate things, but their words did not make their way into the files of the Campaign for Social Justice and have to go unrecorded here.

5.

THE PRESSURE GROUPS

The CCDC

The CCDC (Central Citizens Defence Committee) was formed in 1969 behind the Falls Road barricades, thrown up after the worst violence Belfast had yet seen. It eventually represented sixteen separate ghetto areas. Its chairman was Tom Conaty, a local business man. Other members were Paddy Devlin, MP, SDLP, and Jim Sullivan who had previously been interned. Meetings were usually held in Leeson Street.

The members negotiated with the Army as required and had many tense interviews with it. They also saw Mr James Callaghan when he visited Belfast, at a time when the British authorities were trying to gain control of the 'no-go' areas.

On 18 November 1970 the CCDC inserted a full-page advertisement in the *Irish News* entitled 'Stop! Stop! Stop!'. We welcomed this effort because we considered that published statements were too few on the minority's side. Rarely had any group sat down and gathered their facts together and set them out clearly. The piece drew attention to the fact that large numbers of people had opted out of their responsibilities with an 'I'm alright Jack' attitude. It went on to regret the slowness of the reforms and 'an obvious unwillingness on the part of most Unionists to reform'. It called for 'restraint and non-violence, for vigilance and intelligence'.

The point of view of the stonethrower was explained thus:

As he saw it, there were guilty men in the RUC. This was well known to the Prime Minister and Sir Arthur Young [the Chief Constable]. The Press reports of the Scarman Tribunal discredited a different senior officer every day.

Sir Arthur Young was forced to go. He sees no evidence whatsoever that the RUC will ever be purged of guilty men.

The youth with a stone has ample evidence to convince him that there is discrimination by the police in bringing charges in the magistrates' courts. He could quote examples: After a football crowd had stoned, knocked down and kicked two policemen in Corn Market in August two football fans were arrested. They were charged with being drunk and disorderly. In evidence one policeman said that he was lucky to escape with his life. They were fined £10 and £12 respectively [These were Protestants]. The crowd proceeded to Unity Flats, where there was a confrontation in the course of which two young men [Catholics] were arrested for allegedly throwing stones; they were charged with disorderly behaviour, which at the time carried a mandatory six months jail sentence.

The advertisement went on to declaim: 'Violence is out. Stones, bottles, guns and bombs are out.'

It made a modulated and restrained appeal to the Republicans to stop the violence, since family life and living conditions were deteriorating under so-called protectors. Finally there was an appeal—'Organise your street, men and women, to prevent riots.'

The group was regarded as middle of the road. That this was a reasonable estimate can be inferred from the reaction of the two extremes, Unionists and Republicans, to the 'Stop! Stop! Stop!' insertion. The Republicans issued a long condemnatory statement accusing them of 'trying to sabotage the struggle for freedom'.

The fact that the group itemised some reasons why conditions had depreciated to the level they had was too much for the Unionist side. Major Chichester-Clark issued a statement in which he declared that there were misleading claims in it. 'I utterly reject', he said, 'that Unionism is injustice. The CCDC statement was "incredibly biased, ignorant or tendentious".'

Mr Roy Bradford, MP, said that it was a 'poisonous and slanderous political pamphlet of the most Republican kind'. Mr Brian Faulkner said that 'When they stripped away the outworn propaganda and the biased anti-government clichés which the CCDC contained, what is revealed is a state of affairs which we knew to exist but which had hitherto been hotly denied by the sort of people who now frankly proclaim it.' Unionist reaction to what was a reasonable statement shows just how standards of social justice had sunk in Northern Ireland. 'Stop! Stop! Stop!' was later issued as a booklet having wide circulation. The Campaign mailed it to all our supporters, to politicans and the newspapers outside the country.

When the residents of Unity Flats were accused of having 'a massive ammunition and arms hoard' in a basement of the flats, the CCDC pointed out that there were no basements in the flats. They suggested, with conviction, because of their inside information, that the arms found were planted there.

They further procured an apology from the army for the unprovoked use of water cannon on women flat dwellers. In March 1971 the CCDC strongly condemned the sectarian and anti-Catholic songs by Linfield football supporters passing the flats and the repeated one-sided searches of the flats by the Army.

Unlike other groups the CCDC was prepared in mid-summer 1971 to condemn a booby-trap attempt against the British Army, and it appealed to Republicans as Christians and Irishmen to end their campaign of violence, but when, at the year's end, Army General Tuzo appealed to the Catholics of Belfast to end violence, the group pointed out that General Tuzo was the man who had advised in the past 'Lean hard on Catholics'. The CCDC suggested that it was too much to expect the Catholics to hand over Republicans to the authorities when there was misconduct by troops.

In its role as spokesman for the people, the group pointed out that the spate of violence causing eight deaths in early 1971 in the Clonard area was due to the persistent one-sided searching by the Army and police. This had united the whole community against the troops. The group made a strong attack on Mr Faulkner because of his attitude to Catholics: 'His arrogance and condescension are staggering,' they stated, again asserting their chief role of 'keeping the peace on the streets'. They continued to deal with refugees and the results of intimidation. An indication of the atmosphere prevailing in

Belfast at the time is given in the CCDC advertisement in the *Irish News* on 24 March 1973. It was advice to Catholics on how to attempt to provide against sectarian assassinations. 'Do not open the door of the house after dark; do not stand in groups talking; avoid going out after dark'. People were advised to vary the route to their place of work, not to accept lifts or give lifts in their cars. 'Be careful,' the advertisement said, 'if an incident on the road causes you to slow down. Make sure your taxi is a genuine one. Watch out for prowling vans or cars. If an attempt is made to force you into a car cause a commotion.' Small wonder there was great respect and admiration for the members of the CCDC.

Derry Citizens Action Committee

This was a sixteen membership committee. The chairman was Ivan Cooper, John Hume was vice chairman. The group was made up of older and more conservative people than the local group of the Northern Ireland Civil Rights committee. In the beginning it had one Unionist committee member who soon resigned.

At first its members specialised in sit-downs in the street. I remember in the very early days before NICRA was established, John Hume, an earnest young man feeling his careful way, came to see Patricia who, even at that time, was a veteran of street marching. 'What am I to do?' he asked. 'Sit down', we suggested, and so he did, and very effective it was. Indeed I have always held that if we could have mobilised all or nearly all of the community in massive sit-downs for all the world to see, the battle for rights could have been won by this method alone. Unfortunately, the Irish psyche is such that this did not appeal. More active, perhaps, even violent, methods, were more attractive.

In November 1965 at a time when marches were banned, the Citizens Action Committee held a very large one from Waterside Station. The marchers were held up by police in Carlisle Square. With considerable sagacity and great restraint they broke up and went in small groups to the Diamond where a successful meeting was held without incident.

The New Ulster Movement

The initiative of this group came from a highly principled man, a convert to the Society of Friends named Brian W.

96

Walker. It was founded in February 1969 as a political catalyst to promote a united community based on equality and justice. The chairman was Brian Walker, the vice chairman, Brian McGuigan, a Belfast solicitor, who for years had been active in social concerns in the city. The secretary was Patricia Morrow. The NUM did not claim to be a political body but a movement aiming to liberalise Northern politics by supporting 'liberal minded' candidates in parliamentary and local government elections. It supported the O'Neill candidates in the 1969 general election. One of its aims was to break the link between the Orange Order and the Unionists. Brian Walker spoke out forcefully on 1 December 1970 when he called on the Attorney General to prosecute the Paisleyite Unionist MP, the Rev. William Beattie, under the Incitement to Religious Hatred Act.

The NUM took a very strong line against Rev. Ian Paisley's anti-Catholic pronouncements. It issued a pamphlet exposing the gross sectarianism of his *Protestant Telegraph*, quoting many extracts from that 'newspaper'. In June 1971 the group was agitating for a reform of Stormont, but by November of that year it had gone further in a proposal that Stormont be suspended for three years, and be replaced by a commission, with an advisory council in which all political parties were to be represented. They also wanted the Government of Ireland Act, 1920 to be updated. These appeals were supported by the South Tyrone Parliamentary Association, an affiliate of the NUM. The NUM has always claimed that the Alliance Party was its brainchild, and as soon as the Alliance organisation was complete three members were added to its Executive to join the two NILP and the two Unionists already there.

After Brian Walker left Ireland to direct the Oxfam organisation, we heard no more of the NUM.

6.
THE
NEWSPAPERS

THERE can be no doubt at all that the first friend of the homeless Catholics in Dungannon was the *Dungannon Observer*. Anyone who wants to see what the first marches for civil rights in Northern Ireland looked like has no alternative but to consult the issues of 15 June and 17 August 1963.

Then on 31 August there were large pictures of squatters in their own homes. More pictures on 7 September. The Unionist *Tyrone Courier*, whose owner was a liberal Protestant, told the same story more discreetly, with an eye on his biased readers.

From Dublin there was virtually nothing at first, but then by far the best supporter of the Catholic minority in the long run, the *Irish Press* and the *Evening Press* weighed in, for the first time on 29 August, and then on 3 September 1963.

As time went on we were driven to the conclusion that the people in the Republic of Ireland most interested in civil rights in the North were people of republican leanings. The last mentioned two papers continued to send reporters to interview people involved, and commissioned writers to deal with the whole Northern Ireland problem.

From the point of view of general publicity, and of keeping the anti-Unionist community informed about the progress of the protest movement, it was the *Irish News* of Belfast which played the most important part. It told the day-to-day story as the civil rights movement got under way, and detailed the manoeuvres of the various participating groups within it. The *Irish News* printed every statement and letter we ever sent them as well as many others from interested parties. Pictures, which from early days we realised could best pull at the heartstrings, were rare in the *News*.

After an interval, the Dublin papers added their voices, the *Sunday Independent* having a trenchant contribution every week, written by James Kelly. What riled us greatly was that his articles only appeared in the Northern edition of the newspaper—we all knew the facts in the North, we wanted the rest of Ireland to be informed. The *Irish Independent*, when it eventually recognised the conflict, produced some good reports. Later, in its grand and intellectual way the *Irish Times* delved deeper than any other organ.

A new paper started up. It was the *Tyrone Democrat* giving us all the coverage we could hope for, and daringly striking out with a leading article—something that many local papers did not do, the explanation being that attitudes were so biased that a newspaper took a risk of losing readers if it expressed an opinion. Surely this is an indication of the sort of place we were compelled to live in.

To our astonishment and delight, some interest had awakened on the mainland. The *People* of 20 October 1963 printed a very professional piece of investigative journalism on Dungannon housing. The London *Universe* produced a full-page article on 5 June 1964 with pictures of one of the Dungannon marches. It is noteworthy that not until the violence started did the British press generally begin to interest itself in our doings.

About this time the *Irish Post* made its appearance in Britain. Directed at the Irish exiles there, its modern approach favoured our cause, and it frequently weighed in on our behalf.

Later, with violence at its height, the press of the whole of Western Europe and the USA joined in. Eastern Europe, including Russia, was not averse to making critical comment.

After the British Government and the Unionist Party, responsibility for all that happened must be laid at the door of the Unionist press. With one honourable exception, and for as long as I can remember, the Unionist newspapers in our province have been steadily misleading and misinforming the decent Protestant folk by hardly ever, if at all, attempting to explain why the Catholics expressed grievances. Protests from what representatives we had at local and parliamentary level were either not reported at all or misleading extracts given. This conspiracy of silence resulted in Protestant people being shocked, bewildered and frightened by the events of 1969.

We had one consoling thought through the darkest days of the 'troubles'. There was a newspaper, the *Belfast Telegraph* which was trying very hard to support what it, and we, saw as the right. That it could do this and still enjoy a very wide circulation convinced us that there were a lot of moderate Protestants in Ulster. The only evening newspaper published in Northern Ireland, it is widely read.

In spite of the *Telegraph* frequently nudging the Unionist establishment in what it thought was a reasonable direction, it continued to prosper. The leaders in the paper were headlined 'Viewpoint'. In December 1966 it was calling for the momentum of change to be kept up; in September 1970, and again in October it was calling for reforms; in April 1971 it felt that there were too many marches; in June of that year it called on the Government to listen to reasonable advice from whatever quarter; then with sterling courage in June 1971 it struck at the heart of things by saying 'No bridges can be built whilst a Protestant organisation [the Orange Order] occupies a privileged and powerful position in the party hierarchy.' In March 1965 the *Telegraph* leader writer questioned the shifting of the University of Derry to Coleraine; in April 1965 it supported the Northern Ireland Labour Party's appeal for electoral reform; in December 1966 it was campaigning for fair treatment for the minority. It certainly took its courage in both hands when, in October 1966, it stated categorically that 'the Ulster Constitution Defence Committee and the UVF embrace criminals'. Mr William Craig's sectarian speeches in December 1968 and counter demonstrations in June 1969 both came in for condemnation. In August 1965 the *Telegraph* drew attention to the failure to develop the west of the province; again in November 1965 there was a condemnation of discrimination; housing policy in Derry condemned (28.7.67); slowness of reforms (29.2.68); opposition to the name 'Craigavon' for the new city (7.7.65). The *Telegraph* felt compelled to strike out on the first day of February 1966 about the antagonism it was receiving from right wing Unionism; then on 8 June 1966 it attacked the 'lunatic fringe of

Protestants' and the Paisley movement as 'a palpable challenge to law and order'. Could one have asked for more generous sentiments in a Northern Ireland Unionist newspaper?

Widgery Report

In the USA the *Washington Post* commented thus:

There are still innocent souls abroad who think that Lewis Carroll's King and Queen of Hearts are creatures of fantasy. But the publication of Lord Chief Justice Widgery's report on Londonderry's 'Bloody Sunday' makes it clear that Alice's Wonderland is very much alive.

The King and Queen of Hearts, it will be recalled, presided over the trial of the knave and invented a procedure of sentence first, verdict next, and evidence last. Careful readers of not only Widgery's report but those of two earlier commissions on Ulster can conclude only that Carroll's method has served as a model.

Widgery, Britain's chief criminal judge, not only absolves the Army for the killings on January 30, but even praises the paratroopers for their 'superior field craft and training.'

This of course explains how the paratroopers managed to kill thirteen and wound perhaps an equal number with only one hundred and two shots, while escaping any wounds themselves from the bullets that Widgery thinks the IRA was firing at the same rate.

Equally imaginative is Widgery's treatment of the paratroopers' orders. The only recorded order Widgery finds forbade troopers from invading Rossville Street. They did precisely this, and that is where most of the killing took place. Widgery simply decides that the written log of the military orders was mistaken.

The good judge was equally inventive with the case of one victim on whom 'arms' were found. This man had been examined by two doctors who saw nothing on him. But when the soldiers displayed his corpse, four bulky homemade fragmentation bombs were found stuffed in his pockets. Widgery says he cannot believe the soldiers planted this 'evidence'. On the witness stand they all seemed honest, except, of course for two whose accounts of gunfire were too much even for the Lord Chief Justice to swallow.

Widgery's report is no more ingenious than that delivered last November by Edmund Compton, Britain's former Ombudsman. He was asked to look into charges that Catholics interned without trial were being subjected to torture during interrogation. Compton found that some men had been forced to stand spread-eagled with their finger tips against a wall for hours, that their heads had been bound in hoods, that a noise-making machine had kept up a continual whine, that they had been deprived of sleep and fed on bread and water. But this, Compton assured the world, merely constituted 'ill treatment' and not 'physical brutality'. The distinction, he said, lay in the fact that the interrogators did not enjoy what they were doing nor were they indifferent to its effect on their victims. How Carroll would have relished that.

Between Compton and Widgery came the report of Sir Leslie George Scarman, judge of the High Court of Justice. His tribunal was charged with looking into the 1969 riots in which a Protestant-dominated police force and a now defunct all Protestant auxiliary police got in their licks at Catholic civil rights marchers.

Judge Scarman handed down his verdict earlier this month. With fine impartiality it found everyone not guilty. The IRA was not guilty. Neither was the militant Protestant Rev. Ian Paisley, nor Bernadette Devlin, a leader of the Catholic cause. Most importantly the police and the vigilante auxiliaries were equally blameless. The police, of course, did make a few mistakes, like the failure to prevent Protestant mobs from burning down Catholic houses. But on the whole they struggled manfully to do their duty.

The point is that these tribunals produce reports carefully tailored to suit the government's needs at the moment. Compton was created to clear the Army and the Ulster police of torture charges.

Scarman was issued at a time when London had taken over direct rule of the province and wanted to ruffle the fewest possible feathers.

Widgery was set up to restore the paratroopers' 'good name'.

The *Washington Post* ends by pointing the contrast between such reports and enquiries held in America about My Lai, the Chicago riots and the misbehaviour of the Ohio National Guard. Unlike what happens in Britain, where they 'deliver the verdict desired by the Government of the day', each of these American cases was unfavourably reported—in America. The original British Government reports should be read in full. This is one United States columnist's opinion only.

7.

THE NORTHERN IRELAND CIVIL RIGHTS ASSOCIATION

'HAD WE all known it, the unreported [by the London *Times*] Civil Rights march [at Dungannon] was to be the start of something which would shake Northern Ireland to its foundations, split the Unionist Party and initiate more reforms in two years than I thought possible in ten. Moreover, Westminster, our sovereign Parliament, had Northern Ireland thrust on its plate as never before since the Government of Ireland Act of 1920.' Terence O'Neill, *Autobiography*.

There can be no doubt that the Northern Ireland Civil Rights Association was one of the great movements which from time to time have materialised in Ireland, flowered, and by losing the balance of the many potent forces contained within them, died.

Eighty people attended a meeting in the International Hotel, Belfast on 29 January 1967. Five of our Campaign members were there, and I must confess I knew very few others present. They were obviously concerned people who had been doing some preparatory homework together, and meant business. We learnt afterwards that, six months beforehand, people like Messrs Cathal Goulding, Chief of Staff of the then united IRA and Roy Johnston had been working with others towards a civil rights movement. Johnston, we were told, was a Marxist theoretician.

The meeting proceeded in a businesslike way, and set to work organising a committee as follows: Noel Harris of the Draughtsmen's Union, DATA, was chairman. I was made vice-chairman. The committee appointed were Jack Bennett, Wolfe Tone Society, Robin Cole, chairman of the Young

Unionists, Paddy Devlin, NILP, Michael Dolley, ~~Communist Party~~, Fred Heatley, Wolfe Tone Society, Billy McMillan, Republican Clubs, John Quinn, Ulster Liberal Party, Joe Sherry, Republican Labour, Betty Sinclair, Communist Party. Derek Peters of the Communist Party was appointed secretary. Amongst those present were three members of the London National Council for Civil Liberties: Tony Smythe, Cedric Thornberry and J.C. Sheppard. We affiliated on that day to the NCCL. One of the people present at the meeting was Mr Nelson Elder, a Unionist senator.

At our first meeting a week later we specified our five rather vague aims, which in a way indicated that we were not very sure of where we were going. They were: (1) To defend the basic freedom of all citizens, (2) to protect the rights of the individual, (3) to highlight all possible abuses of power, (4) to demand guarantees for freedom of speech, assembly and association, (5) to inform the public of their lawful rights. We then went on to formulate a draft constitution which was accepted at a later meeting. It was emphasised again and again that there was to be no attempt to subvert the constitution of the State and that the organisation would not deal with the question of the partition of Ireland in any way.

It is interesting to note how long it took to really get our ideas into good order. For instance, when the executive met in Dungannon on 27 April 1969, we presented a much more potent and cohesive image. We set out our demands uncompromisingly. They were (1) One man one vote with each vote of equal value, (2) abolition of the Special Powers Act, (3) withdrawal of the Public Order (Amendment) Bill, (4) introduction of anti-discriminatory legislation, (5) introduction of a compulsory local authority housing points system, (6) disbandment of the B-Specials, (7) disarming of the RUC and (8) a public enquiry into police activities in Derry.

Would it not have been a wonderful world if the authorities had said, 'These are sensible people, these are reasonable requests, let us grant them without delay.' That would have been the end of the civil rights movement and of the killing. Our little province could possibly have moved on into a joyous future. As things turned out, most of the demands were eventually, grudgingly conceded, but in a welter of blood and disorder.

But before that meeting in 1967 we had lost one member of our committee, whom I at least valued, Robin Cole the Unionist. I suppose it was not unexpected that he should go. Once the Unionist Party realised that NICRA was a force to be reckoned with they presumably pulled him out. He gave as his reason for leaving the speech by our first secretary, Derek Peters, at the Annual Meeting in February 1968. Mr Cole accused Derek of a 'lack of objectivity' because he compared 'the fascist South African Government' with the Northern Ireland Government over the Special Powers Act. 'Mr Peters is not prepared to be objective, and I regard this as a deplorable return to a sophisticated form of "gable wall" politics. Personally I would like to see an end to the Special Powers Act, and I feel the Minister of Home Affairs must establish that a crisis situation exists to justify its retention', he said.

From then onwards meetings of the executive occurred at regular intervals. There was a good deal of talk, but little action. There had been eighteen months of rather unrewarding leaflet campaigns and meetings in church halls.

A head of steam was, however, gradually building up all over Northern Ireland. People were aware that the British Government seemed much more concerned about the plight of the majority black population in Rhodesia than about conditions here, and that in spite of great efforts by Paul Rose and Gerry Fitt on our behalf.

At a press conference on 6 June 1968 Lord Stonham, Minister of State at the Home Office, had indicated that nothing would be done by the Government to interfere in the matter of discrimination, plural voting or gerrymander. He said that he 'had no instructions from Mr. Wilson to tell Mr. O'Neill to move faster or further on reforms'.

In Dungannon as elsewhere, the local Urban and Rural Councils continued their intransigence, so much so that Austin Currie felt obliged to draw national attention to our problems when he took possession of an unjustly allocated Council house in Caledon. Soon afterwards he requested to be present with two colleagues at a meeting of the Northern Ireland Civil Rights executive. This was held in late July. To facilitate country members it was held at the house of Kevin Agnew in Maghera. Austin's proposition, put forward by

Michael McLaughlin and John Donaghy, was for a civil rights march.

This new chapter in minority affairs produced a lengthy and serious discussion, chaired by Betty Sinclair. The outcome of this meeting was a press release in which we stated that a new approach to our problems was overdue, that blunt denials were no longer acceptable and that Unionist monopoly of power must be reduced. The executive went on to say that 'a demonstration would take place in an area in which discrimination was clearly evident. This will take the form of a protest march from Coalisland to Dungannon on Saturday August 24th'.

In her book, *The Price of my Soul*, Bernadette Devlin took a much more flippant approach than most of the rest of us. She talked of people in Coalisland 'generally behaving as if they were at a carnival'. In my view most were serious, perhaps a little apprehensive. She talked of 'marchers dropping off at every pub on the way'. But there was only one small public house on the route, and the march proceeded at a spanking pace on its five-mile route. The marchers, about two and a half or three thousand in number, were banned from entering the centre of Dungannon, called Market Square, and we were ordered to skirt the town by Quarry Lane and enter the Catholic area about a mile and a half farther on. It was only when we arrived in Coalisland to start the march that we were made aware of this ban. When we arrived at the outskirts of Dungannon there were about 400 police with tracker dogs barring the way. A rope was also slung between three police tenders near the gates of the local hospital. When the procession reached this police blockade, microphones were erected on a lorry and the marchers sat down on the road. Behind the police barricade about 500 Unionist Party supporters had gathered. Many carried clubs and staves but the police in the area did nothing but exchange greetings with them. Amongst them were prominent Unionist councillors, shouting slogans and singing party songs. The NICRA supporters were addressed by Betty Sinclair, Gerry Fitt, Austin Currie, Erskine Holmes and Jack Hassard. Betty was placatory and reasonable, yet at the same time she inspired us. The men were more militant. As Austin Currie, from the platform of the lorry, looked across the police barricades he compared his position with that of President Kennedy surveying the Berlin Wall. 'Only for the women and children present' Gerry Fitt said 'I would lead the people to the centre of the town'. Jack Hassard explained that the opposition councillors had done all they could through progressive means to obtain a fair method of housing allocation but their claims had fallen on deaf ears.

There were minor attempts to break through the barricade but they were beaten back by police using truncheons. The meeting ended with the singing of the American civil rights anthem 'We shall overcome', and the crowd was advised to disperse quietly. After this a large number of leaders, some of whom we did not even know, adjourned to our house, a couple of hundred yards away, for tea and sandwiches. Later that night a section of the crowd made a detour to Market Square and attempted to 'sit down'. They were batoned by the police.

Erskine Holmes, a member of both the executive of the Northern Ireland Labour Party and that of NICRA, and a speaker at the demonstration, issued a statement condemning the action of the Minister of Home Affairs, Mr William Craig, and the RUC, in preventing a peaceful and non-sectarian demonstration from entering Dungannon.

There was another statement issued by the secretary of the Young Socialists in Belfast, Mr David A. Graham. It condemned the RUC for not allowing the parade to reach the Market Square. It also condemned all those who spoke at the meeting who, without exception, accepted the police decision instead of continuing with the march.

There has been much play made by Unionists of the fact that there were republicans in our civil rights march. Of course there were, they are a segment of Irish life, and probably always will be. They were not there as an organised group, they carried no placards and were not recognisable since they were anonymous marchers. What would the Unionists expect the executive to do about them? The same question would apply to Tomas MacGiolla who was also on the march to Dungannon.

Whether they were republicans or Republicans I do not know, but there were many young brawny men keeping order and restraining militants, among whom were the Young

Socialist Alliance, forever trying to break down barriers and whom many of us regarded as noisy, combative pests.

The Campaign for Social Justice, trying desperately to promote reasonableness in a deteriorating situation, fraught with danger, wrote to Mr Harold Wilson thus:

Dear Prime Minister,

I want to add my views to those of Mr Gerry Fitt, MP, who has already seen you about the Civil Rights march in Dungannon.

(1) Although notification to the police was given a month previously, the proposed route was banned at midnight on the day before the march. Responsibility for the ban was taken by the Minister of Home Affairs. Are we not entitled to claim that this prohibition, coming when it did, was calculated to inflame the passions of the marchers?

(2) The alternative route would have added almost a mile and a half to our march, which after five miles already uphill, would have been impossible for many of us.

(3) Some time after the meeting ended, young people who 'sat down' in the town square were batoned by the police as they sat, whilst shrieking Unionist demonstrators were not even approached!

I can tell you that I found the spectacle of the armed and furious police, with their dogs, most terrifying.

Mr Jack Hassard, the local N.I. Labour leader, has had his life threatened more than once since Saturday.

I am sending you copies of both the Unionist and anti-Unionist local papers, so that you can judge for yourself between them. I only make one point; Mr. Austin Currie MP, did not at any time use bad language as has been alleged.

Our next march will be in Londonderry. I trust you will not think it an impertinence on my part if I suggest to you that the taxpayers in Britain, as well as those here, are paying for a disproportionately large police force, great number of 'B' specials, and even contingents of the British army here in Northern Ireland.

I suggest that the time has come for any political group

to be allowed to demonstrate peaceably anywhere in Northern Ireland.

If the Unionists were to see, even once, that you were deploying your police force and your army to protect the minority here, they would shrink from this kind of publicity from then onwards.

Please let me know that our good Civil Rights people will be safe when they march in Derry.

Yours sincerely,

M.P. McCluskey

for The Campaign for Social Justice.

At this time there were two very active organisations in the city of Derry. One was the Derry Citizens Action Committee, whose members included John Hume and Ivan Cooper. The other was the Derry Housing Action Committee, dominated by Eamonn McCann and Eamonn Melaugh. These last were younger, much more militant and thrusting, and had been organising sit-downs and protest meetings. I attended a get-together in Derry at which members of both associations were present, and it took little perception to see that there was no love lost between them. Members of the Housing Action Committee were closer to the executive of the Civil Rights Association. Thus it was no surprise to us in the governing body of NICRA when we were approached by them in September 1968 about a march in Derry.

The executive of the CRA held a properly constituted meeting. Betty Sinclair was in the chair. We were told that Mr William Craig, the Minister of Home Affairs, had placed a ban on marching within Derry's walls. A majority decision was taken not to attempt to break the police barricades in Derry on 5 October—the day when the Derry people, mainly the Housing Action Committee, had decided to hold the march. The plan was to withdraw from the barricade if we were stopped, and hold a meeting, as we had done so successfully in Dungannon a month before.

Frank Gogarty, Fred Heatley and I were delegated to go to Derry on 4 October to inform them there of our decision. We were meeting the Derry Civil Rights Association, which, I got the impression, was little more than the Housing Action

110

Committee wearing other hats. (It is noteworthy that John Hume never joined the Derry CRA)

The meeting was tempestuous and attended only by very militant people who overwhelmed our efforts, and in the end we agreed to support the Derry Civil Rights Association and break the police ban. Although I did not attend the march on 5 October because of the way the Derry people had rejected the Civil Rights Association decision, I now have to admit that the militants could claim a success, since at that time every Westminster politican had been carefully briefed again and again by our Campaign for Social Justice as to the true situation in Ulster, and were showing every sign of doing nothing about it. It seemed therefore to have required a brutal orgy to secure world attention which might lead to reforms. It began to dawn on me that, if the Northern Ireland Catholics had been waiting for our reasoned arguments and carefully collected statistics to influence events, they might have waited for a further fifty years.

Mr Craig's ban on the march changed the whole situation because it brought into the civil rights movement opposition Stormont MPs, Queen's University students and a large number of Catholics who up till then had been tepid about civil rights.

Gerry Fitt had persuaded three Westminster Labour MPs—Russell Kerr, Mrs Anne Kerr and John Ryan—to attend as observers. The world press and television was there in force. John Hume, Ivan Cooper, Eddie McAteer, Kevin Agnew, Gerry Fitt and Paddy Devlin positioned themselves in the front row as they made ready to start the march from the Waterside Station. Their intention was to make their way to the Diamond where an open air meeting was to be held. The crowd was warned by District Inspector Meharg about what would happen if the ban was breached.

All started forward singing their way up Duke Street where they were stopped by the police, who promptly attacked, clubbing Fitt and McAteer who were incapacitated. Betty Sinclair at this stage climbed on to a chair and tried to cool tempers. It looked then as if the marchers would abandon their aim of proceeding. The police again attacked with batons and watercannon. The marchers retreated but were set upon at the other end of Duke Street by another police contingent. There was mayhem as the crowd tried to escape. The police must not have realised, or perhaps did not care, that practically the whole world was looking on as the watercannon hosed women and even babies indiscriminately. Some of the marchers were trampled underfoot, and some beaten as they lay on the ground. The MP John Ryan was aghast. He particularly spoke of one woman over sixty who first had her glasses removed by one policeman and was then batoned by another. This lady was not even taking part in the demonstration.

The copy that every newsman present in Derry on that day sent to his paper contained a series of anecdotes telling of the unbelievable ferocity and stupidity of the RUC. Fergus Pyle of the *Irish Times* headed his piece, 'An old city faces a new sorrow' and that about summed it all up.

Even today, as an introduction to many documentaries about Northern Ireland, we are treated to flashbacks of policemen scrambling over bodies, truncheons flailing, as they dispersed the Derry demonstrators.

As in Dungannon the month before, it was inevitable that some hotheads would seek revenge, which indeed they did. They set to on the Protestant Commemorative Monuments in Butcher Street, then on into the Protestant ghetto off the Diamond where, armed with bottles and stones, they attacked anyone they saw. The inhabitants responded and another sectarian upheaval had begun. Later the riot squad followed the crowds back to the Bogside, where the first barricades to prevent police entry were being erected.

Ulster was now in a bigger mess than ever.

By now most provincial towns which had a sizeable Catholic minority were organising a local civil rights group. Later in October of that year Strabane Civil Rights Association was formed. On 27 October twelve of its members set out on a fourteen-mile march from Strabane to Derry to show their solidarity with the Derry Civil Rights Association. They only got half way when they were attacked and beaten up by a crowd at Maghermason in Co. Tyrone. The placards they were carrying were seized and torn up, and poles used to beat the marchers, augmenting the sticks which their assailants already possessed. Some marchers were thrown to the ground, and an attempt was made to knife one person. Earlier, as they passed Bready, they were stoned and opponents yelled at them 'Up Paisley' and 'Up Craig'. Eventually they reached Derry Guildhall where their Chairman, Laurence O'Kane, attempted to present a letter to the Unionist Mayor of Derry. This gentleman was nowhere to be found in spite of a previous letter to him telling of the group's intended arrival. The marchers were received by Ivan Cooper, representing the Derry Citizens Action Committee.

On their way the police shadowed the marchers but made no attempt to protect them.

As the minority community gradually pushed for its place in the sun, the Protestants were finding it very difficult to adjust to the changing situation. The television was opening up to what in Britain had long been standard practice. Civil rights leaders had to battle their way forward in the changing environment. This was the kind of thing that happened:

In mid-October there was a current affairs programme screened on Independent Television from the Belfast studio at Havelock House. Taking part were John Hume, Ivan Cooper, Eamonn Melaugh, Finbarr O'Doherty (Derry), Rory McShane (Newry), and Patricia, as well as some people not involved in civil rights, to provide a contrary view. A crowd of Paisleyite extremists, some 200-300 strong, laid siege to Havelock House. As he left, Austin Currie was kicked and punched and treated to a flood of obscenities, as indeed was anyone else that the crowd recognised. Gerry Fitt had to wait for more than an hour before he could be smuggled out of the building via the back door by two Special Branch men.

The Armagh committee for Civil Rights—like Strabane, only recently formed, but with a solid middle-of-the-road membership—wanted to show their new organisation's capacity and passed on a request to us at the centre for support of a march on 30 November. This was readily given.

By now Rev. Ian Paisley had decided to take a hand in affairs. He issued a call for 'every Loyalist in Ulster to assemble in Armagh on Saturday to take control of the city' so as to prevent civil rights demonstrators from marching. Describing the civil rights movement as 'a front for the IRA', Rev. Paisley alleged that arrangements had already been made for many 'hooligans' to cross the border to take part in what was hoped would be a full-scale civil riot. 'We intend to take over the city and be in control of it. They are not going to move around here the way they did in Londonderry.' He and the local hardliner, Douglas Hutchinson, made 'an aggressive and threatening' [Cameron report] approach to the RUC demanding that the march be banned. A tatty handbill was circulated in the town saying 'Board up your windows. Remove all women and children from the city on Saturday 30th November.' Posters were everywhere, they read 'For God and Ulster SOS to all Protestant Religions. Don't let the Republican IRA and CRA make Armagh another Londonderry. Assembly in Armagh on Saturday 30th November. Issued by the UCDC' [Ulster Constitution Defence Committee]. Rev. Paisley's lieutenant, Major Ronald Bunting, made strenuous attempts to mount a counter demonstration so that both it and the Civil Rights Association march would be banned, but without success. [It was notable that the police in Armagh were trying harder than heretofore to be fair. They removed many of the UCDC posters].

At 1.00 a.m. on the morning of the march thirty cars drove into the centre of Armagh and parked. Rev. Paisley, Bunting and about a hundred supporters stayed in their cars till morning, when they proposed to hold a 'religious service'. The police had roadblocks in place around the city. Protestant weapons removed from cars that morning included two revolvers and over one hundred other weapons, including bill-hooks, scythes and other sharpened metal objects. In spite of police precautions, crowds of Paisleyites could be seen in the city carrying staves and clubs. Rev. Paisley carried a black-thorn stick and Bunting a walking stick.

Thomas Street, part of the march route, was blocked by a truck. Paisleyites sang hymns continuously. By now Market Street, on the Civil Rights Association route, was crowded with Protestants. The police, knowing that they would be unable to clear a way, erected barricades to keep the two sides apart. We marchers, numbering about five thousand, were compelled to hold our meeting at the police blockade. Only by good stewarding the same troublemakers as at Derry, namely the Young Socialists, were prevented from breaking through to the Paisleyites.

When the main demonstration had broken up and most

CRA members and supporters had dispersed, a clash occurred in Catholic Cathedral Road between young civil rights supporters and Paisleyites. The police made baton charges. A disturbance broke out when a group of Paisleyites carrying a Union Jack and pickaxe handles were returning to their buses. An armoured car, fitted with a watercannon and steel helmeted police carrying riot shields, went into action. Some people required hospital treatment as a result of these activities.

A BBC Panorama team was later attacked and television crews generally were reviled. At the close of the day Rev. Paisley and his supporters staged a triumphal march over part of the area denied to us, singing their sectarian songs and shouting abuse at policemen.

Understandably we of the executive were angry that once again our properly notified march had been aborted. The Campaign, in order to keep Westminster fully informed, again wrote to Mr Wilson thus:

Dear Prime Minister,

I am sending you a report of a speech made by Mr William Craig which, some people say, was an important reason for the Rev. Ian Paisley and his followers deciding to take the law into their own hands and to occupy the centre of Armagh last Saturday.

On that day the Civil Rights Association was to march through the city along a route previously agreed with the police. Later the County Inspector announced that he had not received enough reinforcements to carry out his task. This is inexcusable since Paisley supporters were in Armagh since 2.00 a.m. the morning of the march, and because there are 3,000 regular police in Northern Ireland, as well as innumerable Specials.

Mr Craig's speech was provocative and sectarian. Indeed, I am sure you will read into it some contempt for both the Westminster and his own Government, and especially for the 'reforms' which have been suggested for Northern Ireland. On the platform was also the deputy Prime Minister.

Our point by point commentary on these 'reforms' has already been sent to you. It has been widely approved of.

The 'reforms' are totally inadequate, and satisfy very few here except *all* the members of the Unionist party. This itself condemns them.

Some members of the subordinate Parliament here seem determined to precipitate a civil war. Mr Craig has been working hard to involve our fine Civil Rights organisation, which is made up of people of all beliefs, in a sectarian struggle (a policy which has worked well for fifty years). Already the activities of Unionists have damaged the good name of Britain.

The kind of unpleasantness your Government is allowing us to endure here at a local level does it little credit.

For example, the young wife of Austin Currie, MP, has had several dreadful nights, with thugs screaming epithets outside her house in the country, at a time when her husband was absent on political business. This lady, who only recently has had a baby, comes from a respectable home, and is unused to such treatment.

I am heartily sick of the evil anonymous letters I receive, and the many death threats against my husband and myself, as I am of the intimidation that decent Protestants are suffering to prevent them speaking out for justice.

We have no law preventing intimidation or incitement, because, let us face it, many Unionists regard both as political weapons.

When you read about Armagh and become aware that British, Irish and even Swiss camera teams were afraid to film the Rev. Paisley's mob, you must see the resemblance to the beginning of Hitler's political movement.

On Saturday 23 November last, the young students of Queen's University came to Dungannon to hold a meeting in order to form a local branch of their People's Democracy.

Thugs, some of whom I am reliably informed were armed, broke it up, and later laid siege to the Post Office, where one of the finest members of your own party in Northern Ireland, and also a Protestant, Jack Hassard, is employed. The police gave little help, and the meeting had to be abandoned. Photographers and journalists were assaulted and cameras broken. The mob subsequently attacked the restaurant where the meeting had adjourned to, assaulting the owner and his pregnant wife.

Last Saturday 30 November on their way to the Civil Rights demonstration in Armagh, a group of courageous people again held an unannounced, surprise half-hour meeting in Dungannon. As the meeting ended, Paisleyites from the town rushed forward to break it up—again, not in Nazi Germany, but in Northern Ireland, British Labour controlled! I know you will understand that it is not presumption on my part when I make suggestions about what could be done to help us here. Surely I would propose what I thought was least likely to cause local disorder or harm the Socialist cause anywhere.

(i) Some liberal Protestants have suggested, as I previously have done to you, that the British Army would need to carry out police work here. Mr Craig is engaged at present in calling up his sectarian and excessively bigoted 'B' Specials. He intends to rule by fear, and to stiumulate the IRA who have been restrained for longer even than we had hoped.

(ii) Some senior police officers here should be English, to counteract the *gaulieter* mentality of so many of the Royal Ulster Constabulary.

(iii) Finally, and most important of all, Mr Faulkner has worked very hard indeed to find new industry for the province. Almost all of this he has placed in Unionist areas, and, to be sure, the main jobs were given to Protestants. He and his friends would not easily let this go or allow Ulster's prosperity to diminish—-therefore the safest and most potent pressure weapon you have is the fiscal.
We are all hoping you will use it in time.
Yours sincerely,
M.P. McCluskey
for The Campaign for Social Justice

Even though we had not yet achieved a planned march to its destination, 1968 ended with some encouragement that our publicity efforts, with the help of the media, were beginning to bear fruit on the British mainland.

At its Annual Conference in Margate, 1968, the National

117

Union of Students passed a motion supporting the civil rights movement. This body, the membership of which at that time was close on four hundred thousand, emphasised that the struggle should be pursued through non-violent means. This was something with which most of us were in agreement. We had realised that our success was greatest when violence was being directed against us—that was when the sympathy built up. Unarmed marchers with placards being assaulted by screaming men or even women, attacking from the sidelines, drew support for us. People sitting quietly in their armchairs watching the television screen and seeing the expressions on the various faces had no difficulty in making a judgment in our favour. The Students' report on the Special Powers Act was prepared by the NUS executive and was one of the items discussed at their conference.

The Ulster Constitution Reform Committee meeting in Cheshire in November stated that its aim was to 'uncover the Ulster pit and offend the British public with its stench'. The Committee added that 'Dr Paisley and his colleagues are fanning the flames of religious hatred to gain political power for themselves.'

Meanwhile the Prime Minister received a telegram from the secretary of the East Scotland Irish Association calling on him to take control in Northern Ireland.

Glasgow Campaign for Civil Rights in Northern Ireland was given a true picture of life in the North by Betty Sinclair, who addressed a meeting on our behalf.

Twelve members of the staff of Sunderland Technical College sent us a telegram congratulating us on what we had already achieved, and promising us support in the future. The signatures on this telegram made it very clear that they were English men and women and not Irish exiles. And we had word too of a proposed social justice march in Birmingham starting from the Church of England Cathedral with the Vicar, Rev. A. Howell, among the marchers.

It was only in December that Dungannon civil rights activists found time to organise a local Committee for the town. It turned out to be a stirring, exciting and at the same time frightening night.

There were about 800 of us gathered in St Patrick's Hall. Outside were about 400 Paisleyites, with steel-helmeted police between them and the hall. A barrage of missiles flew between the opposing factions. What annoyed me then and has always been a source of resentment in this kind of confrontation, was the fact that the police faced the Catholics, with their backs to the Protestants.

The meeting began without two of the speakers, John Hume and Austin Currie who were delayed by a court hearing in Derry. When they did arrive they were given a five-minute standing ovation—the first time I had ever seen anything like this in Northern Ireland.

For a fuller description of events I could not do better than reproduce the letter the Campaign sent to the Home Secretary of the day. There is a possiblity that he may have read it himself because when he visited Dungannon on behalf of the Labour Party in 1970 he complimented us on the high standard and amount of the publicity he had received from us (the Labour Party was out of office at the time—he could, I suppose, afford to be frank!).

7 December 1968
Dear Mr Callaghan,
   On Wednesday last, 4 December, I was asked to be one of a platform party at a meeting in Dungannon to elect a local Civil Rights Committee. We were aware that the Paisleyites had been out in force the evening before, as they thought that was the date of our meeting.

I was unhappy all day because after the dreadful happenings in Armagh, I feared there would be trouble.

The organisers requested the police for protection. The meeting was a huge success, everyone was moderate in their pronouncements, my husband and I were warmly applauded when we stated that we accepted the Constitution of Northern Ireland, and that we would regard it as a social injustice to attempt to alter it without the approval of the majority of the people.

The meeting was covered from beginning to end by a BBC team headed by Martin Bell, as well as by other television and press reporters. During the meeting a large crowd of Paisleyites had assembled. I have been informed that the police made no attempt to disperse this menacing crowd.

When we left the hall we had to run the gauntlet of this mob and were protected mainly by our own stewards.

In the interests of all of the truth, I must inform you that before our stewards could control them, a few youths threw stones back at the Paisleyites—this, I suppose is human nature.

A reporter was shot at, his camera being damaged.

Martin Bell informed us afterwards on BBC 2 that he also was attacked.

I must further inform you that many have complained to me that the police on duty that night exchanged jokes with the Paisleyites.

My Protestant Labour councillor colleague, Jack Hassard, a World War 2 veteran, who topped the poll in our 'Catholic' ward, had his car smashed by an axe that night. His life and that of his wife and family has been threatened so many times that he has just announced his resignation from politics.

My own life has been threatened many times also.

How long must all this go on? How long must we suffer this intimidation, when all we are doing is asking for the rights which, said the Prime Minister in 1964, we were entitled to?

Meantime, Mr Craig is making provocative speeches in Belfast, Clogher, County Tyrone, and the night before last in Dungannon.

He is trying hard to whip up a sectarian conflict. This is not what the people of Civil Rights want, and I know all the leaders intimately.

As you are aware, Mr Paisley claimed on Tuesday last that these dreaded 'B Specials', all extreme Protestants, were largely his followers.

Please send me some reassurance at least.

Yours sincerely,

M.P. McCluskey

for The Campaign for Social Justice.

There is no joy in telling of NICRA's next endeavour, the Newry civil rights march on 11 January 1969. It ended in disorder and arson.

When the march was announced, Mr Paisley's lieutenant,

Major Ronald Bunting, intervened by threatening a counter demonstration. The police promptly re-routed the march. Immediately the temperature began to rise. Since Newry is a largely Catholic town, the local bishop Dr Eugene O'Doherty expressed the view that the original route had the approval of all sections of the people of Newry.

On the day of the march, when the participants arrived at the first crash barriers at the corner of Monaghan Street and Merchants Quay, the civil rights leaders sought to retain control by addressing them through a loud hailer. One of those appealing for non-violence was Michael Farrell of the People's Democracy. Tom Keane, Chairman of the local People's Democracy formally demanded of District Inspector Edgar that the marchers use the planned route. This was refused.

The crowd surged forward. A police tender was set on fire. Other tenders had their windows smashed as the mob crowded round them. The organisers made a further attempt to get the crowd to disperse without success.

At Merchants Quay another tender was set alight. The police allowed it to burn without attempting to intervene. Stewards grappled with marchers, trying to prevent them entering tenders to drive them away. Two hours after the first attack on the barriers, the police had not intervened. A watercannon held in reserve on Merchants Quay had not been brought into action. In all, five police tenders were burned. Another which would not burn was pushed into Newry Canal. Some students sat on the tenders to try and prevent them being driven off and burned, but were over-whelmed. A Queen's University student, William Bennett, writing to the press afterwards, told how he had remonstrated with a ringleader of the 'bully boys' not to set the police tenders on fire, with the argument that as a citizen of Newry and a ratepayer he had paid for these tenders. To this the other retorted that he was not a Newry citizen.

By this stage the police were being showered with missiles. The civil rights organisers dropped a plan to seal off the town by means of sit-downs on the main roads and instead attempted to take over some of the public buildings, including the Post Office and the Labour Exchange.

The next morning the *Sunday News* carried a large picture of civil rights leaders, with arms locked, trying to hold back the mobs. They included three of the greatest friends of true civil rights in Dungannon, Paddy Fox, Michael McLaughlin and John Donaghy, their expressions all showing ineffable sadness.

Later on the night of the Newry debacle, Gerry Fitt laid his finger firmly on the nub of the matter, when in a statement he said, 'The Government was well aware that the eyes of the world, through press and television, were focused on these incidents, and the police, far from taking any action to prevent what happened, appeared to condone the burning of their vehicles. But the Government did not succeed in their objectives of smearing the Civil Rights movement. In fact not a single Protestant resident or business premises was interfered with or damaged,'—'It was significant', he commented, 'that no arrests were made at Burntollet but over twenty-three were arrested in Newry.'

The Inspector General of the RUC, Mr Anthony Peacock, said on 5 February 1969, that the police had 'evidence of IRA support for the civil rights movement. I do not think they are organising it, but it fits in with their long term plans for uniting Ireland forcibly. We know that at least two of them, including the president of Sinn Fein, have attended civil rights meetings in Belfast,'—'The police were satisfied that there was no armed Protestant organisation....' Harry Diamond, MP, declared that the Inspector General's statement 'could be seen as a scandalous party political intervention by a public official'.

There was great encouragement for us when, on 28 January 1969, the Presbyterian Church of Ireland issued a statement thus:

> Whatever the faults of demonstrators, a far greater disservice has been done to Northern Ireland by those who have banded themselves together to prevent, by physical resistance, the peaceful expression of opinion, instead of answering it with greater reason and self discipline. By violence of speech and action, by personal vilification and harassment, they have dishonoured the cause they professed to defend. By mob action they have seriously compromised not only the principles of law and order but

122

also those whose difficult task it is to uphold law and order without fear or favour—both Government and police.

Such treatment of those who were protesting against what they believed to be wrong has been a grevious betrayal of the Protestant and Presbyterian principles of civil and religious liberty, and respect for conscience. We believe that many still do not realise the irreparable damage which has been done to the witness of the Gospel and to the Protestant and Presbyterian name both in Ireland and overseas. Avowed enemies of christianity could not have done more damage to the faith than things which have been said and done under the banner of religion.

The statement went on to declare that 'It was an unhealthy thing for any political force or party to restrict its member-ship, in theory or in practice, to any one church or group of denominations,' ... 'It is an unhappy legacy of our history that the Roman Catholic section of the community is dispro-portionately represented among the socially and economically depressed.' There was more in this vein, all very humane and reasonable.

In February 1969 Frank Gogarty was voted into the chair of the central executive of NICRA. The next big set piece demonstration was at Omagh on 12 April. Patrick Fahy, chairman of the local Civil Rights Association, secured our blessing for the protest and having informed the police in the required manner the local group set off. Despite the presence of 400 police, Paisleyite militants succeeded in having the march re-routed. At one stage the rival groups were within eighty yards of each other, and a policeman and a civilian were injured when a scuffle broke out between police and counter demonstrators. Two lines of police had earlier separ-ated the 1,500-strong marchers and a few hundred Paisleyites in the town's Market Square.

Long before the marchers gathered at their starting-point the counter demonstrators had taken up positions on a narrow part of Market Street, many of them waving Union Jacks and some wearing Orange Order sashes.

When the marchers reached Dublin road corner they found their way blocked. They sat down on the road while officials of the Committee walked forward to talk to District Inspector Dandale, who told them it was obvious that the march could not go through.

There and then the speeches were made. Patrick Fahy began by assuring those on the other side of the barrier that those he represented did not aim to replace one system of discrimination by another, the rights of all would be secure. Eamonn McCann said that they must make demands for those things that would serve the interests of the working classes. He appealed to disillusioned Protestants for support. Austin Currie suggested that the opposition were using the Union Jack as a cheap political rag. He reminded his listeners that notice of the march had been given, no re-routing had been ordered, yet their march had been stopped. Claude Wilton, chairman of the Derry Citizens Action Committee, said that he was an ordinary Protestant who had rebelled. It was their common battle to seek equal rights and opportunities for all. Michael Farrell, the People's Democracy leader, said that Captain O'Neill's mask as a liberal had slipped. Ivan Cooper, Frank Gogarty, Phelim O'Neill and Patsy McDonald added their weight to the appeal for equality by also speaking.

After listening to the speeches for an hour and a half the crowd by-passed the counter demonstration and made its way to the Courthouse. As they marched into Drumreagh Avenue the counter demonstrators pushed forward but were held back by a cordon of police, in front of which stood the march stewards. The counter demonstrators then rushed back up Market Street, in an effort to meet their opponents at the junction of Bridge Street and High Street, but they were again held back by a line of police.

There was a tense moment as a struggle broke out between the counter demonstrators and the police but the line of crash barriers held firm. As the civil rights crowd sat down on the Courthouse Hill a small group of Loyalists tried to outflank the police but were halted. On the roof of the Courthouse three groups of people were flying Union Jacks. Shortly afterwards both the civil rights protestors and the counter demonstrators dispersed quietly.

Of course many more civil rights marches were held, but nothing like the number of Protestant parades. To refer back;

the Minister of Home Affairs at the Stormont parliament, in answer to a question from John Hume, reported that more than 1,300 parades, marches or processions were held in 1968 by the Orange Order, the Apprentice Boys and the Royal Black Preceptory. This at a time when there had been less than a dozen civil rights marches, mostly in predominantly Catholic areas, and every one of these begrudged by the Protestant community.

By this stage there was a local Civil Rights Association in most towns. As a group they tackled local abuses as they occurred. The Magherafelt CRA pinpointed how the local Rural District Council abused housing allocation procedure. The Dungannon Group dealt with employment discrimination in the South Tyrone Hospital. The Maghera Association produced statistics to expose the misdeeds of the local Rural Council, the Mid-Ulster Hospital and the Telephone Exchange. Lurgan Civil Rights Committee held a 'teach-in' at which young Protestants were praised for their support. The fact that Protestants suffered discrimination, also, was stressed.

With so many disparate elements in NICRA it was inevitable that a smooth progress would not occur. The first 'split' was announced by the press on 15 March 1969. John MacAnerney, secretary, Fred Heatley, treasurer, Betty Sinclair, a past chairman, as well as a fourth executive member, Dr Raymond Shearer, resigned. The dispute came about because the People's Democracy, on the initiative of Michael Farrell and without previously consulting the executive, arranged a march through Protestant east Belfast to Stormont and indicated that they expected the Northern Ireland Civil Rights Association to take part.

John McAnerney described the march as lunacy. 'This route is notorious for the number of people who have been done to death in the past forty years. I strongly suspect that those who proposed this march have no intention of really walking along this route. One of them said to me: after all, we can rely on it being banned.'

The four who withdrew also stated that the Northern Ireland Civil Rights Association was 'being infiltrated by a political party, forcing it into decisions which are preventing the aims for which the Association was founded'. Dr

Raymond Shearer, in a personal statement, pointed out that the march was to be conducted on People's Democracy lines only, that to attempt to traverse 'eight miles of solidly hostile streets was folly'. He went on to say that the PD representative on the Council denied that they were a political party (they had just fielded eight candidates in the Stormont election of February 1969). However, Kevin Boyle admitted to Raymond Shearer that they were indeed a political party, and that they hoped eventually to be the effective opposition at Stormont. Dr Shearer's fear was that the People's Democracy was trying to take over NICRA.

'A vote was taken concerning participation in the march, the result, "seven for", "seven against". The chairman, Frank Gogarty, gave his casting vote for participation,' Dr Raymond Shearer concluded.

On 22 March a conference was called to deal with the impasse. Frank Gogarty berated both sides who had allowed hostility to develop between the People's Democracy and the Civil Rights Association. Betty Sinclair announced that she was rejoining the executive.

Still the antagonisms rumbled on, one speaker objecting strongly to the People's Democracy preaching class war and the take-over of Catholic schools. 'These were not Civil Rights Association objectives.'

It was with a heavy sense of responsibility and some foreboding that we of the central executive contemplated Saturday 22 March 1969. Six civil rights parades were to be held in protest about a new Public Order Act proposed by the Stormont Unionists. It turned out to be a day of triumph for the protesters, who carried through the demonstrations as peacefully as they could, although at various flashpoints there were scuffles and a few arrests.

In Enniskillen police blocked off East Bridge Street to 700 civil rights marchers. The marchers sat down and held a meeting on the spot, after refusing to accept an alternative route. Townspeople peered from behind boarded-up windows of local shops as the protesters walked the few hundred yards from Jail Square before coming to a halt at the East Bridge which spans the River Erne. The marchers chanted slogans and waved banners as one of their leaders, Bowes Egan, argued with a District Inspector of the RUC. Paddy Devlin and James Kennedy, both MPs, and James Lynch stood silently by. Bowes Egan claimed that there were only a few loyalists in the Diamond and that the police would have been well able to prevent any trouble along that route.

In Armagh about one thousand demonstrators gathered in the Market Street where they staged a sit-down and chanted 'We shall overcome'. There were some minor scuffles and five arrests of demonstrators and Paisleyites.

There was a small demonstration in Newry, in which about 300 people took part. The crowd staged a sit-down in the main square and sang civil rights songs. There was only one minor incident when a car tried to push its way through the crowd.

In Derry 500 extra police had been drafted in. The demonstration turned out to be the quietest ever in the city. Apart from one short vicious struggle at the War Memorial the parade went off quietly. There were about five and a half thousand marchers who passed through the familiar route, Duke Street, over Craigavon Bridge to Carlisle Road and the Diamond. The cause of the fracas at the War Memorial was a counter demonstrator, surrounded by his associates, waving a Union Jack. A Land Rover containing a detained marcher was attacked with stones and coins. The usual leaders—John Hume, Ivan Cooper and Claude Wilton—led the parade. The only damage was a few smashed windows.

Lung power won the day for 200 Paisleyites against only thirty civil rights demonstrators in Belfast. With only a couple of minor scuffles the affair turned out to be more farcical than dramatic.

The character of the civil rights movement was gradually changing, possibly maturing. A forty-car motorcade left County Fermanagh on 11 June 1969 to expose a Unionist move to safeguard two County Council seats in the reorganisation of local Councils. This had been promised in the heralded Downing Street Declaration. The method the Unionists proposed to use was to build fifty new houses, not in Newtownbutler, where they were required, but three and a half miles away in the rural area of Donagh. This would ensure that the two Newtownbutler seats on the County Council would be returned by Unionists. Larry Murphy, the press officer of the Fermanagh Civil Rights Association, explained that 'the Unionists hold the village seats on marginal majorities. If the new houses were built in Newtownbutler there is a strong possibility that the seats would be lost, for most of the people on the housing waiting list are Catholic. Donagh however returns two Nationalist Councillors with very good majorities, so the Unionists won't be scared of losing two seats.'

The motorcade passed through the various Fermanagh towns. A police escort was provided through Belfast to Stormont where representations were made. There were other attempts at boundary manipulation to which the Civil Rights Association drew attention, such as in the case of the crossing of the County Tyrone border to Unionist Fivemiletown by the Fermanagh Council to pick up the necessary votes in order to secure the Unionist majority. The division of County Derry into two areas, one of which stretched into County Antrim, was equally suspect, the Civil Rights Association pointed out.

In Dungiven a new NICRA tactic was put to the test. Three thousand Orangemen marched through the predominantly Catholic town on 28 June for a banner unfurling ceremoney. Scores of extra police were drafted in as busloads of Orangemen from all parts swelled the normally small Orange parade.

Dungiven's population, from behind closed doors and shuttered windows, saw their civil rights placards and posters being ripped down by squads of Orangemen, some wearing their sashes. One poster said 'We are allowing you to march because we believe in civil rights for all.' An NBC cameraman was struck as he was filming the marchers.

Among those who stayed behind closed doors was Ivan Cooper, the kingpin of the Derry Citizens Action Committee and Member of Parliament for the area.

Moderate members of the Northern Ireland Civil Rights Association had a premonition of impending disaster when banner headlines appeared in the *Sunday Press* of 29 June 1969, 'Platform Row by C.R.' It was referring to events at a demonstration of three thousand supporters in Strabane on the previous day.

Eamonn McCann accused the members of the Stormont opposition of selling out to the Government by accepting Capt. O'Neill's timetable of reform, and he coupled with this the name of Austin Currie. He also attacked Senator Edward Kennedy as 'mouthing emotionalism' and questioned his attitude to the Vietnam War and the American Negro Rights struggle. The chairman of the meeting, Ivan Barr, a member of the Northern Ireland Civil Rights Association executive, called him to order for making a political speech. Other speakers listed grievances arising from job and housing discrimination but Miss Bernadette Devlin described this as sectarianism and went on to censure the Nationalist Party. 'I was elected an MP to Westminster as a Unity candidate but if this is to be the same kind of unity as Austin Currie's the sooner you get rid of me the better. Let there be no mistake about it, I follow Eamonn McCann's policy.'

The Belfast branch of the J.F. Kennedy Association condemned Mr McCann for a biased attack saying that both Ted Kennedy and his two brothers had always identified with Dr Martin Luther King and the senator had frequently called for the withdrawal of troops from Vietnam.

Mr James Callaghan and Lord Stonham came to Belfast at the end of August 1969. Their aim was to consult with as many separate groups as possible. It was arranged that some members of the executive would have an interview with Lord Stonham. I was one of the chosen representatives.

When the meeting assembled I was horrified to discover that there were two extra representatives for the Northern Ireland Civil Rights Association present whom I had never seen before. This was the first time such an irregularity had occurred. Had I only known it, this was to be the first shock of many. What could I do? To create a fuss would have done more harm than good, so I had to accept them. One of these people took an aggressive approach to Lord Stonham. Truculence was a poor disposition on such an occasion. I showed Lord Stonham a copy of *The Plain Truth* and asked if he had seen it before. He had not, but promised to read the copy I gave him. To my intense satisfaction, a few days later I had a letter from him requesting a further eight copies.

In the book *John Hume* by Barry White, I am reported as having said to Lord Stonham concerning discrimination, 'The next time I have a case of discrimination I won't send it to you. I'll burn a street of houses.' I cannot imagine myself being so militant, especially on such an important occasion. I have no recollection of saying anything like that to him or anyone else at any time.

In the very fluid situation of Northern Ireland it was a

wholetime job safeguarding the Northern Ireland Civil Rights Association flanks. We found it necessary in the executive to disown the Monaghan Civil Rights Association, where a civil rights office was opened and literature from the South became available. We made it clear that we never had organised any meetings south of the border, nor did we intend to do so in the future. In a separate news item in the *Tyrone Democrat* of 31 October 1969 a Fianna Fáil spokesman, referring to a controversy concerning a meeting in Cork, is alleged to have said that 'All these Communists are coming down from the North'. This indicated that the Republic of Ireland did not realise that we in the civil rights movement were working together, and provided that any one group did not dominate, we were happy to continue in this manner.

If the background had not been so serious some civil rights activities would have verged on the absurd. In the right-wing *Impartial Reporter* newspaper of Enniskillen, on 25 February 1970, there was a picture that one can be sure no Unionist would have ever considered imaginable. It showed James Lynch of Roslea, our Campaign member, Councillor Jim Donnelly, and Mr Frank McManus, chairman of the Fermanagh Civil Rights Association, seated *on the dais of the Fermanagh Council Chamber*. At the time when this photograph was taken there was uproar, with the opposing groups singing 'We shall Overcome' and 'The Sash'. The occasion was a motion proposed by Jim Donnelly and seconded by Philip McCarron for the abolition of the Council. There was a serious and responsible contribution to the debate by the anti-Unionist members, who covered most of the administrative misdeeds by the majority. This was countered by the usual stonewalling tactics, when the Unionists listed all the good things that happened and refused to deal with the injustices. In the end the motion was, of course, lost by twenty-eight votes to ten. Whereupon the opposition members left the chamber, promising never to return. The Chairman, Captain J. Brooke MP (later Lord Brookeborough) announced an adjournment. Shortly afterwards the doors of the Chamber swung open and in marched a group of twenty-two civil rights and People's democracy members led by Mr McManus. They took up the principal positions reserved for the Unionist majority members. There was stamping of feet, cheering, jeering and applause. Eventually, after a request by the police, the demonstrators left quietly, under protest. They had held up the Council for about an hour. The demonstration had a sequel when on 5 October of that year police took into custody twenty people associated with it who refused to pay fines. Among these were Frank McManus, our Jim Donnelly and James Lynch of Roslea.

James Lynch who died some time after his prison sentence had been completed, was the father of the village of Roslea. This fine local representative had fought unsuccessfully for years to have a sewage system installed, but was always thwarted. (A frequent ploy of Unionists to prevent houses being built where the occupiers were likely to be Catholics was to deny sewage, and thereby to deny houses.)

The Annual General Meeting of the Armagh Civil Rights Association for the election of office bearers was scheduled for mid-January 1970. John Donaghy and I were delegated by the central body to act as scrutineers. Anticipating a left-wing takeover I wrote to Cardinal Conway's secretary, Father James Lenny (later Bishop Lenny) telling him of my concern. I asked him to persuade a few solid tradesmen and their wives to attend this open meeting and vote for moderate candidates. I stressed to him not to involve the local 'gentry' because there was bitterness amongst working people that these had distanced themselves in the struggle for justice. One person who should have known a lot better was heard to say that 'there was no housing problem in Armagh'. This of course was nonsense. I recall being brought by Tom McLaughlin to a house where there was such overcrowding that the only bedroom the tenants possessed accommodated, not only the man and his wife, but all their children—I vividly remember that there were so many beds in the room that I could not see the floor!

After an emotive and persuasive speech by Michael Farrell to a relatively young audience, a vote was taken. The incorruptible Donaghy and I counted the votes. The moderates lost virtually all the positions on the local executive by six or seven votes. My motives had obviously been doubted, and not for the first time, by the Catholic establishment.

Within a week the Red Flag was flying from a window of the Republican Club at Ogle Street in the Primatial City of Armagh.

Meetings of the Civil Rights Association were held in Belfast in the late evenings, often in Frank Gogarty's house, where his kindness and generosity were boundless. I often wondered what Mrs Gogarty, a gentle Frenchwoman, made of these large-scale invasions of her privacy.

At this time the strain of attending the meetings and trying to follow all that was going on was almost insupportable. Up until now there was no trouble dealing with innovatory ideas: Unionist politicians do not pose this problem! Now we had to cope with clever young people whose motives at every meeting were now suspect.

One of the reasons why the central executive had changed so much was that, with typical and regrettable Irish impulsiveness, John McAnerney and his three colleagues had left the executive in March 1969. The four people who replaced them were elected in contravention of the constitution at an Extraordinary General Meeting. Three further co-options had then been made to add to the previous co-options which had occurred since the last Annual General Meeting. The result was that the Belfast tail was wagging the country dog.

To attend meetings John Donaghy and I drove the forty miles from Dungannon, picking up Bríd Rodgers on the way in Lurgan. We were at that time the only three members of the executive who did not owe allegiance to any political party. Added to the physical distance from the centre and anxiety to keep in touch and have some control of events, there was the further problem of my medical practice behind me. I was at that time the press officer. Before we left the meeting for home the press release was composed to be given to the papers after the meeting was over by the assistant press officer Kevin Boyle. At least twice when we arrived home there was a different press statement on the midnight news from the one to which we had been a party.

Civil rights meetings often lasted till 2 a.m. This was a common occurrence, both centrally and at area meetings, a stratagem the People's Democracy shared with the 'Looney Left' of the British Labour Party and leftists trying to take over trade unions. Other civil rights members had businesses to superintend and family commitments to fulfil which compelled them to leave at a reasonable hour. When they did, the militants proposed suspension of Standing Orders and went on to carry resolutions which mature adults would not have countenanced. Added to this, meetings of the executive had become frenetic, there were tensions between members and, as we were soon to learn, information was being suppressed.

Frank Gogarty, the chairman, was emotional by nature, although the kindest of men. I remember once saying to my fellow passengers on the trip to Belfast, 'These people are in such a fervid state that I would not be surprised to find when we arrive that they had levitated to half way between the floor and the ceiling.'

At this time the Campaign for Social Justice had been notified by friends in the USA, and very aggrieved friends at that, that the First Annual Conference sponsored by the National Association for Irish Justice was to be held in New York on 7, 8, and 9 November. That Conference was to be attended by Bernadette Devlin, Frank Gogarty, Eamonn McCann, Kevin Boyle and Michael Farrell. What shocked and surprised traditional Irish-American people and clubs such as the Ancient Order of Hibernians was the leftward orientation of the new American movement. Consequently the eighteen organisations which made up the Irish Action Committee had come together and banned the Association for Irish Justice to which, in the early stages, some of them had belonged. This National Association for Irish Justice had described itself as the American Affiliate of the Civil Rights Association of Northern Ireland. It was socialist rather than nationalist.

Brian Heron, its leader, was himself a revolutionary. He had played an active part in the grape pickers' strike in California and had attempted to organise the Greenland fishermen into a militant union. He supported the Black Panther Movement. The office of the National Association for Irish Justice in East 23rd Street, New York was also the office of Mr Cathal Goulding. In short the NAIJ existed to promote revolution in Ireland, north and south.

Mr Proinsias MacAonghusa (*Irish Times* 9.11.69) interviewed Mr Heron. He asked for an explanation 'as to what happened to funds collected in the United States by Miss

Bernadette Devlin MP. Miss Devlin appeared to be sponsored by the NAIJ while on a fund-collecting tour for non-denominational relief work in the North.—According to his version the money had been divided into three parts and deposited in a Belfast bank, one part for direct relief work, the second for civil rights, the third will help in the defence of political prisoners'.

At the first opportunity I asked to see the minutes of the meeting where the National Association for Irish Justice was appointed by the Civil Rights Association as the only organisation to act on its behalf in the United States. None was produced.

On 4 December 1969, with the deck lifting under our feet, we three felt it necessary to make public our anxiety about the way the Civil Rights Association was tending. In our joint press release we told how Frank Gogarty and two other members of the executive, Kevin Boyle and Michael Farrell, with other People's Democracy colleagues, had departed as representatives of NICRA, on a speaking tour organised by the National Association for Irish Justice, without telling the other members of the executive of their plans, nor was there a minute available to inform the other members.

We felt, and said it openly, that the country membership should be aware of these things, since they made up the bulk of the movement. We reminded people of 'the savage attacks by speech and leaflet of People's Democracy on Ivan Cooper, Gerry Fitt, Aidan Corrigan, John Hume, Austin Currie and on the Nationalist Party generally'. Whatever the views that might be held in some quarters about this party, it had much loyal country support. To antagonise this was divisive of the civil rights movement. We objected to 'the hawking of shoddy news sheets at Provincial Council meetings'. We ended our statement by declaring that we would soldier on till the Annual General Meeting on 14 February 1970.

John Donaghy followed this up by an interview he gave to the *Tyrone Democrat*. He pointed out that all but five members of the central executive came from Belfast, where there was relatively little civil rights activity compared to the provinces. John objected strongly to Michael Farrell, an executive member, using the civil rights platform to put over his own political views. All he asked of the People's Democracy members on the executive was 'to do as the Republicans and other political groups had done, i.e. not to use civil rights platforms for political gain'. John Donaghy went on to counter various accusations by Mr Farrell against himself and myself of lack of militancy, being right-wing Tories in search of power for ourselves, and not being prepared to help working people. He reminded Mr Farrell of his long history as a Dungannon Councillor and a civil rights activist. He recalled that he had attended an executive meeting forty-eight hours prior to the departure of the party for the USA, when the trip was not mentioned. He ended by complaining about how frequently he had requested financial statements from the executive without result. Needless to say the *exposé* by the three of us produced a strong reaction. In a press release the Northern Ireland Civil Rights Association executive condemned us 'in the strongest possible terms'. The press release went on to say that 'a detailed refutation of the points raised would be issued shortly'. We have no record in the Campaign files of this happening.

We attended our last executive meeting in the run up to the 1970 Annual Meeting due to be held on 14 and 15 February. In the two days before applications closed for membership eligible to vote in the 1970 elections to the executive, the numbers went from 380 to 560. (To elicit numerical precision at this stage was very difficult, but eventually Bríd Rodgers prised the membership list from the secretary and it had jumped as detailed.)

John McAnerney, a former secretary of NICRA, observed to the press that 'it seems pretty evident that there has been a takeover by people who are not really out for civil rights, but who use the movement for putting forward their extreme left wing views'.

Before the Annual General Meeting was held Bríd Rodgers, John Donaghy and I indicated with 'sadness in our hearts' that we had decided not to stand for election to the executive, because, as we said, 'the civil rights movement had ceased to be what it originally was—a broadly based movement commanding widespread respect. It had lost its sense of unity and its mass support.'

The People's Democracy let it be known that they would not seek seats on the executive but would continue to be

135

individual members. Also declining to be executive members were Andrew Boyd, John McAnerney, Fred Heatley and Tom Conaty, all of Belfast, as well as Joe O'Hagan (Lurgan), Aidan Corrigan and Mary Hughes (Dungannon), and P.J. Rafferty (Carrickmore) who withdrew for personal reasons.

The meeting itself was large, and at times turbulent. To our great annoyance the press was excluded. Before the voting for the fourteen-strong executive took place we saw a sheet with a list of names being circulated among Republican Club members.

The outcome of the election for the 1970 executive was a takeover by pro-Goulding Official Republicans and Communists. Kevin Agnew (275) Republican Clubs; Frank Gogarty (263) republican; Malachy McGurran (251) Republican Clubs; Ann Hope (247) Communist; Liam McMillan (233) Republican Clubs; Madge Davidson (231) Communist; Denis Cassin (218) Republican Clubs; Ivan Barr (206) Republican Clubs; Vincent McDowell (201) republican; Mrs Edwina Stewart (201) Communist; Dalton Kelly (199) republican; F. Patterson (167); John D. Stewart (132) Northern Ireland Labour Party; Rebecca Mc Glade (124) republican. Subsequently Mr Kevin Agnew was elected chairman and Frank Gogarty vice-chairman.

During the meeting a proposal by Michael Farrell calling on members to oppose injustice in the Republic of Ireland, on a vote of ninety to eighty-eight, was referred back to the new executive. By the time the resolution was put to the meeting 300 of the 500 of the original attenders had left for home.

The 1970 Annual General Meeting was of course a watershed for the civil rights movement. Letters to the press (mostly unsigned as is customary in Northern Ireland, because people do not want to invite a brick thrown through their front window, or worse) regretted that the executive's main aim from now on seemed to be a socialist all-Ireland republic. Because of the loss of responsible middle-of-the-road direction, some letters said, the concern was now no longer for reform but for revolution.

From then on, by not resigning from the movement we three were able to hold a watching brief on NICRA activities. After the 1970 AGM, as onlookers, we watched the executive blunder along, often at cross purposes. Here are a few isolated events, as small groups, making piecemeal efforts, allowed NICRA to wind down.

There was a newspaper statement by the chairman of the Dungannon Civil Rights Committee, Aidan Corrigan, on 16 February 1970, in which he attacked the People's Democracy. The subject was a debate on the Ulster Defence Regiment. The PD claimed that Austin Currie had absented himself deliberately from the meeting when in fact he had been misinformed about the date. When the meeting took place the People's Democracy 'attempted to shout down Jack Hassard, a respected Protestant and a tried and tireless civil rights worker, when he spoke. The People's Democracy also made personal attacks on Messrs Hume and Currie. The Armagh PD are unwelcome and unwanted at future civil rights meetings.' declared Aidan Corrigan.

On 1 March the People's Democracy announced that they would seriously consider not participating in civil rights marches because of the sectarian-type speeches made in Enniskillen by the chairman of Northern Ireland Civil Rights Association, Mr Kevin Agnew, and Mr Aidan Corrigan. Mr Cyril Toman, another PD member, claimed that 'the executive of Northern Ireland Civil Rights Association had been elected by underhand methods following an alliance between what was now termed Official Sinn Fein and the Communist Party'.

On 13 March the Northern Ireland Civil Rights Association organiser, Mr K. McCorry, speaking in Toome, described the People's Democracy as 'ultra Left' and the Dungannon group as 'ultra Right', at a time when people were calling for the bickering to stop.

On 16 April NICRA announced that the retention of Stormont was its official policy. This was supported in a further statement by the Communist Party of Ireland—'the abolition of Stormont would solve nothing.' This drew a shoal of indignant letters to the press.

Twice on the night of 12 May 1970 Frank Gogarty's house was attacked with stones. Most of the windows in his house had previously been broken, and one side of the house had already been almost completely boarded up. When his appeal against a mandatory six months prison sentence was lost on 26 February 1971 Frank Gogarty was sent to gaol. Knowing him, I can assume that Frank lost his head during a relatively minor incident. Some time after this, Frank Gogarty died.

A branch of the Campaign for Social Justice Northern Ireland was formed in Birmingham and another in Coventry. We were unable to prevent them using our name without vexatious and time-consuming litigation. Another branch, which was formed in Manchester, ceased to use the Campaign's name when we requested this.

The Birmingham 'branch' was in effect a civil rights organisation of sorts. It sponsored a march in Enniskillen on 28 November 1970. By pressing the SDLP to participate, these people helped to widen the split between the moderates and the militants in the civil rights movement because this Fermanagh march was an almost completely republican event.

Frank McManus was jailed in a most selective way by the Northern Ireland judiciary. He was given a six months prison sentence in late January 1971 for taking part in a banned march. Three members of the Northern Ireland Civil Rights Association executive and other prominent marchers were not prosecuted. Some marchers were fined one pound.

The Annual General Meeting of the Dungannon Civil Rights Association was held on 24 February 1971, having been previously adjourned because of the small attendance. There were about 100 members present. There were many disputes from the floor. Jack Hassard accused the Civil Rights Association of alienating Protestants by talking too much about a united Ireland and he described Mr Kevin Agnew, Chairman of the Northern Ireland Civil Rights Association as 'another Enoch Powell' for his advocacy of 'sending planters back from whence they came'. Jack Hassard reminded those present that he had taken part in the first civil rights march to Dungannon and had then warned that 'under no circumstances should the civil rights movement become a sectarian organisation'. He said that he had appealed to Catholics to join the Ulster Defence Regiment but by their not doing so 'we've handed over the UDR to the B-Specials. This has been a catastrophe from the Catholic point of view'. Mr Agnew asked, 'Who as an Irishman wants to take an oath of allegiance to the Queen, to wear the UDR uniform and get a gun—especially if you can get a gun without it?'.

A new committee was elected. Mrs Bríd McAleer, one of our Campaign members and a civil rights pioneer, declined to go forward on the grounds of ill-health. Mr Kevin McCorry the Civil Rights Association organiser, warned that the general situation of the country 'was not good' and that the new committee had an added burden because of the unhealthy situation in Dungannon of the civil rights movement, with various groups and sections sniping at one another.

The next day Ivan Cooper MP issued a statement warning that the Civil Rights Association was being wrecked by some of its own members abusing the platform. Referring to the Dungannon meeting he re-emphasised that it was never the function of the civil rights movement to work for the re-unification of Ireland. 'Non violence is an important base of the movement, that seems to have been lost in the past twelve months. The unity which we once had has been smashed to pieces by a handful of people who have used civil rights as a political weapon.'

At a Northern Ireland Civil Rights Association conference in Dungannon on 24 October 1971 the delegates supported the role of civil disobedience and the rent and rates strike. The conference called on all supporters to refuse to pay radio, television and dog licences and to withhold payment for gas, water and electricity, while farmers were urged to withhold land annuities. It was advised that savings be withdrawn from post offices and other Government schemes.

The conference agreed to arrange other militant activities including disruption of local councils and post offices by sit-ins and pickets. Little came of all this but, needless to say, the Unionists poured scorn and condemnation on the proposals that were made.

Jim Donnelly's wife Margaret, a delicate, retiring lady, was 'kicked and punched senseless' by police on 8 March 1972, as she and her husband were getting into their car after court proceedings. Her husband was similarly attacked and two men who went to their assistance also came in for police treatment. Jim had to carry his wife to the nearby Catholic church and call a doctor. James and Margaret Donnelly were defendants in court proceedings which resulted from an anti-internment protest in Enniskillen on 18 February (*Fermanagh News* 11.3.72).

The Northern Ireland Civil Rights Association said in a statement on 1 December 1972 that it could not lend its support to a conference called by the County Antrim executive of the Association because it had been arranged without its approval. The conference was due to be addressed by Mr Frank McManus MP, Mr Aidan Corrigan and Mr Michael Farrell, three people who, the Northern Ireland Civil Rights Association pointed out, 'were not its members and have consistently tried to destroy the association and sow confusion among our supporters'.

One of our last communications was a sad little letter in the *Irish Times* from Northern Ireland Civil Rights Association headquarters at Marquis Street, Belfast, signed by Edwina Stewart and Madge Davidson. This pointed out that when Frank Gogarty was on the platform at the inaugural meeting of the Irish Civil Rights Association in Dublin, with Mrs Maire Drumm, he was not representing the Northern Ireland Civil Rights Asssociation because he had resigned from the executive the week before.

By this time no original civil righter would have given the existing emasculated segment of NICRA the time of day. What had begun as a roaring lion was now only a squeaking mouse. But civil rights had done most of what it had set out to do. Things were far from perfect in Northern Ireland but they were a great deal better. Minorities at any time and in any place are always at some disadvantage. It is the job of the politicians, with patient determination, to oppose abuses and fight for minority rights. Opposition politicians must continue to do this in the future as far ahead as one can see.

8.

BERNADETTE DEVLIN

PITY anyone who attempts in Northern Ireland, to write something about Bernadette McAliskey, née Devlin!

As she herself emphasises, she was born in Cookstown of decent underprivileged Catholic parents. She displayed early her combative nature which so often goes with a stocky physique.

She was lucky enough to be among the earliest stream to have free secondary and third level education.

It was the British Labour Party which provided this great amenity for Catholics. Those with brains—and Bernadette was well provided with that commodity—could, for the first time, promote themselves even from the least affluent section of the community. I often wonder whether Bernadette, or indeed many of those other younger political figures who have so successfully forced Ulster Unionists away from the grudging obscurantism of earlier years, ever give credit to the British Labour Party for what has been made possible for them.

Bernadette secured her secondary education in St Patrick's Academy at Dungannon, then went on to read Celtic Studies at Queens's University, Belfast, later switching to Psychology which she studied for a time.

She became involved in various societies and in the beginning conformed to the picture of a country girl tasting what for her was the big city, and the big university. Needless to say she found her feet in the Debating Society. At this time her opinions were swinging between republicanism and socialism. Eventually she gravitated to the group of young militants who later became the People's Democracy.

At that time the Northern Ireland Civil Rights Association

was in the second year of its not very thrusting activity. NICRA was not militant enough for Bernadette or her friends. They were moving along beside it, but not of it.

1968 and 1969 were certainly Devlin years. In October 1968, as an emissary for the People's Democracy, she confronted the Rev. Ian Paisley in his home, attempting to persuade him that they were both concerned with the same problem, namely the disadvantaged working-class people, both Protestant and Catholic. 'In his blinkered way he is quite bright but we got nowhere,' she said afterwards. Rev. Paisley agreed that there were injustices, but said to her, 'I would rather be British than fair.'

The operation of the Dungannon march and the nuances that led up to it were too subtle for her youthful comprehension, but what came later, the Derry march of 5 October, was the catalyst which matured her as it did many others of her generation.

She was horrified by all she saw, especially, as she says in her book *The Price of my Soul*, 'the evil delight the police showed as they beat the people down'. She herself escaped being attacked. Later she took an injured person to Altnagalvin Hospital where she got the impression from the staff, rightly or wrongly, that they thought 'the injured people got what they deserved'.

Her next outings were on the People's Decocracy marches. These were prevented from going through Shaftesbury Square on their way to the city centre. Then she was off with her fellow members to picket Mr William Craig's house to show displeasure at his having banned the march of 5 October. They received personal abuse from Mr Craig.

Worse was to follow, she joined the Burntollet march where she was savaged by the Paisleyite mob, one man attacking her with a piece of flat wood armoured with two nails. Later she was knocked down and beaten as she lay on the ground.

Then in February 1969, a spate of party politics. She contested the South Derry seat against Major Chichester-Clark, then the Minister of Agriculture, later to become Prime Minister of Northern Ireland. She lost by six thousand to his nine thousand odd votes. A very creditable performance.

Her real opportunity came when she was nominated and won the Mid-Ulster seat at Westminster. At that time she was everyone's darling. We were delighted with her dynamism and her absence of posturing. We hoped that from then on she would consolidate her position, fusing together the disparate elements of minority life. Unfortunately this did not happen.

When Bernadette was nominated for the seat, apart from her relatives she could only call for help on her left-wing associates from Queen's University. These latter had little rapport with rural mid-Ulster. She possessed neither a political organisation nor money.

There was a concerned and socially conscious citizen of republican persuasion, in Maghera, Mrs Betty Noone. She came to Bernadette's assistance, gathering a group of practical people around her. Mrs Noone and her friends worked very hard for Bernadette. When she was elected she ignored these good friends. At the least estimate they surely could have contributed something. In her book she dismisses them with the relentless cruelty of youth.

Patricia made a judgment that she would not be able to influence Bernadette, and she did not try.

Introduced to the House by Paul Rose and Gerry Fitt, her maiden speech at Westminster was a huge success. Ignoring the 'convention', which had been so successfully ignored before her by Gerry Fitt, instead of saying a few conventional words, she lambasted all those who deserved it. The press lionised her as did an almost incredulous British public—at that time we were winning hands down.

Thereafter things did not go so well. Bernadette gathered around her, in her smart Belgravia flat, a 'coterie' who were of no use to her, or to those of us who helped to put her into Westminster. Rose and Fitt found her a difficult colleague. Furthermore her political agent had no time for them. A few women MPs who tried to be friendly were rebuffed. Relations depreciated further when Paul and Gerry tried to co-operate with her in drafting Amendments to the Ulster Defence Regiment Bill. She was determined to paddle her own canoe, and produced her own Amendments.

Paul Rose is Jewish and, understandably perhaps, was angry when she declared her support for El Fatah, an extremist pro-Palestine organisation.

She thought little of the Campaign for Democracy in Ulster, a group which did more to provide our Campaign for Social

Justice with a platform in Britain than any other—at a time when Bernadette was still a schoolgirl. Indeed, relations between her and this large group of Westminster MPs were virtually non-existent.

Although the publicity she was enjoying was bringing in a great deal of money from television appearances, lectures and the like, she found the media attention hard to bear. Indeed she seems to have revealed the only faintheartedness in her makeup when dealing with the rapacious newsmen of the British popular press.

By August 1969, Derry, like Belfast, was going through one of the worst periods Northern Ireland had known. It was in a state of near anarchy. The police and the Bogsiders were in a fight-to-a-finish situation. Bernadette joined in and helped to place the first barricades in position, thereby beginning to set up the first no-go area in what was later to be called 'Free Derry'. The world was treated to television shots of her racing round the area in jeans and sweater urging the people to greater efforts through a loudhailer, organising the filling of petrol bombs, and screaming at the defenders to man the barricades. At times she wore welders' goggles to protect her against the CS gas being used against her. There was an eyecatching shot in the newspapers of Bernadette breaking a flagstone to use as ammunition.

She said afterwards that she did what she did because she felt that the police were out to get her. She was concerned also for the survival of the Bogside as a Catholic 'ghetto'.

This Derry episode had a further emotive outcome for her and her followers, still more for most of the Northern Ireland Catholics. Court proceedings were started against her. The result was that she was found guilty on three charges of incitement to riot and one of rioting. She was sentenced to six months gaol. She appealed; in vain. Her barrister, Sir Dingle Foot, QC, attempted to bring her case to the House of Lords. His main arguments centred on a group's right to self-defence, an MP's right to protect people she believed to be in danger, and the relevance of disallowed evidence about the police. The Chief Justice of Northern Ireland, Lord MacDermott, rejected the application. There was condemnation of her sentence from many quarters including Norman St John Stevas, the Tory

MP. The French newspapers, *L'Aurore* and *Figaro* also disapproved. But to emphasise her martyrdom, the inept law and order arbiters of the province, after first arranging that she should surrender herself to the police in Derry at an agreed time, stopped her car on a windswept country road and she was bundled away to commence her sentence.

Gaol, her opponents said hopefully, would teach Bernadette a lesson. They were wrong. She came out after four months, committed to a militant revolutionary socialism, as she confided to Mary Holland in an article in the London *Observer*. She was seeking a grass roots movement of the left, saying that she did not see herself as an Irish MP but as a Socialist MP. These, too, were the views she propounded in her book, *The Price of my Soul*. They shocked many Catholic conservatives who were, and still are, in the majority. Her book detailed a sort of Marxist manifesto, Bernadette style. She had little time for traditional Nationalism, the Catholic Church (as at present constituted), for the reigning Pope, for Cardinal Conway, even for the various Governments of the Republic of Ireland. This in spite of the fact that these Governments are democratically chosen by the total voting population. For example, Barry Desmond in the Irish Dáil, speaking in December 1972 at a debate on the Offences Against the State Bill, denounced Bernadette for a statement she made in Liberty Hall. She said, 'If the Bill is passed through the Dáil may the hand of the President who signs it wither as he signs it, and may every one of his dead comrades who fought and died for this country, appear before his dim eyes and curse his beating heart.' Great rhetoric, but damaging to what many held dear.

She frequently referred in the book to the problems of the oppressed Protestant working class. It is very doubtful indeed if there was more than a handful of these who saw things as she did. She objected to 'Catholic slum landlords marching virtuously beside the tenants they exploited, in civil rights gatherings'. She claimed, 'Only if it is an all-Ireland working class revolution are there enough of us to overthrow the powers that be,' and again, 'Basically I believe that the parliamentary system of democracy has broken down.' Again and again she praised Eamonn McCann and Michael Farrell, the latter being the leader of the Young Socialist Alliance, members of which seemed to hold ideas far to the left even of Bernadette's.

A final quotation to demonstrate her philosophy, culled from the *Irish Times* of 22 January 1970:

> It is up to Mike Farrell and Eamonn McCann to say 'That's what you're thinking and that's what we're thinking and this is what we've got to do about it.' I know we've got to have control of our own lives, control of our factories but somebody like Farrell or McCann knows how to spell out how it's done. They know the principle of private ownership which has got to be destroyed—they know how to get from the profit margin to workers' control.

In all this she revealed sentiments which relatively few shared.

Particularly stung by the book's content were the good nuns of St Patrick's Academy, Dungannon, who gave Bernadette her education and a lot more. They were so incensed as to issue a circular in which they said 'Bernadette Devlin's references to this school, in her book *The Price of my Soul*, have shocked all of us....Bernadette has hurt two of her best friends, who are lifelong friends to each other....With regard to corporal punishment this school could stand the strictest scrutiny.' The document was signed by three nuns and thirteen lay teachers, some men, some women.

In Paris in November 1970 she declared that she would advocate armed guerilla warfare against Northern Ireland to get better conditions for workers. Her aim was a workers' socialist republic. 'We are not interested in liberal democracy.' She was addressing a mass rally sponsored by 'Secours Rouge', and was accompanied by Seamus Costello of Sinn Féin, Eamonn McCann and Frank Gogarty.

A manifestation of her republican feeling was shown when she helped to found the Irish Republican Socialist Party, the IRSP. This eventually became the political wing of the ultra-extreme INLA. Bernadette has always denied that she had links with this latter body.

It was the same sort of strong gut feeling for the people of Northern Ireland, and for Derry in particular, when, in Westminster Parliament, she reacted in a way which shocked the British, who regard their Parliament as a sacred institution. The House was discussing 'Bloody Sunday' in Derry. Mr Reginald Maudling, the Home Secretary, claimed that the troops had fired in self-defence. Bernadette, who was on the platform on that awful day, was on her feet immediately. She called Mr Maudling a 'lying hypocrite'. Thereupon she crossed the floor and boxed his ears. After living with a half century of mealy-mouthed Nationalism most Irish people forgave her.

America proved to be a very attractive setting for her. In the beginning she was a thoroughgoing success. In the early days citizens of the USA with an Irish background seized upon the same features that so delighted us when Bernadette first appeared on the scene.

In March 1971 she was scheduled to speak at Nevada State University in Las Vegas. She had a bigger audience than Jane Fonda, who had appeared the previous night. Fifteen minutes before she was due to speak, the doors were closed. Hundreds were locked out. More than three thousand had paid a dollar admission charge.

The older members of the audience were angry, and showed it, when she harangued them about the American way of life, the almighty dollar and the injustice of jailing Angela Davis, a black power militant.

She condemned injustices in Northern Ireland and the brutality of the police both there and in America. She condemned also the injustices perpetrated against the Viet Cong. She called John D. Rockefeller 'an exploiter of the American people'. She got laughs when she referred to the Catholic Church, expressing standard left-wing censures. Bernadette was paid two thousand dollars a lecture and she talked in thirty-eight universities in twenty-eight days. Of the money received she had to pay thirty per cent booking fees as well as other expenses, of course.

Mayor John V. Lindsay of New York presented Bernadette with the Golden Key of the City. She later turned it over to the Black Panther organisation—'As a gesture of solidarity with the black liberation and revolutionary socialist movement in America. To these common people to whom this city and this country belongs, I return what is rightfully theirs, this symbol of the freedom of New York.'

The United Ireland Committee issued a statement saying that this 'was a flagrant act of discourtesy which offends the vast majority of the Irish people both here and throughout the world'.

The American Irish Action Committee, which represented eighteen Irish organisations in the USA, had banned the National Association for Irish Justice, mainly because of its association with the Black Panther movement. When Bernadette was to visit the United States in November 1969, not one of the eighteen associations was notified about it. This was greatly resented. They said that the proposed million dollar target for Ulster riot relief would have been raised for her project but for the association with the National Association for Irish Justice.

When she returned from this fund-raising tour she announced that £40,000 had been collected. The *Sunday News*, however, reported that only £20,000 had materialised because hundreds of Irish Americans had cancelled donations. One of the fund's trustees, Mr P.K.O'Doherty, claimed that many Americans had been annoyed by Miss Devlin's anti-American speeches. Also she had snubbed Mayor Daley of Chicago. On the date of the *Sunday News* report, 3 May 1970, less than £10,000 had been distributed in the city of Belfast. The newspaper then went into further detail.

Some of this bad publicity had by now rubbed off in Bernadette's own constituency. At first meetings were few and far between, although great enthusiasm was shown for their MP. Later, quibbles began about how she had carried out her mandate. She was reminded that she had given a great deal of her time to Derry city. There were questions about her private life which she declined to answer.

By this time our Campaign for Social Justice had been disbanded, but a chapter about Bernadette Devlin would be incomplete without mentioning two further incidents in her tempestuous career.

There was a Westminster election in February 1974. The Mid-Ulster seat was won by the Unionist John Dunlop with 26,044 votes. Ivan Cooper, SDLP, received 19,372, Bernadette Devlin, Independent Socialist 16,672 votes. Thus, as I see it, because Bernadette received less than Ivan Cooper, she can be considered to have split the Nationalist vote on this occasion.

Some time after this, an attempted assassination by shooting at the hands of Protestant paramilitaries left her and her husband for dead. They were discovered by the British Army and rushed to hospital. Both recovered slowly. Bernadette is a survivor.

9.

PROTESTANT FUNDAMENTALISM, PAISLEY AND PAISLEYISM

'BUT beyond any shadow of a doubt no single man in Northern Ireland bears a greater share of the blame for all the horror that took place than Ian Paisley, leader of the Protestant extremists'—Max Hastings, *Ulster 1969*.

This chapter, indeed this whole book, will have been worthwhile for me if it succeeds in persuading some people living outside Northern Ireland, people who probably have never set foot in the place, that they should think of the province as a region different from anywhere else in the world.

Religious fundamentalism teaches that every word in the Bible must be taken literally. This of course rules out Darwin's theory of evolution. Many of its followers accept St Paul's admonition to his converts not to have any dealings with unbelievers. Strict Protestants adhere to these teachings to the letter, avoiding where possible their Catholic fellow countrymen.

The Protestant majority in Northern Ireland is descended from Scottish and central English planters. It seems to be a racial characteristic that they cannot tolerate a dogmatic approach to religion, being Protestant to the backbone. They are so Protestant that they cannot even accept the tenets of the three main Protestant Churches, the Church of Ireland, the Presbyterian and the Methodist. They forsake these bodies in large numbers and worship in small halls dotted throughout the countryside. For years every Saturday the *Belfast Telegraph* carried advertisements for services the next day at over two hundred places of Protestant worship, three-fifths of them held by denominations and sects outside the three main Protestant Churches. By nature these people are evangelical, revivalist and puritan. That Catholics can accept so much explicit doctrine puzzles and annoys them. They even resent the constraints that Catholicism imposes on its members. These are sincerely held views, which one would not attempt to deny them.

The appointments and furnishings of Protestant churches are generally austere. The services are run in a stern and serious way, with the congregation singing enthusiastically. The Rev. Ian Paisley was not the first of his kind of Protestant minister. Apparently it does something for the psyche of some people to be bawled at by their cleric. They have in the past erected a statue in Belfast, called the 'Black Man', to one of their divines, 'Roaring' Hugh Hanna.

Some years ago I attended a Presbyterian service which happened to be a funeral. It astonished me that there were no facilities provided for the congregation to kneel down. I said to myself 'These people are too independent-minded to kneel even to God.'

When I lived in Dungannon my next-door neighbour was such a person. He was a veterinary surgeon, upright, reliable and hardworking. His day commenced an hour before mine. We had a completely happy, if somewhat formal relationship, and though he never smiled he was civil to a degree. The only time I saw him in an angry mood was the morning after a massive IRA bombing attack on the town. We both stood in the street, deep in broken masonry, debris and crunching glass, surveying the desolation of our bombed houses—for both of us it was the thirteenth time (not because of who we were, but because we lived on the main shopping street of the town). He turned to me in a fury, 'You are responsible for all this!'

I discussed religion with him once or twice. He lent me a religious book, but we were poles apart. Like most fundamentalists, he loved the blood and thunder of the Old Testament. I suggested to him that perhaps it would be more appropriate to stress the New Testament with its gentler message—after

151

all he would not depend on last year's newspapers or veterinary journals. His answer was typical, a retreat into platitudes.

Living next to him provided the opportunity for our children to meet Protestant playmates. With the segregated schooling and general apartheid of Ulster, the only Protestant children ours ever met were at the ballet classes patronised by both sections of the community. I well remember our children, when they were very young, coming to me in astonishment to tell me that on a Sunday this neighbour was not allowed to have a bottle of stout or read a newspaper.

It is not surprising that in this inflexible environment a person such as Rev. Ian Paisley would be acceptable to many. My first appreciation of his existence was when he behaved in a most scurrilous way at a religious debate in the Oxford Union. He held up the equivalent of a Catholic Host and ridiculed it. This kind of raw Protestantism I soon discovered was one of his hallmarks.

In their book, *Paisley*, Moloney and Pollak tell an almost unbelievable story—unbelievable in that anyone could go so far as to even suggest such things, of how Rev. Paisley accused Cardinal Leo Josef Suenens, Catholic Primate of Belgium, of having presided in 1970 over a Catholic theological congress in Brussels, largely attended by young women, which had turned into a celebration of sexual potency and fertility worship, 'So what the Cardinal arranged for the young, mostly girls, of Brussels, was a show of phallic worship, which symbolises the generative power contained in the semen.' All this denunciation and more was put in a letter to the Church of Ireland Dean of St Anne's Cathedral in Belfast, the reason being that the then retired Cardinal Suenens was scheduled to preach in the Cathedral.

Ian Kyle Paisley was born in Armagh in April 1926, the son of a Baptist minister. He trained to be a parson of the Reformed Presbyterian Church in Belfast, then he became the pastor of Ravenhill Evangelical Mission Church. He was ordained as a minister there. (Orthodox Presbyterians maintain that he was never properly ordained). From then onwards he revealed that he was a politician as well as a churchman.

He began to organise a group called the National Union of

Protestants which concerned itself with religion, politics and discrimination in employment—needless to say, to Protestant advantage. From the first, when he addressed meetings he was abusively anti-Catholic, which went down well with his previously brainwashed audience. Slogans like 'Popish tyranny versus Protestant tolerance' were used to advertise his meetings.

He next interested himself in Stormont politics, supporting Protestant hardliners. While supporting his favourite candidate for the 1949 elections in the New Lodge area he was involved in his first sectarian skirmish. His group was stoned in this Catholic ghetto.

He disagreed with mainstream Presbyterians in a dispute over the use of the Protestant church at Crossgar, Co. Down. He regarded its approach as too modernistic and conventional. The outcome was that he resolved when the opportunity presented itself to strike out on his own and establish the Free Presbyterian Church.

About this time he quarrelled with the Orange Order because the Protestant Lord Mayor of Belfast attended the funeral of a Catholic alderman. He still continued to speak at Orange meetings, however, sowing discord among its members. A favourite theme was his antagonism to the World Council of Churches, a Romeward move, as he saw it, although the Catholic Church was not a member, only sending observers to the World Council of Churches in later years.

On the night of 17 June 1959 an event occurred in which Rev. Paisley sowed the first of the dragons teeth for which he was responsible. Many people at this time held the opinion that the Unionist Government welcomed his confrontation tactics because it kept bitterness alive, thereby helping to consolidate Protestant voter support. Had the Stormont authorities acted on this occasion to discipline him or had the British sovereign power stepped in to warn that a line should be clearly drawn, much sorrow would have been avoided in Northern Ireland.

The occasion was a meeting of Ulster Protestant Action in Shankill Road, Belfast. They were addressed by Rev. Paisley. His speech was inflammatory and resulted in a riot in which Catholic houses were attacked and daubed with slogans.

There was also looting. He boasted later about 'a great meeting'. He was not prosecuted.

Rev. Dr Donald Soper, former president of the Methodist Church, came to Ballymena to hold a meeting. Rev. Ian Paisley and his supporters prevented him from speaking. The function ended in a riot. 'The most animal-like meeting of any I have spoken at', Dr Soper said afterwards. Rev. Paisley was taken to court and fined for disorderly behaviour, the fine being paid by a supporter because the Reverend said he would go to gaol rather than pay. From an early date his aim seemed to be a gaol sentence as it would increase his appeal in feuding Northern Ireland.

In October 1962 he led two other Free Presbyterians on a protest outing to Rome, giving as his reason the attendance of the World Council of Churches at the Second Vatican Council. Unlike the abetting Stormont authorities, the Italian Government dealt strongly with these troublemakers. They were hounded by the *carabinieri* and their passports taken from them. There was no protest possible.

In 1964 the Republicans decorated their office window in Divis Street, Belfast with the flag of the Irish Republic as part of their election campaign. Rev. Paisley threatened to march his supporters to remove it, thus forcing the police to act. It was removed on two occasions and the march did not take place. The incident however, caused militant Catholics to gather in order to repel him and his followers. There was rioting with water cannon and petrol bombs both used. Divis Street is in the heart of the Catholic 'ghetto' and for Protestants to suggest that the flags were an incitement there was nonsense.

By endorsing the formation of a new group, the Ulster Constitution Defence Committee, Paisley became associated with some very violent men. The secretary, N. Doherty, was afterwards linked by the police with the UVF and the latter's helper, W. Mitchell, was later exposed as a UVF gunman. Doherty, a close associate of Rev. Paisley, organised the Orange Defence Committee.

A further example of how not to run a country was displayed by the Unionist Government when Rev. Paisley introduced a further tactic, the counter march which, when it

154

was not nipped in the bud, led to many excesses and much violence on later occasions. The matter developed thus:

The Republicans were to hold their parade for Easter 1966. Rev. Paisley set up a counter-demonstration. The Government, hearing of this, banned the Republican parade (both demonstrations were illegal since they had not been properly notified beforehand). This generated much nationalist resentment.

Again, in 1966, Rev. Paisley led a parade through a Catholic area in Belfast, the Markets and Cromac Square. The marchers carried placards attacking the Catholic Church. There was rioting lasting several hours. Later that evening Rev. Paisley led his followers to where the Presbyterians were holding a social function. They hurled abuse at the guests, who included the Governor, Lord Erskine, and his wife. This lady later had to receive medical treatment for her heart complaint.

Newspapers as far apart as the *New York Times*, the *Frankfurter Allgemeine Zeitung*, and the *Daily Mail* of London, as early as June 1966 were calling for Paisleyism to be confronted by the Unionist Government, but nothing worthwhile was done.

In 1967 the students of Queen's University formed a Republican Club and proposed a march. Rev. Paisley assembled five hundred of his Union Jack-waving mob to block the route. The RUC re-routed the students; this was another blow against what passed for democracy in Northern Ireland.

Paisleyite obstruction of the Dungannon and Armagh civil rights marches has already been documented. He received a gaol sentence for his part in the Armagh demonstration, but was released as part of Major Chichester Clark's amnesty when he became Prime Minister.

In the same way Rev. Paisley and his followers blocked the People's Democracy marchers at Shaftesbury Square. When the Burntollet march arrived in Derry they were to be met by Rev. Paisley and his lieutenant, Major Bunting, who prepared for their arrival by holding 'a religious service'.

The explosions of March-April 1969, which Captain O'Neill claimed forced him from office, were carried out by Stevenson and McDowell among others, who were senior members of Rev. Paisley's Ulster Constitution Defence Committee and the Ulster Protestant Volunteers.

Stevenson occasionally acted as Rev. Paisley's bodyguard. Out of Ulster Protestant Action, which Rev. Paisley had helped to set up, the UVF developed.

The Cameron Report indicated that Rev. Paisley had a heavy share of direct responsibility for the Northern Ireland disorders.

The Church which he founded had by 1986 spread from Ravenhill Road to include 59 congregations, 49 of which were in Northern Ireland, and the other 10 in the Republic of Ireland, England, North America and Australia. For many years Rev. Paisley has been associated with Dr Bob Jones, the South Carolina fundamentalist preacher, who ran the Bob Jones University in Grenville, South Carolina, USA, founded by his father. The university awarded Rev. Paisley a doctorate of divinity in September 1966.

The Democratic Unionist Party, which he founded with the help of Mr Desmond Boal, a Belfast barrister, gathered together the most extreme section of the Protestant working class. Virtually all party decisions were made by himself.

He set up two fundamentalist newspapers, *The Revivalist* and the *Protestant Telegraph*. The *Revivalist's* main object was to lambaste more liberal Protestant sects and to attack Catholicism. The *Protestant Telegraph* went further. There Vatican plots were detailed, 'sexual licences' of the Catholic Church exposed. There were sneering references to nuns: 'The older nuns are raving, while the younger ones are craving'.

'Protestants have always had to stand the diabolical hate of Popery. This hate, when Rome is in power, manifests itself in open and bloody persecution. Rome is a past-master in the use of weapons of torture—the boot, the rack and the thumbscrew—and equally a past-master in the use of weapons of murder—the dagger, the poisoned cup, the bullet and any other murderous missile'.

'Do you know that the nephew of a Roman Catholic prelate attending the Second Vatican Council, during a visit to Rome, saw his uncle unholy seduced by a most unholy woman in the very heart of that most holy of all cities?'

'A spiritual Brothel (the Roman Catholic Church). When to this the same Church nurses, tolerates and promotes clerics who are not only agnostics but even blasphemers, then such a Church is nothing but a spiritual brothel, harbouring theological prostitutes and ecumenical pimps'.

'The Rome-ward rot—The whole world shall go a-whoring after the Beast. This Bible prophecy has come true in our day. All around us are the glaring evidences of the harvest of the carefully-sown seed of Romanistic apostasy'.

When the Moderator of the Presbyterian Church of Scotland met the Pope he was later described as 'drunk with the wine of the Roman whore's fornication'.

When Pope John XXIII died, Rev. Paisley said, 'This Romanish man of sin is now in hell.'

The Rev. Paisley alleged, both in the USA and in the Ulster Hall, Belfast on 17 August 1969, that the Passionist Monastery in Belfast was used as an arsenal for guns, including machine guns.

Referring to Catholics in Derry agitating for better housing he said, 'Catholics would be happy to live in a pigsty provided it was near to the Papist Chapel.' In one of his religious services he advocated taking away grants from Catholic schools and that family allowances should not be given from the fourth child onwards. In a BBC interview he called the Pope 'the Roman Anti-Christ', and the Catholic Church 'the harlot of Babylon'.

It is distasteful to have to produce these views and sayings, even for the record.

Captain Terence O'Neill summed up the Paisley phenomenon when he said, 'The activities of Paisleyism had a parallel in the rise to power of the Nazis.' He branded Paisleyite activities as 'the sordid techniques of gangsterism'—but then Captain O'Neill was unable to quell the man and was himself eventually deposed by his Unionist colleagues.

It is surely not surprising that the activities touched upon in this chapter, and they were only a fraction of what occurred, embittered many Catholics. Such recent occurrences make it difficult for many Catholics to give wholehearted allegiance to the Northern State.

10.
THE
PARAMILITARIES

THE REPUBLICANS

To study unalloyed modern Republicanism one has to look intently at its progenitors, the leaders of the 1916 Easter Rising. The closest one can approach them is to study the *Capuchin Annual* of 1966 when a Souvenir copy to celebrate the Fiftieth Anniversary of the Rising was issued. This is not an easy thing to do because the Annual of that year is a collectors' item.

These Republicans were a group of cultured intellectuals, and included a university lecturer, two poets and an author of repute. From the beginning of the Rising they were isolated in the General Post Office in O'Connell Street, Dublin. The odds against them militarily were twenty to one although it is most unlikely that they themselves calculated their disadvantage. Their gesture of defiance against Britain, and their attempt to awaken dying nationalism in their own countrymen lasted one week. Then they surrendered to prevent further bloodshed.

What the *Capuchin Annual* does, and it does it with heart-breaking poignancy, is to detail their last hours. There are photostats of their farewell letters to loved ones. The story is also told of their final contacts with their spiritual advisers, the Capuchin fathers. Consider one of their number, spending a last hour with his priest in the cell in Kilmainham jail. Because it was dark, the cell was lighted by a candle. This burned out. He did not complain. His resignation was total.

Soon they all faced an English firing squad. Even so many years afterwards, it makes the heart ache to think of poor James Connolly, one of their number, with his broken leg, being carried out, tied to a chair, and shot in a sitting position.

Setting aside for a moment the claim of some that the sacrifice of their own lives—for that is what it was, was unnecessary, and progress would have occurred without it, one cannot but honour their quixotic idealism.

It is most inappropriate, and very hurtful to the minority community, for Ulster Protestants to denigrate those men—one has in the past read with resentment vituperative comment about them. They would do well to accept that many reasonable people regard the 1916 leaders as heroes.

After this brief reflection on early modern Republicanism, we can now go on to consider the violence of the 1950s. There were raids on army barracks in England early in the decade, but the stolen guns were recovered. In 1954 successful raids were made at barracks in Armagh and Omagh. In 1956 there were bombings and shootings, mainly on the border with the Republic. Six policemen were killed. These attacks carried on till 1962, but had very little general support. The violence gradually petered out without achieving anything.

In the summer of 1969 when the police and Paisleyites started attacking Catholic districts in earnest, there was no Republican presence in Belfast to come to their aid. It has been said that there were only five or six guns in West Belfast. In December of that year the Goulding socialist type Republicans and the 'physical force' section split into the Official Republicans and the Provisional Republicans. The Provisionals established a political wing called Sinn Féin, administered by Gerry Adams, Martin McGuinness and Danny Morrison.

With the Unionist Government obstructing reforms and whole streets being laid waste by the Paisleyites, the 'Provos' gradually became a strong fighting force.

The Social Democratic and Labour Party (the SDLP) and the Northern Ireland Civil Rights Association embarked on a programme of civil disobedience. NICRA sponsored 'days of disruption' to try and bring life in the province to a halt by non-violent means. Unlike India under the leadership of Mahatma Ghandi, these efforts were poorly supported. One is forced to conclude that a more violent approach had greater appeal to the Irish temperament.

159

Republican violence then really got into its stride. Mr Roy Bradford, Minister of Development before Britain was compelled by Unionist intransigence to suspend Stormont, on 28 April 1972 declared on television that 'the Republicans had abolished Stormont'. This was, to a great degree, correct.

Here was another watershed, but the Provisional Republicans did not realise that they should have then changed gear. They ought to have known that with the reforms at last beginning and being worthwhile, killing people would achieve nothing more. The minority had clearly begun to gain equal rights. From then on, the Republicans were fighting only for a United Ireland, which, generally speaking, the world thought should be a majority political decision. The British public has always had a great regard for their Army. The killing of 'our boys' caused furious resentment. Irishmen killing each other drew far less tears. Also there was almost uninterrupted murder of men of the RUC and UDR, members of both groups being as Irish as the Provisionals. Kidnappings and the killing of personages like Lord Mountbatten have resulted in great damage to the tourist industry. The limited resources of the Irish State have been heavily strained by policing requirements along the border with Northern Ireland. None of this tragic loss of life has achieved anything.

Undoubtedly it was a gross injustice to partition Ireland. Nevertheless most unionist-minded people have lived all their lives in a divided Ireland, so to bundle them into an all-Ireland Republic against their will would be further injustice. Killing Irish policemen or UDR soldiers, because they support the status quo, is indefensible. These men and their friends passionately reject a united Ireland, and until they are persuaded otherwise they should not be harmed. As things stand now, bitterness—understandable bitterness—has continued to grow and must last at least a couple of generations even if violence were to cease forthwith.

From 1969, Republican extremism grew worse and worse, financed by robberies of banks and post offices, more frequently in the Republic of Ireland. Another source of money was from well-meaning but extremely deluded Americans locked in a time-warp situation in which their world was the world of 1916. For them, the excesses of the Black and Tans occurred only yesterday. Repeated appeals from both Fianna

Fáil and Coalition Governments to them have fallen on deaf ears.

Supporters of Unionism—even, occasionally, others, by mistake—were mown down. Although a warning was given before civilian targets were bombed, there were errors here too like what happened at the 'La Mon' restaurant, Belfast, where diners were indiscriminately slaughtered. Later the world saw on their television sets ambulance men and police collecting human remains in plastic bags after the bombing of a Belfast omibus station. The higher echelons of the judiciary were a Republican target. New Catholic members of the judiciary who, thanks to the pressure of civil rights movement had been elevated, were also murdered.

This book could be filled by lists of excesses by the Republicans in the same way as it could be filled by the injustices previously carried out by the Unionists. Unfortunately 'two wrongs do not make a right'.

Not satisfied with the level of violence, a breakaway group, the Irish National Liberation Army (INLA) was formed to indulge in more extreme excesses. Its political wing was named the Irish Republican Socialist Party (IRSP). It was Marxist, anti-British and anti-Protestant.

The Irish reputation worldwide was by now taking a severe beating, and people who regarded the Unionists and the British as the evil forces were now turning against the native Irish.

In the 'ghettos', the Republicans took over the administration of 'justice' with kangaroo courts. Knee-capping became a favourite punishment. The *Irish Times* of 20 August 1981 records the case of a teenage boy who arrived in hospital after 'a court' had decided that his arm should be sawn off at the elbow as a punishment for an alleged crime committed against the Nationalist community.

At this time I received a letter from Tom Enright of New York, a Republican sympathiser, who was our indulgent host when Father Faul and I attended the hearings on Northern Ireland at the House of Representatives in Washington. Tom told me how one day he was working in his garage when a driver pinned him between two cars, seriously damaging both his knees. 'Now,' I replied, 'you can appreciate how much I hate knee-capping.' I never heard from Tom again!

There was tarring and feathering of girls who had consorted with British soldiers, and shaving of women's heads. When a mob in West Belfast attacked someone for something they disapproved of, they often used *camáns*, the hurley stick of Ireland's historic game.

Then the depths were plumbed for me, and I am sure for many others previously proud to be Irish, when dozens of Republican prisoners smeared the walls of their cells with their own excrement. This they kept up for weeks on end. Their aim in doing this was to be treated as political prisoners. In this they were unsuccessful. Some of these later went on hunger strike and died for their convictions, which made one realise something of the depth of the tumultuous feelings that motivated them.

THE LOYALIST PARAMILITARIES

It is a most difficult task to disentangle the various Protestant organisations, and their relationships with each other, because, at times, some of them merged. At other times they presented an almost reputable facade, some members finding it useful to belong to the Unionist Party. Diffused through them all is an element of bigotry, violence and, in some cases, even murder. A common sentiment they have shared was a desire to safeguard Protestant privilege, and to apply varying degrees of pressure to squeeze out Catholic residents from predominantly Protestant housing estates. The Rev. Ian Paisley can be discovered moving on the fringe of many of them.

The Ulster Protestant League, formed first in the early thirties 'to safeguard the employment of Protestants', was at that time deeply involved in the sectarian riots of 1935. A policeman, J.W. Nixon, who had been discharged from the force, was an enthusiastic member of the Ulster Protestant League and later became a Stormont MP.

By 1956 the League, reactivated as a result of IRA activity, sheltered some very disreputable characters like E. Lusty who was also a member of the Unionist Party.

Also- in the fifties, at a meeting attended by J. McQuade (later an MP at Stormont), C. McCullough (later a Unionist senator), Frank Millar (whose son became secretary of the Unionist Party), B. Spence (brother of Gusty Spence, later

jailed for the Malvern Street murder) and the Rev. Ian
Paisley, a new organisation, Ulster Protestant Action, was
formed. These people and others organised themselves for an
attack should the IRA move against Protestants. They possessed a few guns. They also concentrated on keeping Catholics out of jobs. At a rally sponsored by Ulster Protestant
Action in June 1959 the Rev. Ian Paisley spoke to a meeting
which ended in the worst riots of that year in Belfast. In 1961
Ulster Protestant Action contested, rather unsuccessfully,
seats on Belfast Corporation.

Another organisation was subsequently set up, the Ulster
Constitution Defence Committee. It too had the Rev. Paisley
as an early member. It grew out of Ulster Protestant Action.
One of its members from the beginning was a man called Noel
Doherty. Within it, again under the influence of the Rev.
Paisley, the Protestant Volunteers was formed. These two
organisations developed side by side, the Ulster Constitution
Defence Committee, as far as one can make out, dominating.
They included in their ranks many members of the B-Specials.
They ran counter to the Orange Order which they regarded as
too meek and mild. These groups regarded journalists as
enemies, the Rev. Paisley describing them as 'the whirring
multitudes of pestiferous scribbling rodents'. The two groups
were linked when they were involved in a series of explosions
which helped to bring down Capt. O'Neill.

Another group, this time within the Orange Order, was the
Orange Defence Committee. Its main aim was to stimulate
the Order into a more aggressive stance.

The Ulster Loyalist Association was an umbrella group of
right-wing Unionist Party members, started by Mr William
Craig, MP. It was anti-Paisley. Its meetings sought to prepare
Ulster Protestants for a violent outcome of the current
troubled situation.

The Ulster Workers' Council was a splinter group of Ulster
Protestant Action. Its main success, a very large one, was to
organise the Ulster Workers' Strike in 1974, which brought
the British Labour Government to its knees, exposing for all to
see the lack of courage of Mr Harold Wilson and his Secretary
of State for Northern Ireland, Mr Merlyn Rees. It also
succeeded in breaking up the power-sharing executive created
at Sunningdale.

The Red Hand Commandos were started by a dubious East Belfast resident, John McKeague, a Free Presbyterian and a homosexual. The group was mainly composed of teenagers. It was involved in bombings and sectarian assassinations in Belfast.

The Shankill Defence Association was another group led by McKeague which was very active in the pogroms in Belfast in 1959.

The Loyal Citizens of Ulster was a small group of mainly UVF and UPV men (Ulster Protestant Volunteers) led by the eccentric Major Ronald Bunting. One of its activities was to harass and attack the Burntollet march of the People's Democracy.

Tara was set up by W. McGrath, who himself believed that the Northern Ireland Protestants were a lost tribe of Israel. McGrath was imprisoned for sexual abuses which occurred at the Kincora Boys' Home, where he was a housefather. He had been involved with Rev. Ian Paisley as far back as the Divis riots in 1964.

The Ulster Freedom Fighters were established in May 1973 and were responsible for a number of sectarian killings. They were said to be an offshoot of the UDA.

The Orange Volunteers were originally associated with Mr William Craig's Vanguard movement, and were active in the Ulster Workers' Strike and probably had ties with the UVF.

By far the most militant and lethal group in Northern Ireland since the troubles began was the Ulster Volunteer Force. The name first appeared to describe a faction providing Sir Edward Carson with his main source of manpower in opposition to the Home Rule Bill in 1922. In as far as one can risk giving such assemblies credit for it, this was an above-board grouping. However it was brought into being again in 1966 by men from the disintegrating Ulster Protestant Action. The leading lights in the formation of the UVF were William and Gusty Spence. The titular head of the group was Gusty, while William, who had previously been election agent for Mr James Kilfedder, MP, Speaker of the new Ulster Assembly, was credited with being the brains of the early movement. Many of their associates had criminal records, and they built up a large file of sectarian assassinations and bombings. Three of their number, two of whom were known to Rev. Ian Paisley, murdered a harmless young Catholic, Peter Ward, outside a public house in Malvern Street, Belfast. One of the murderers was Gusty Spence who, with the others, received a long jail sentence. After the Malvern Street murder the UVF was outlawed; the embargo was subsequently lifted, only to be re-applied in 1975.

The most horrendous desperadoes of the UVF were known as 'the Shankill Butchers'. Catholics were captured, beaten, clubbed and dispatched by having their throats cut. Police, finding the victims, hardened as they were by what had been happening in Belfast previously, were nauseated. One unfortunate victim, left for dead, survived, and after his recovery was driven around loyalist areas by police. He managed to identify his torturers who were given life sentences when they were brought to court.

The Ulster Defence Association emerged in 1971 as an umbrella organisation encompassing a number of smaller groups. After many false starts, disputes and allegations of the use of protection rackets, they were firmly taken over by A. Tyrie. They held marches in paramilitary garb. Members of the UDA were undoubtedly involved in murder and bombings. That they were never proscribed has been a source of resentment to the Catholic community, because they were by far the largest paramilitary organisation. The UDA played a large part in the successful Ulster Workers' Strike. (For the uninitiated there is another organisation operating in Northern Ireland, the Ulster Defence Regiment. This is a Government sponsored military force, almost entirely Protestant in composition, but under the direct control of the British Army. There are no prohibitions about Catholics joining the UDR. There is a great risk of assassination of its members, especially Catholics, by the Provisional IRA who regard the UDR as a special target. It is noteworthy that several members of the force have been convicted of sectarian murder of Catholics.)

One of the most repulsive and contemptible of paramilitary activities has been their strategy, if it could be dignified thus, of sectarian killings. Both sides have indulged in this but the bulk of it has been by loyalists. Innocent people, mostly working-class, going to their place of work or even after they had arrived, have been shot. In the same way, employers of either religious persuasion, who were working for the security

165

forces, have suffered in the same way. The vast majority of these people have had no firm political commitment, they were soft targets who happened to be in the wrong place at the wrong time, easily identified and murdered.

In the subculture of the two opposing paramilitary groups it has leaked out that they hold covert meetings to share out areas of influence, and sort out their differences. Both sides are said to operate protection rackets.

There are some distinguishing characteristics between them as to how they run their wars. This is presumably due to the fact that they hold different religious beliefs (or more likely in their youth have had different religious teachings). They also have a different racial origin. In recent times there has been some imitation—Protestants have lately suffered knee-capping.

Where the police in their searches have found home-made machine guns their owners have been virtually all Protestants, demonstrating that community's higher mechanical skills. Meanwhile Republican activists have mastered the intricacies of electronic bomb detonators.

When Protestants bomb a Catholic public house or social club they give no warning. The IRA setting bombs almost always give a warning which in a few cases may be late or garbled.

I was discussing the killing of a Catholic with a Unionist notability in my local area. His concern was not so much for the murdered man as for the foolish boy who had spoilt his life by having to undergo a long prison sentence.

The ten heroic Republican foot soldiers, in what I would describe as their misplaced idealism, fasted to death. Protestant hunger strikers gave up in two or three days when they realised that their aims would not be achieved. This has happened on many occasions, and can now be regarded as the norm.

11.
A SHORT DIARY
OF EVENTS

Since the aim of this book is as much to present a point of view as to tell a story, precise dates are few and far between, although exact references are available. Where I suspect that the person mentioned might later indignantly deny what I have stated or suggested, names of newspapers and dates are added. The Irish are notoriously critical and difficult to please, especially in political matters, thus I do not expect my views to be shared by all, or even by some of my own side.

It would be impossible to give a full history of all the relevant events between 24 May 1963 when the Homeless Citizens League was formed in Dungannon, and 26 March 1973, when we wound up our own Campaign for Social Justice in Northern Ireland. We ceased our endeavours after William Whitelaw's White Paper, which forecast the 1973 Constitution Act, thereupon passing future endeavours to the politicans.

To tackle this chapter, and having to leave out so much, is intensely frustrating. Indeed it is unfair to a great many people whose personal suffering, struggles and heroism must go unrecorded. For completeness, and because of their importance, I have included the Sunningdale Conference and the Workers' Strike in this chapter. They were both later events.

During most of the time covered here, horrible sectarian killings took place, mostly of Catholics. There is no way it would be possible to document them all here, since they occurred from the beginning to the end of our story.

For more details of the events I list here it will be necessary to consult the books given in the bibliography. In some cases I have added details where they are needed to fill in the picture, and to make my case.

1963   Captain Terence O'Neill (later Lord O'Neill of the Maine) had been Prime Minister of the Stormont Government since March 1963. At that time the Tories were in power in Britain, the Prime Minister being Sir Alec Douglas-Home.

1964   15 February 1964, Mr Harold Wilson said that Labour, when in power, would bring in the Racial Discrimination and Incitement Bill and make whatever minor amendments might be necessary to it.

16 October, Mr Wilson became Prime Minister. The Ulster Protestant Volunteers were formed in that year by Mr Noel Doherty, a colleague of Rev. Ian Paisley, as a working-class paramilitary organisation.

1965   14 January, Capt. O'Neill met Sean Lemass, the Taoiseach of the Republic of Ireland, at Stormont. This was very badly received by many Protestants.

3 May, Sir Frank Soskice, the British Home Secretary in the Labour administration, excluded Northern Ireland from the Race Relations Act.

1966   The UVF was re-formed in May 1966 and proscribed in July of the same year.

1967   27 January, the Bishop of Ripon, Dr John Moorman, was forbidden to speak in St Anne's Cathedral, Belfast because the Orange Order objected to him as a noted ecumenist, and because of the risk of civil disorder if he was granted permission to give an address.

29 January, the Northern Ireland Civil Rights Association was formed.

On 27 April Capt. O'Neill explained that he found it necessary to dismiss Mr Harry West because, in spite of his advice, Mr West had purchased a farm at a time when he was in possession of privileged information that part of the farm was to be used to develop St Angelo Airport. This development was to be assisted by Government funds.

1968   21 June, Austin Currie squatted in a house in Caledon which had been allocated to a nineteen-year-old unmarried Protestant girl, the secretary of a

1968   solicitor who was an Armagh Unionist councillor. Austin was protesting against this and the eviction of a Catholic family from a similar house a few days before.

24 August, the first civil rights march was held from Coalisland to Dungannon.

5 October, the civil rights march in Derry.

9 October, the People's Democracy (the PD) was formed.

11 December, Capt. O'Neill sacked Mr William Craig. The latter had committed many indiscretions; the banning of the civil rights march in Derry on 5 October and subsequent bans on further Derry marches were inexcusable. When he advocated a Unilateral Declaration of Independence for Ulster Capt. O'Neill was forced to act. After leaving office Craig frequently advocated UDI for Northern Ireland.

1969   4 January, the Belfast to Derry People's Democracy march reached Burntollet. That evening the barricades went up in the Bogside, followed by rioting and the use of water cannons.

In January the Cameron Enquiry was set up by Capt. O'Neill, 'to investigate the causes of violence since 5 October 1968 and the conduct and aims of those bodies involved in the current agitation'. A week after the setting up of the Enquiry Mr Brian Faulkner resigned from the Stormont Government. (The results of the Enquiry were published in September 1969. It criticised William Craig, Rev. Ian Paisley and his associates, and the RUC for its handling of the situation. It supported the minority's accusations of housing discrimination and discrimination in appointments to public bodies. It condemned the manipulation of local government electoral boundaries. Lord Cameron further stated that he understood nationalist objections to the B-Specials.)

11 February, Capt. O'Neill's bid 'to woo moderate support' collapsed when the executive of the Unionist Party, meeting in Glengall Street, Belfast, rejected a Catholic, Mr Louis Boyle, as a candidate for the South Down seat at Stormont. Mr Boyle was one of only two or three Catholics in the Unionist Party.

24 February, at the general election to Stormont, Rev. Ian Paisley improved his position. Capt. O'Neill did not do well. John Hume was elected to the Foyle seat in Derry, beating Eddie McAteer. Ivan Cooper won in mid-Derry.

19 April, there was one of the many riots in Derry: 'On that day seven or eight policemen smashed down the door and forced their way into the house of Samuel Joseph Devenney, aged 43 years. They beat him with batons on the head and kicked him. Samuel Devenney's son Fred was also hit with a baton. A policeman hit Cathy on the legs with his baton, another kicked her. Another of his daughters tried to lie on top of Samuel to protect him. She was lifted off by the hair. Samuel was then seized and thrown across the floor. His face, head and hands were covered with blood.' (Extract from the inquest held when Samuel Devenney died of coronary thrombosis some three months later.)

30 March, an electricity sub-station at Castlereagh was blown up.

17 April, Bernadette Devlin was elected to Westminster.

20 April, an electricity pylon at Kilmore was damaged by an explosion.

21 April, the main outlet to the Silent Valley reservoir, the principal water supply to Belfast, was blown up.

24 April, a water main at Dunadry was disjointed by a bomb.

(On 16 February 1970 five men were charged with blowing up the water main at Dunadry, near Belfast. The Crown claimed that the pipe was blown up to cause disruption in order to bring down the Prime Minister, Capt. O'Neill, and to promote the release from prison of Rev. Ian Paisley and Mr Ronald Bunting. The defendants were John McKeague, William Owens, Derek Elwood, Trevor Gracey and Frank Mallon. Another UPV member, S. Stevenson, was associated with a man named T. McDowell in various bombings including one at Ballyshannon in the Republic of Ireland, where McDowell was himself killed by his own bomb. Stevenson, when he was brought before the courts, admitted his involvement in various bombings. He pleaded guilty, declaring that he was the Chief of Staff of the UVF. He also agreed that he helped to form the Ulster Protestant Volunteers at the behest of the Rev. Ian Paisley. Details of all these manoeuvres are to be found in the book *Paisley* by Maloney and Pollak.)

28 April, Capt. O'Neill resigned and was followed in office by Major James Chichester-Clarke.

31 July, a rent and rates strike was begun in Dungannon.

2 August, a vicious riot occurred in Belfast when a crowd of more than a thousand Paisleyites, flinging stones, bottles and other missiles, laid siege to Catholic occupied flats at Unity Walk. They were opposed by the Catholics. A police force, inadequate in size, could not cope with the disorder. A policeman was stabbed.

12 August, the Apprentice Boys march in Derry was held. By right it should have been banned. John Hume and his associates pressed the then Minister of Home Affairs, Mr Robert Porter, QC, as well as Capt. O'Neill to that effect without success. The Protestant marchers threw down pennies on the Bogside district. The Bogsiders replied with nails and stones. There was rioting and the 'battle' of the Bogside had begun. 'Free Derry' was established, the first no-go area. By now CS gas was being used by the police and petrol bombs by the rioters. After three days the police were exhausted and on 14 August Major Chichester-Clark called in the troops.

Also on 12 August the 'battle' of Belfast began in the Falls Road area with attacks on Hastings Street police station. The B-Specials were called out. Barricades were set up and fires lighted on the roads. Petrol bombs and broken paving stones were hurled at the police. The police then attacked the mobs. Protestants from the Shankill joined in. By now many buildings were on fire. The shooting then started, probably from both sides, though it is agreed there were only a few guns and little ammunition in Catholic hands. The

1969 B-Specials went into action on the Protestant side. The police brought out their armoured cars, mounted with heavy machine guns. These raced up and down the Falls Road shooting wildly. The police, who were being sniped at, panicked and sprayed machine gun fire indiscriminately. A nine-year-old Catholic child was hit and had half his head blown away.

In Ardoyne people were sheltering behind barricades made of looted timber, steel and commandeered lorries and buses. Police and Protestants, working in unison, were on the attack. Here also there were many fires. There were a few Catholic snipers. Many people received bullet wounds from police fire.

During the night six men died in Belfast and over one hundred were injured. More than a hundred homes had been destroyed and more than a dozen factories. Some factories were burned to silence snipers who were operating on their roofs. Three hundred houses were damaged by petrol bombs. One Protestant was killed. The next day the Army was brought in. It was welcomed by the Catholics.

There was no army presence in Ardoyne. Thus the Protestants attacked and burned houses in several streets. In the Clonard area they destroyed all the houses in the Catholic Bombay Street. When the Army personnel first arrived they were totally confused and only of limited help. They, and not the police, offered some protection to Catholics. The police sided with the Protestants in most areas. Only one soldier was slightly injured in the whole 'battle'. The Army claimed that the soldiers did not fire a single shot in the entire two days of fighting. The Catholics were the main sufferers in the whole episode.

At this time Jack Lynch mobilised a few army reserves and army emergency medical centres on his side of the 'border'. He also demanded a United Nations peace keeping force. By now many Protestants were certain that they were about to be invaded from the South. Major Chichester-Clark promised that the police would investigate police atrocities.

It was after dark one evening at this time when Bríd

1969   Rodgers, John Donaghy and I, as members of the executive of NICRA, arrived to attend a meeting in the Catholic redoubt in Leeson Street, Belfast. It was held in the Long Bar. The atmosphere was one I had never experienced before or since.

Consider these people, involved, whether they liked it or not, in continuous rioting for several days on end, and menaced by the Protestants, but now safely behind the barricades with all fear and reserve gone.

After a close scrutiny by the vigilantes we were admitted to this district of tiny outmoded kitchen houses, teeming with life, full of bonhomie. The children were still playing on the streets, little groups of adults quietly conversing.... The visit convinced me, if I needed convincing, that our civil rights work was worth while. That work could no longer be seen as the production, in lonely isolation, of dry statistics for the Campaign to publish. Here were the reasons for it all. It was satisfying, too, to know that, compared with previous upheavals in Northern Ireland at least this time the world could not dismiss what was happening in Belfast or elsewhere as 'those wild Irish fighting again'. Now people who mattered could lay their hands on *The Plain Truth*, the first of many publications in which the Campaign and others traced the reasons for what was now happening (see Appendix and Select Bibliography).

19 August, Major Chichester-Clark met Messrs Wilson and Callaghan in London. Two senior civil servants from London were sent to Belfast to supervise affairs. An Enquiry into the police and the B-Specials under Lord Hunt was set up.

20 August, the British Government made the Downing Street Declaration in which equal rights were acknowledged, a Central Housing Authority was set up, local government was to be reformed and an Ombudsman appointed. It was affirmed also that discrimination in employment would be ended.

10 September, the army built the 'Peace Line' barricade—a minor Berlin Wall of steel between the Falls and Shankill Roads.

10 October, Lord Hunt reported. The B-Specials were disbanded and the RUC disarmed. Sir Arthur Young was put in charge of the police, who were to be denied armoured cars with machine guns. The RUC uniform was changed. The slow improvement of standards in the RUC had at last begun.

12 October, the Hunt Report had produced an electric effect on the Shankill Protestants who organised and started to move down towards the centre of Belfast where Catholic Unity Flats were situated. The police and army halted them. A fierce battle ensued. They shot two policemen, one died, a constable, Victor Arbuckle. The army shot two Protestants. The army had twenty-two men wounded, sixteen by gunfire. Their tolerant attitude towards the Protestant community was forced that night to change because of the intensity of the battle. The Shankill had learnt the price of excess.

A Tribunal of Enquiry under Lord Justice Scarman was set up to investigate the riots in July and August and the sabotage of the water supply in April. Its main hearings took place later, during the year 1971. Those various investigations were not a substitute for what should really have been done, which was to abolish Stormont, since without this nothing could really change. What subsequently happened supports this contention. However, Lord Scarman looked meticulously into the various matters which came within the ambit of his Enquiry. He sat for many months.

When he investigated Dungannon he heard of B-Specials on the nights of 11 and 13 August running amok with rifles and machine guns. He heard how no prosecutions were carried out against Orangemen who tore down civil rights banners in Dungiven on 28 June 1969.

The Scarman tribunal heard, on 11 May 1971, that the arms register, which had a record of guns and ammunition issued to the B-Specials in Dungannon in August 1969, was burnt.

John McKeague, chairman of the Shankill Defence

Association, told the Tribunal that he directed the use of guns, petrol bombs and stones against Catholics on the Crumlin Road on the night of 15 August 1969.

Only three specific incidents are described here. The files of the *Irish News* should be consulted to appreciate the width and depth of the Enquiry, and to learn the facts. Lord Scarman, himself British, was commissioned by a British Government to sum up an entirely Irish situation and present findings which the British Government would accept.

In November the Republicans split into the Official IRA (Cathal Goulding, Billy McMillen, Thomas McGiolla, Malachy McGurran), and the Provisional IRA (Sean MacStiofáin, Billy McKee, Daithi O'Conaill, Joe Cahill, Francis Card, Joe Martin, Seamus Twomey). The 'Officials', who were strongly Marxist, were nicknamed the 'Stickies' because their paper Easter Lily was held in place by an adhesive backing, whereas that of the 'Provos' was secured with the traditional pin.

The 'Provos' continued with the aim of a thirty-two county Republic to be achieved by violence.

In January the UDR was formed, as a unit of the British Army. Neither side was pleased.

24 January, part of the leader in the *Irish News* went as follows:

On January 19th two members of the Peoples' Democracy were charged, following a four-month prison sentence on Mr Niall Vallely, with disorderly behaviour in Armagh last November. Meanwhile, the person or persons who shot John Gallagher in Armagh in the sight of hundreds of people go free. On January 19th and 20th no less that fifty-one individuals in Enniskillen were charged arising out of incidents in the town on July 26th last. Meanwhile the people who burnt over four hundred homes in Belfast; who burnt and looted sixty-four Catholic owned public houses; who were responsible for the death, among others, of a nine-year old child, go free. On January 22nd the indescribably objectionable Public Order Bill was driven through that supposedly revising body, the Senate Committee, a mammoth list of seventy-four amendments from the Opposition having been totally rejected.

In other words the minority was entirely dissatisfied with the reluctant reformers of the Stormont Parliament.

18 June, Mr Wilson lost the election to Edward Heath. Mr Reginald Maudling was made Home Secretary. At this time the Stormont Government brought in a new measure which laid down a mandatory minimum six months jail term for rioting or disorderly behaviour, to the great anger of Sir Arthur Young who was trying to settle things down. One of the first victims was Frank Gogarty, chairman of NICRA. The new law was repealed on 17 December.

27 June, there was very serious rioting in many areas of Belfast with gun battles in Ardoyne and Short Strand, between Catholics and Protestants. Seven people were killed. There were incendiary attacks on shops in central Belfast, looting on the Crumlin Road. Ballymurphy police station was taken over by rioters.

3 July, the army raided a house in the Falls Road area. They found arms and ammunition but were pinned down by rioters. Pitched battles; buses burned; C.S. gas; nail bombs; petrol bombs; hand grenades.

A curfew was imposed. The army was firing continuously. Four civilians were shot and one killed by an army vehicle. When morning came the curfew was not lifted and the population claimed that the army had decided to starve them out. House-to-house searches produced arms but also great bitterness among the population because of the destruction caused. The Provisionals received a flood of recruits and were now regarded as the defenders of the general public in Catholic areas.

21 August, the SDLP was formed.

23 September, Sir Arthur Young resigned, because of right-wing pressure. (His work was generously praised by Gerry Fitt, Ivan Cooper and Paddy Devlin in Stormont on 11 November 1970.)

1971   10 January, trouble started in Ballymurphy. Rioting lasted for a week. There were house-to-house searches.

3 February, there were army searches in Clonard and Ardoyne. This caused severe rioting for two nights. This spread to New Lodge Road. On 10 March three Scottish soldiers were shot after being lured to a public house.

18 February, in Stormont John Hume said, 'of the 108 registered gun clubs only about 40 are affiliated to recognised sporting organisations. Thirty out of the 108 have been formed in the past eighteen months.' Many guns belonged to the recently disbanded B-Specials. The great majority of non-sporting guns in Northern Ireland were held by Protestants.

27 February, two policemen were shot dead in Ardoyne. This was caused by alleged police partiality on the day before when they associated with the Protestant rioters, joking with them and arresting twenty Catholic women and six Catholic men.

28 March, Major Chichester-Clark resigned and was replaced by Mr Brian Faulkner.

13 April, Protestants broke through a police cordon and attacked Catholics. The Army fired on this Protestant crowd. That night St Matthews Catholic church was the target. Soldiers were attacked with petrol bombs.

30 April, the Minister of State for Home Affairs, Mr John Taylor, a hardline Unionist, doubtless made more hardline after he was gunned down on an Armagh Street by the Official IRA, revealed in Stormont that 102,112 guns were held on licence in Northern Ireland.

5 May, Mr Taylor stated that 11,953 weapons were held legally in the police division of North and East Down; 818 in Central Belfast; 764 in Springfield and Andersonstown; 1,375 in Shankill, Oldpark and Ligoniel; in Antrim Road, Greencastle, Newtownabbey, 2,970; in Newtownards Road, Dundonald, Holywood, 3,650; Castlereagh to Dunmurry, 3,632; South Down and South East Armagh, 7,065; Mid-Down and East Armagh, 8,434; East Tyrone and West Armagh, 9,085;

1971   Fermanagh, 6,838; Mid, South and West Tyrone, 6,987; North West Tyrone, North West Londonderry including Derry City, 5,110; North, Mid and South Derry, 10,283; North and part of Mid Antrim, 9,628; Mid-Antrim and South Antrim, 11,725.

22 May, after Catholic girls employed at Gallaghers tobacco factory had been locked in a lavatory and later assaulted by a Paisleyite gang, a riot developed in the New Lodge Road area. Paddy Kennedy, describing events in the Stormont Parliament, told how a ferocious attack was made on the people by the soldiers, using batons and rubber bullets. Mr Kennedy pointed out that out of a work force of almost 5,000 at Gallaghers, there was only one Catholic male employee. These were Scottish soldiers who have always had a poor reputation for impartiality and restraint in the Northern Ireland situation. It was claimed by Gerry Fitt that the soldiers at the riot declared, 'You got three of ours, now we are going to get you.' This was a reference to the murder of three Scottish soldiers at Ligoniel on 10th March.

7 and 8 July, severe riots in the Bogside. Two unarmed Catholics, Seamus Cussack and Desmond Beattie were shot dead. The SDLP issued an ultimatum, that unless the Government set up an independent enquiry they would leave Stormont. It did not, so they left. This was really only part of the reason for their going. By that date not one of the reforms had been sincerely accepted by the Unionist Party or the Unionist Government. The Downing Street Declaration was so far a Declaration without conviction. This point of view was backed up by the Foreign Minister of the Republic, Dr Patrick Hillery, speaking at the United Nations.

7 August, severe rioting in Belfast.

9 August, internment introduced. 342 men were interned, mostly republicans of the 1952 vintage and civil rights leaders. (By 8 February 1972, 750 were interned. 2,447 persons had been arrested under the Special Powers Act since August 1971. Most were Catholics.) Internment led to very severe rioting. In

1971   Belfast, where Protestants intervened in force, whole streets were burned down, about 300 houses in all. Again there were barricades, bombs, CS gas and gunfire. There was rioting in Belfast, Newry, Derry, Armagh, Strabane and Crossmaglen as well as elsewhere. Eight thousand Catholics fled to the Republic. Three thousand were housed in eight army camps, in convents, schools and monasteries. Gormanstown camp was one of the largest sites. The police training centre in Templemore was also used. Eighty-two Protestant refugees went to Liverpool. In the two years up to internment 66 people had been killed. In the 17 months after internment 610 were killed, including 146 soldiers. Some internees were treated with unspeakable brutality. It would be an injustice to the men who suffered if I attempted to summarise. The Campaign for Social Justice's *Mailed Fist*, Andrew Boyd's book *Brian Faulkner*, and even the British *Sunday Times* of 17 October and 24 October gave full details and should be read. The British set up one of their Enquiries, the Compton Enquiry. Only one of the internees attended personally to give evidence, so the conclusions are thus diminished but nevertheless, give much food for thought.

12 August, there were heavy black headlines in the *Irish News*—'Bryson Street Dies in Scorched Earth Exit'. This introduced one of the most bizarre incidents of the 'troubles'. Belfast had an acute shortage of housing accommodation yet the situation was so bad that Bryson Street had to be eliminated. It was an unbelievable sight as almost one hundred comfortable, eminently habitable dwellings were reduced to charred ruins or wrecked so that they could never be occupied by the other side. The army stood guard on one side and the RUC on the other as vans, lorries and forklift truck were used to move the furniture, the aim being to produce a 'no man's land' separating the minority Newtownards Road pocket at St Matthew's Church from the Unionist section of the area. Both sides approved of the action because tension and disturbances had been a feature since the beginning of 1969.

1971　　From August onwards in Derry it became increasingly difficult for the army to enter the Bogside due to barricades. Eventually the area became a 'no-go' area for the army. The Republicans controlled the area.

In September the Democratic Unionist Party was formed. Also formed at that time was the UDA. It has been alleged that some of its members formed the dreaded UFF (the UVF had been in existence since 1966). The police were also re-armed about this time.

30 September, a Belfast jury failed to reach a verdict on the first prosecution under the new Prevention of Incitement to Hatred Act. Before the City Commission in Belfast were John McKeague, Hugh Close and Hugh Johnston. They were accused of publishing offensive songs in a book entitled *Orange Loyalist Songs 1971*, which was quoted at the trial thus: 'Taigs were made to kill, Hell is up the Falls, Falls was made for burning, Skulls were made to crack'. The Act was never made use of again, the reason for its failure being that the Bill was badly drafted. There was a requirement to prove that the person intended to stir up hatred. The mistake was to leave it to the jury to decide whether there was or was not deliberate incitement. Not till March 1987 was a new Bill placed on the Statute Book in which it was only necessary to prove that hatred was likely to be stirred up.

In October the assembly of the Northern Irish People (the Dungiven Parliament) was set up.

In the last days of 1971 and into 1972 the British authorities attempted to muzzle the press in its reporting of Northern Irish affairs. The subtle phrase 'balanced reporting' was used. A group of BBC producers and journalists, who stated that they were remaining anonymous because of fear of dismissal, called for a total ban on their staff visiting Northern Ireland 'if BBC censorship and pressures were not lifted immediately'. The BBC withdrew permission for the reporters and producers to talk to some civil rights leaders and some Roman Catholic priests.

Independent Television was experiencing the same difficulties. The *Irish Post*, the *Irish Press* and the *Sunday*

1971   *Times* all reacted strongly, as did the *Universe*. The matter had come to a head when Mr Reginald Maulding, the Home Secretary, attempted to ban an enquiry programme in Northern Ireland, presided over by Lord Devlin. Mr Brian Faulkner did his best to prevent the programme going out, but eventually it was transmitted.

1972   13 January, it was announced that all undergraduate work at Magee University College, Derry, was to cease and all students were to be transferred to the New University of Ulster at Coleraine. (This was subsequently countermanded.)

18 January, a six-hour search by hundreds of British troops took place in Belfast. They were seeking seven internees who had escaped from the prison ship *Maidstone* in Belfast harbour. Doors were forced in with crowbars and sledgehammers, especially in the Markets area. None of the escapers was found.

25 January, Magilligan Strand march. This march was organised by the Derry CRA. 4,000 anti-internment marchers were prevented from approaching Magilligan camp. The soldiers fired rubber bullets, often at point-blank range. Twenty people were injured by truncheons. Some were kicked and batoned on the ground. Ivan Cooper, MP, was hit on the head by a plastic bullet. John Hume and Mr McAteer condemned the army as brutal.

30 January, Bloody Sunday. A civil rights march to be addressed by Ivan Cooper, Bernadette Devlin and Fenner Brockway was arranged. As it progressed through Catholic parts of Derry a stone-throwing riot occurred. The army pinioned the marchers between two groups of men. The Paratrooper group opened fire and killed thirteen marchers and injured twelve others. The army alleged that they were first fired on but this is very, very doubtful. Another British Enquiry was set up, the Widgery Enquiry. The Catholic community was so incensed that at first they were tempted to boycott the hearings. Eventually wiser counsels prevailed. By attending they forced Lord Widgery into an even more contemptible set of conclusions.

1972   12 February, Mr William Craig formed the Ulster Vanguard Movement, promoting the use of the Ulster flag which became more popular with militant Protestants than the Union Jack. Mr Craig declared that he 'was establishing a loyalist army ready for action if the need arose'. The new movement had support from the Harland and Wolff shipyard workers, the B-Specials, the Orange Lodges, the Apprentice Boys of Derry, some young Unionist Associations and the Ulster Defence Association. Paramilitary garb was worn by some. Not one of these loyalists was ever interned.

After 'Bloody Sunday' the violence escalated. The economic life of Northern Ireland was now severely affected. The British Government informed Mr Faulkner that they were going to take over security. He resigned.

24 March, Edward Heath suspended Stormont and installed William Whitelaw as Secretary of State. Both these acts were, even at this late hour, greatly appreciated by the minority.

Violence continued in April and May. On 29 May the Official Republicans declared a truce but the Provisionals did not.

7 July, William Whitelaw met S. MacStiofáin, D. O'Connaill, Martin McGuinness, Seamus Twomey, G. Adams and Ivor Bell together with a legal adviser Myles Shevlin. A truce was arranged. This only lasted two days and was followed by even greater violence.

21 July, Bloody Friday. A huge bombing blitz by the IRA of Belfast city centre overwhelmed the various organised forces, and was horrible butchery. Men shovelling human remains into plastic bags were seen on television.

31 July, 'Operation Motorman' was a mass invasion of the 'no-go' areas by the army, which at that time stood at over 20,000 men in Northern Ireland. The army consolidated its position in Derry and Belfast by commandeering large buildings. This reduced the number of explosions and shooting incidents.

1973   8 March, the British Government had promised a poll every ten years to discover the degree of desire for the status quo or a United Ireland, the Border Poll. The first was held on 8 March. There was a boycott by the Nationalist population. The vast majority of those who voted favoured the Union, and 57.2% of the electorate voted. The results indicate that up to 40% of the electorate did not wish to remain linked to the United Kingdom. 6,463 voted for Northern Ireland to join the Republic. There were 5,973 spoiled votes. Total electorate 1,035,000. 591,820 voted for union with Britain.

The Republicans and the SDLP both advised their followers to boycott the poll. There were some who did not agree with this advice because, if followed, the opportunity for a test of real opinions would be lost.

In March William Whitelaw proposed that there should be an Assembly set up comprising seventy-eight members with a power-sharing Executive. Westminster was to retain control over law and order and elections. There was provision in the proposals for a Council of Ireland to establish the existence of an 'Irish Dimension'.

The new proposals first appeared in the form of a White Paper in March 1973 and were implemented by the Northern Ireland Constitution Act which repealed most of the extant clauses of the Government of Ireland Act, 1920. It was this particular initiative which made us in the Campaign decide that we had achieved our main aims, and that our publicity work should come to an end.

28 June, elections were held for the Assembly. Those in favour of the proposal won 51 seats, the opposition 27 seats. Mr Faulkner led the pro-Assembly Unionists. The SDLP participated although internment was still in existence. The Executive had 11 members—6 Unionists, 4 SDLP, 1 Alliance. There were 5 non-voting members—2 SDLP, 2 Alliance and 1 Unionist. Mr Faulkner was the Chief Executive; his deputy, Gerry Fitt.

1973   In December, in order to discuss the Council of Ireland, a special meeting was held in Sunningdale, England. The general body of Unionists would not accept the Sunningdale idea and Mr Faulkner took with him to England those Unionists who did. He renamed them the Unionist Party of Northern Ireland, UPNI. The Alliance Party would assert that, at the various negotiations at Sunningdale, the SDLP pushed the Unionists too hard on the Irish Dimension, and were insensitive to Unionist psychological stresses and strains stemming from the loss of their Parliament at Stormont.

1974   In January William Whitelaw was replaced by Francis Pym. He was a poor substitute since he appeared to have no comprehension of the Northern Ireland situation. In February, because of the miners' strike in Britain, Edward Heath called a general election which he lost to Mr Wilson.

14 May, the Ulster Workers' Council was set up by Mr Harry Murray from the Harland and Wolff shipyard. These people organised a well-prepared strike. After 14 days the Executive collapsed because there was paralysis of many parts of the economy. Electricity was severely rationed, as was petrol. Those workers who wanted to attend their places of employment were intimidated and many factories closed.

The new Labour Government failed miserably to confront the enormous pressure and aggressions which were present for all to see. The army's efforts to control the workers were restrained from above and Britain capitulated. This was a very serious turning-point in the affairs of Northern Ireland. It would perhaps have been too much to expect a more determined reaction from Mr Wilson.

Indeed, things for the Catholic minority did not begin to move again until the Tories returned to power and Margaret Thatcher took charge.

ENVOI

THERE are people living in the Republic of Ireland, especially in the remoter parts, who talk nostalgically about 'the fourth green field', and think that Ireland should be united forthwith. Pluralistic ideas are beyond many of their spokesmen. They are so steeped in Irish nationalism that they are incapable of making observations on the situation here without annoying the Ulster Protestant community, even citizens who are neither Orangemen nor Unionists. I can assure them that a simplistic approach has no place in the thinking about Northern Ireland. It is a very particular, even peculiar, place.

It should be appreciated by outsiders that in order to survive, many Catholics have had to conform to a small degree to the ethos of the majority. This makes them slightly different people from their brothers and sisters down south.

The Protestant majority have developed, over the years, their own inward-looking, isolationist attitude, referred to as their 'siege mentality'. Just as it is a safe assumption that every Northern Irish Catholic suffers to some extent from an inferiority complex, in the same way every Protestant feels to some extent threatened. This explains many of the things they have done, and still do. The fact that they feel Irish and British at the same time does not discomfort them.

The least civilised Protestants and Catholics have each their own completely unacceptable solution to the Irish problem. The Protestants suggest that all Catholics should be expelled to the Republic. The Catholics propose that the Ulster Protestants should emigrate to Scotland. It would surely be a lesser place, a mediocre province, if either of these were to happen.

The stern resolve of the Protestant community to remain as they are has been the cause of all the trouble in Northern Ireland. They have indulged in mass religious discrimination to counter the menace, as they see it, of the increasing number of Catholics in the province who would eventually vote them into a united Ireland. To understand this is not to excuse, in any way, the grinding injustices they imposed to keep Ulster as it is.

Because they see it as a further impulse towards the equality of the two communities most nationalists have welcomed the initiative of Dr Garret FitzGerald, his colleagues, and the Labour members of the Coalition Government, who negotiated the Anglo-Irish Agreement. Following it, it is a great comfort to feel that Charles Haughey's Government of Fianna Fáil has played its part, and comforting, too, to see that the two sovereign Governments have already achieved some small success by working together.

There is one small group of people in the Republic of Ireland whose approach to the Anglo-Irish Agreement causes resentment amongst Northern Catholics. They are those who, probably to curry favour with some group, have made it clear that they disapprove of the way the Agreement was negotiated, because the Unionists were not consulted as the negotiations proceeded.

Unionists already had their opportunity to contribute to the solution of all our problems, three chances in fact, which they rejected. Firstly they turned down the Sunningdale Agreement. Later, there was a Convention in 1975 to negotiate power-sharing which they aborted. Again, trying for the third time, Mr (later Sir) Humphrey Atkins's Conference in 1980 was torpedoed by them.

It would have been too much to expect that the pragmatic, no-nonsense Margaret Thatcher, upon whom they had so often heaped abuse, should have wasted time arguing with them as the Agreement was negotiated. They are people who for over sixty years had steamrollered opposition of even the gentlest kind.

It is obvious that the present situation of bitterness, cruelty and murder will have to pass. Sooner or later the two communities will have to do what they find most difficult; compromise, and sincerely co-operate in running their own affairs together.

The police, trying to overcome their more than inauspicious past, will have to continue to endeavour to be fair to all sections and to react very strongly to those of their number who show bias, while the minority community must acknowledge generously police evenhandedness, because without a successful police force this country would not be a place even to contemplate living in.

Considering the weakness of purpose of past Labour Governments we can thank our lucky stars that in Margaret Thatcher we have a person of resolve who would never, as Mr (later Sir) James Callaghan did, increase the Westminster seats available to Northern Ireland from twelve to seventeen, in exchange for a morsel of political power.

Even at this late stage, in certain areas of employment religious discrimination against Catholics is still almost total. The Fair Employment Agency has not yet been provided with real teeth. The British Government is optimistic indeed if it expects real progress when these discrepancies are still occurring.

The second of the two scraps of paper (see p. 60) which Patricia always refused to surrender to the Campaign for Social Justice files must surely point a moral. It is a press photograph taken in the very early days of the Campaign, before the Northern Ireland Civil Rights Association was formed. It shows a surgeon, John Ward, a gynaecologist, John Watson, John Donaghy, Jack Hassard, Patsy McCoey and Patricia, and also among the group Ken Magennis, later the Westminster Unionist MP. They were on their way as a delegation of the Dungannon Community Council to see Mr Brian Faulkner.

Here were responsible Protestants and Catholics going together to Stormont to petition Mr Faulkner to abolish the Dungannon Urban Council because of its misdeeds. At that time Ken Magennis was an involved and concerned united community man. Now as a Unionist representative he feels he should take a completely one-sided line.

Surely we are all entitled to seek an explanation and the explanation should not be sought from Ken Magennis alone but from deep in our own hearts.

It has been noted more than once that the middle class has been slow to support civil rights. To a degree this is an excusable human instinct. The same tendency has been seen among the blacks both of the USA and of Africa. Presumably after fighting their way out of the 'ghetto' or from some less auspicious environment, and having achieved middle-class status, they want to forget that they, or perhaps their parents, were members of the dispossessed.

Looking back over these last tragic years there is one inescapable reality. It is this. Complaints by the minority, and later full documentation of the facts by our Campaign for Social Justice, were not acted upon by the politicians of either of the two main British parties when they were in power. Had they intervened promptly to put things right in Northern Ireland at a time when the Republican movement was still a small rump, the grim price that has already been paid, both in lives and money, in an attempt to heal the situation, might have proved unnecessary. Further, delay has so embittered many people, and so clouded their judgment, that they have not been prepared to accept that considerable improvement has already taken place.

Finally, this farewell must extend to that little band of amateurs, who by choice did not associate with any political party but rode the tiger when they came together to form the Campaign for Social Justice in Northern Ireland. Being true amateurs, these people did not count the cost. The Campaign was run from start to finish on an absurdly small sum of money which was collected by Peter Gormley and carefully husbanded by our treasurer, Conor Gilligan. Printing and postage were the only two items on which Conor would agree to spend money.

There was a warmth, dedication and even sometimes humour in our very serious and responsible deliberations—taking part were tired men after a full day's work, sometimes even splitting hairs in their efforts to be absolutely fair and absolutely accurate. Patricia and I salute them.

Appendix I

NORTHERN IRELAND
THE PLAIN TRUTH
(SECOND EDITION)

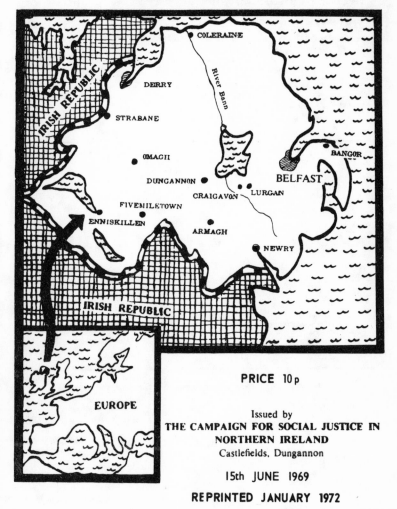

PRICE 10p

Issued by
**THE CAMPAIGN FOR SOCIAL JUSTICE IN
NORTHERN IRELAND**
Castlefields, Dungannon

15th JUNE 1969

REPRINTED JANUARY 1972

All the facts given here are correct for the date given. Once
Britain intervened there were big changes.

"I AGREE with you as to the importance of the issues with which your Campaign is concerned, and can assure you that a Labour Government would do everything in its power to see that the infringements of justice to which you are so rightly drawing attention are effectively dealt with."

— Mr. Harold Wilson, writing to Campaign for Social Justice in September, 1964.

"WE work closely with our colleagues of the Northern Ireland Labour Party. Like them we deplore religious and other kinds of discrimination; and we agree with them that this should be tackled by introducing new and impartial procedures for the allocation of houses, by setting up joint tribunals to which particular cases of alleged discrimination in public appointments can be referred, and indeed, by any other effective means that can be agreed."

— Mr. Harold Wilson, writing to the Campaign for Social Justice in July, 1964.

Section 75 of the Government of Ireland Act, 1920, by which the Parliament at Westminster set up the Northern Ireland State, says:

"Notwithstanding the establishment of the Parliament . . . of Northern Ireland . . . or anything contained in this Act, the supreme authority of the Parliament of the United Kingdom shall remain unaffected and undiminished over all persons, matters and things in Ireland and every part thereof."

CAMPAIGN FOR SOCIAL JUSTICE

IN NORTHERN IRELAND   CASTLEFIELDS, DUNGANNON.

Committee:

MRS. BRIGID MCALEER B SC.	PETER GORMLEY M.B . F.R.C.S.	JAMES MCCARTHEY LL B
CLLR MRS. PATRICIA MCCLUSKEY	CONOR GILLIGAN F.R C S.	CONN MCCLUSKEY M B.
MRS MAURA MULLALLY	BRIAN GREGORY B.A . F.R.I.B.A.	HUGH P. MCCONVILLE P T
CLLR. J. J. DONNELLY	JOHN MCANERNEY	SEAN MCGIVERN

PRINTED BY BETHLEHEM ABBEY PRESS, PORTGLENONE, CO. ANTRIM

NORTHERN IRELAND

THE PLAIN TRUTH

(Second Edition)

Since 1920, when Ireland was divided, the Republic of Ireland has been a separate independent state, while Northern Ireland has remained an integral part of the United Kingdom. It is now loosely termed 'Ulster,' although there were nine counties in old-time Ulster, three of which are now in the Republic of Ireland. The British Parliament in London first legalised this arrangement by the Government of Ireland Act, 1920 (H.M. Stationery Office, London). London has since ruled Northern Ireland through its subordinate Parliament at Stormont, Belfast.

Both London and Stormont have always been at pains to present the province as a happy, contented place, whereas in fact it contains a minority which has always been very hard pressed, and indeed denied rights which most of the free world has come to accept as a matter of course.

The outside world was largely unaware of what was going on in Ulster mainly because the British press had always been discouraged from printing stories about it. Some years ago when a British television group had a series of documentaries suppressed, the leader of the reporting team, Alan Whicker, declared "No country deserves the Government you have here. This is the only place in the world where you can't report honestly without silly people kicking up about what is only the truth."

Since the 5th October, 1968, when a peaceful Civil Rights march was broken up by the police, the world has been looking at Northern Ireland on television, and reading about her in the press, first with incredulity, and then shock.

Civil Rights activities have been opposed by various groups of militant Protestants. These people already have their civil rights, and do not wish to share them with others. They have caused the recent unrest by opposing democratic demands for change. This opposition has been effected mainly by violent counter-demonstrations, and by arbitrary police bans on Civil Rights marches in certain places, e.g., in the city of Londonderry.

This booklet attempts to explain the situation in Northern Ireland, and to detail the discriminatory injustices from which the minority has been suffering there for almost fifty years.

There are roughly one and a half million people living in Northern Ireland, of whom two thirds are Protestant, and who generally support the Unionist Government. The remaining one third are Roman Catholics, who generally support a variety of opposition parties.

Out of a total of 52, the Unionists hold 39 seats in the Stormont Parliament. They are closely linked with the Conservative (Tory) party in Britain. The Unionist Party is a sectarian one. Down the years it has discouraged Catholics from joining and at present only a dozen or so belong to it. It is dominated by the Orange Order, a secret society having many points of similarity with the Dutch Reformed Church in South Africa. Virtually all of the Government, including the present Prime Minister, Major Chichester-Clark as well as most Unionist parliamentarians, are members of the Orange Order.

Six Nationalists, four Labour and three Independent members make up the Parliamentary opposition.

Northern Ireland also sends twelve M.P.'s to the London Parliament (Westminster). For many years they were all Unionists, boosting Conservative voting strength there. This is a main reason why the British Conservatives, who were in power most of the time, did not insist that the Stormont Government should modify their repressive and discriminatory policies towards the political minority.

One of these London seats was taken from the Unionists in 1964, and is now held by the redoubtable Gerry Fitt. In April 1969, a twenty-one year old Civil Rights leader, Bernadette Devlin, took another seat from the Unionists to become the youngest M.P. in the London Parliament.

Before Fitt's and Devlin's day, the Republican party dominated minority politics as far as Westminster was concerned. It took a logical enough view that Irishmen had no place in an English Parliament, and that asking favours of the British, either in their own Parliament or elsewhere, was both degrading and a waste of time. This was the policy of 'abstention.'

POPULATION CONTROL

Outsiders looking at Northern Ireland, and listening to Government claims that it is a democratic State, and that Unionists have been the peoples' choice all along, find it hard to understand why there has never been a change of party control.

It is correct that the Unionists have always had a majority, but mainly because of a ruthless and far-seeing plan to contain their opponents' numbers.

All down the years the percentage of Catholics (anti-Unionists) has been strictly regulated by allowing only the same percentage to remain, and forcing the rest to emigrate by denying them jobs and houses.

At the present time in Northern Ireland the Roman Catholic primary schools contain 51% of all the children (Capt. O'Neill's own figure given in 1968), because the Catholic birth rate is almost twice that of the non-Catholic. If these children were to grow to maturity and remain at home, the Unionists grasp of affairs would be shaken in a very short time. That a good percentage of these potential anti-Tory voters is got rid of is shown by the graph page 3 (Figures from the Government Census, H.M. Stationery Office, Belfast). It will be noted that the drain occurs principally at voting age.

In 1951 Catholics were 37.7% of the under 30 years population. Ten years later in 1961 they had fallen to 35.4% of the 10 to 39 years age group, which corresponds to the under 30 years population of 1951.

In this ten year period Catholics, although originally only 37.7% of the age group, account for 55.6% of the total decrease of population due to death and emigration. In effect this meant a drop of 16.7% of the total Catholic population under 30 years in 1951.

From the Registrar-General's births and deaths report, it can be seen that the death rate is negligible, the main drain is in emigration.

The comparative figures for Protestants are: in 1951 Protestants were 62.3% of the under 30 population, ten years later, in 1961 they had risen to 64.6% of the 10 to 39 age group, which corresponds to the under 30 population of 1951. In this ten year period Protestants, although originally 62.3% of the age group account for only 44.4% of the total decrease of population due to death and emigration. In

NORTHERN IRELAND

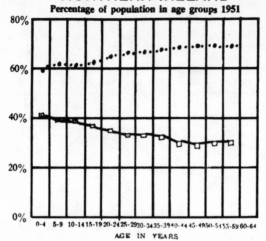

Percentage of population in age groups 1951

80%

60%

40%

20%

0%

0-4 5-9 10-14 15-19 20-24 25-29 30-34 35-39 40-44 45-49 50-54 55-59 60-64

AGE IN YEARS

Population percentage decrease in age groups during the period 1951 — 1961

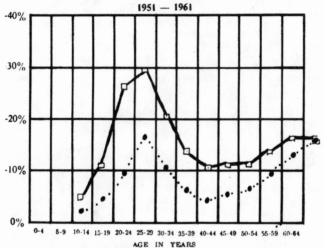

-40%

-30%

-20%

-10%

0%

0-4 5-9 10-14 15-19 20-24 25-29 30-34 35-39 40-44 45-49 50-54 55-59 60-64

AGE IN YEARS

□————□————□ Catholic   ● . . . ● . . . ● Protestant

(FIGURES FROM CENSUS, H M STATIONERY OFFICE, BELFAST)

effect, this meant a drop of only 8.1% of the total Protestant population under 30 in 1951, and contrasts with a drop of 16.7% for the total Catholic population under 30 in 1951.

Or to put it another way, the official Census shows the Catholic proportion of the total population to have remained static, 33.5% in 1937, 34.9% in 1961.

From 1937 to 1961, the last year in which the Census required a declaration of religion, a total of 90,000 Catholics emigrated from Northern Ireland. For non-Catholics the total was 69,000, or 8% of their 1937 population. The Catholic percentage was 21.

"The difference in economic opportunity is a regulator maintaining the status quo." This is the formula for these facts, given by two English Quakers, Barritt and Carter, in an impartial survey entitled ''The Northern Ireland Problem.' '(Oxford University Press).

JOB DISCRIMINATION

Reference to the back pages makes it very clear that it has always been Unionist policy, not only to control the numbers, but to keep the Roman Catholics as 'second class citizens' in their own land. They have been rightly referred to as 'the white negroes of Ulster.'

Even the opportunity of menial work is denied first to them. As a result of this they make up by far the greater proportion of the dole queues. The Campaign for Social Justice asked a parliamentarian to request names of all on unemployment benefit in one town so that a percentage figure could be arrived at, but the Government refused this.

In a town of half and half Unionists and anti-Unionists which we surveyed, the anti-Unionists predominated on the unemployment register in a ratio of about ten to one.

But it is in the higher ranks that the politico-religious discrimination is most serious because the lack of opportunity here forces emigration of the best Catholic brains.

In this publication the figures we present are not earlier than 1968, unless otherwise stated.

Starting with the Government itself:

The Departments of the Northern Ireland Government fall into two categories:

(a) The Technical and Professional grades, people like engineers, lawyers, doctors, accountants, etc., who work in government and (b) Civil Servants proper, who administer the Province.

All these people are listed in the British Imperial Calender and Civil Service List, published each year by the Stationery Office.

We have analysed the 1961 edition.

(a) The Professional and Technical Grades.

	Total	Catholics
Cabinet Officers	5	—
Houses of Parliament	6	—
Ministry of Finance	62	3
Ministry of Agriculture	29	1
Ministry of Commerce	9	2
Ministry of Development	32	2
Ministry for Education	7	—
Ministry of Health and Social Services	35	3
Ministry of Home Affairs	8	—
Exchequer and Audit Department	10	2
Parliamentary Draughtsmans Office	6	—
	209	13

(b) Administrative Grades of the Northern Ireland Civil Service:

(The figures for Catholics are in brackets).

	Assistant Secretary (plus)	Principle Officer	Deputy Principle Officer	Total
Cabinet Secretariat Prime Minister's Department Government Information Service	4 (—)	2 (—)	2 (—)	8 (—)
Ministry of Finance	9 (1)	16 (1)	31 (4)	56 (6)
Ministry of Agriculture	7 (—)	13 (3)	18 (—)	38 (3)
Ministry of Commerce	6 (—)	12 (1)	19 (3)	37 (4)
Ministry of Development	7 (—)	19 (3)	25 (1)	51 (4)
Ministry of Education	5 (—)	10 (2)	16 (2)	31 (4)
Ministry of Health & Social Services	11 (—)	22 (—)	45 (1)	78 (1)
Ministry of Home Affairs	4 (—)	8 (1)	8 (—)	20 (1)
All Departments	53 (1)	102 (11)	164 (11)	319 (23)

Our information is that employment in the Civil Service is controlled by two bodies, the Placing Authority and the Establishment Authority. They are such Unionist preserves that the Campaign was not able to find out even the names of those on them !

THE PUBLIC BOARDS

The Government administers a large segment of public affairs through its official bodies, the members of which it appoints itself. Where an occasional Catholic is given this important function, not only is he hopelessly outnumbered vote-wise, but also those chosen are often known to be Government collaborators, who would be unlikely to insist on minority rights in a way that members elected by the minority itself would do. The parallel with Mr. Ian Smith of Rhodesia choosing tribal chiefs to advise him is surely apparent. Herewith the membership details of the main ruling bodies, with religions:

	Total Membership	Catholics
Electricity Board for N.I.	5	0
Housing Trust	7	1
Craigavon Development Commission	9	1
Economic Council	18	2
Hospitals Authority	22	5
General Health Services Board	24	2
Medical Advisory Committee to the Ministry of Health	11	1
Pigs Marketing Board	14	2
Milk Marketing Board	13	1
Seed Potato Marketing Board	14	1
Agricultural Wages Board	15	2
Youth Employment Service Board	18	3
Fire Authority	16	0
Child Welfare Council	22	6
Ulster Folk Museum Trustees	20	1
Tourist Board	11	3
Advisory Council for Education	16	5
Council for Education Research	27	5
Youth and Sports Council	20	6
Industrial Court	22	1
Lowry Commission to redistribute Four University Parliamentary Seats	5	0
1969 Commission to Overhaul Stormont Parliamentary Boundaries	3	1

DOCTORS

The Hospitals Authority administers Northern Ireland's 97 hospitals, practising religious discrimination in the way it chooses the specialist doctors who work in them (1967 figures) viz.:

There are 387 specialists, only 31 of these are Roman Catholic. Of the 387, 61 hold teaching posts at the University. Of the 31 Catholics, three hold University posts. Excluding the University appointees only 8.5% of Hospital Authority specialist jobs go to Catholics. (In general practice doctoring, where the patients are free to choose their own practitioner, one third of the G.P.s are Catholic, thereby reflecting the general population percentage. Chemists, barristers and solicitors, where free enterprise prevails, show identical trends).

These hospitals are run by Management Committees. Total Committee members: 456, 72 are Roman Catholics, i.e., 15.7%. Again the Roman Catholic members are chosen for their 'reliability.' Noteworthy is Londonderry, seven Roman Catholics out of 21. The population of Derry is 65% Roman Catholic. Of the total 50 matrons of Hospitals, only six are Catholic, i.e., 12%.

Government Health Service:

Chief Medical Officer and deputy Chief, both Protestants. Medical Referees: Full time, there are eight, all Protestants. Part-time, 50, only six Roman Catholics (Referee figures were obtained in 1969).

Not one Catholic is employed as Chief County or Borough Medical Officer of Health. Neither is there a Catholic employed as Deputy Chief Medical Officer of Health.

There is no Borough or County Chief Dental Officer who is a Catholic. There is no County or Borough Public Health Inspector a Catholic. Of all the sixteen Public Health Inspectors only three are Catholic.

POLICE (a) Royal Ulster Constabulary

Complement, just over 3,000, 10% of which are Catholic†; 50 Officers in R.U.C. six are Catholic; 120 Head Constables, 16 are Catholic; 400 Sergeants, 50 Catholic (1967 figures). Upkeep, £6.7 million* in the coming year, of which over £5 million is pay and allowances.

(b) Ulster Special Constabulary

This is a sectarian part-time force 11,300 strong. All members are Protestant. They are mainly recruited from members of the Orange Order. As recipients of Unionist patronage these constitute a private Unionist army. They have the right to retain their firearms in their own homes. There have been several documented cases of vicious attacks by members of the Ulster Specials on peaceful Civil Rights marchers, and on other anti-Unionists. Specials in mufti have been found in possession of firearms at counter demonstrations to Civil Rights marches. The Government has recently augmented its full-time police force with well over 1,000 of these men—upkeep—£972,700 in the coming year.

† A Ministry of Home Affairs spokesman recently stated that this figure was 11%.

* The pound sterling (£1) is worth 2.4 American dollars; 2.14 Australian dollars; £5.10.0. is equivalent to 100 Indian rupees.

POLICE BRUTALITY

Up to October 5th, 1968, with some notable exceptions, relations between the police and the minority, were normal.

At the first Londonderry Civil Rights march the Royal Ulster Constabulary sealed off the marchers in Duke Street in front and behind and batoned them indiscriminately. Gerry Fitt, M.P., was wounded on the head. Edward McAteer, M.P., in the groin. A girl was batoned on the mouth. The people were hosed with water cannons. This was all witnessed by two British Labour M.P.s, John Ryan and Mrs. Anne Kerr. While this was going on, police not actively engaged were laughing. (See report in the "Listener," a B.B.C. publication, 24:10:68).

(Minister of Home Affairs — Mr. William Craig)

At a later date student marchers at Burntollet Bridge received scant protection from the R.U.C., who fraternised freely with the Paisleyites led by Major Bunting. Students were stoned, beaten with nail-studded clubs, and thrown into a stream. Threats of rape were made on the women. (See report in "Sunday Times," London, 27:4:69).

In January 1969, police, some alleged to be intoxicated, broke into houses in Lecky Road, Derry, and, using obscene and sectarian abuse, attacked the citizens indiscriminately with batons and kicks. As a result, 190 formal complaints against the police were documented.

Again, demonstrating its particular brand of "democracy," the Ulster Government ordered an Enquiry to be carried out by police officials themselves ! The Government has refused to make the results of this Enquiry public.

(Minister of Home Affairs — Capt. William Long)

In April 1969, in Derry, the police were caught at a disadvantage and were stoned by a mob and some injured. Police later invaded Catholic homes and rendered many men, women (including a semi-invalid) and children hospital cases !

(Minister of Home Affairs — Mr. R. Porter)

At demonstrations the police always face the Civil Rights groups, and turn their backs to the militant Protestants, with whom many police are on terms of easy familiarity.

We are well aware that a stable society depends on a responsible and esteemed police force. Successive Unionist Ministers of Home Affairs have, for their own ends, allowed a sadistic minority of policemen to destroy the reputation of the force.

THE LAW	Protestants	Catholics
High Court Judges	6	1
County Court Judges	4	1
Resident Magistrates	9	3
Lands Tribunal Members	2	0
Commission for National Insurance (with relatively few Protestants unemployed)	3	0
Clerks of Crown and Peace	6	0

Under Sheriffs	6	0
Crown Solicitors	8	0
Clerks of Petty Sessions	26	1
Summary Jurisdiction Rules Committee	6	3

THE SCHOOLS

School Inspectors.—There are 53 Inspectors of County and Voluntary Schools, five are Roman Catholic.

LOCAL EDUCATION COMMITTEES

These bodies run the schools. There are eight, one for each County and one each for Belfast and Londonderry. Total membership 223. Only 39 are Roman Catholic (17%); there are 36 Protestant and four Roman Catholic clergymen members. Roman Catholics are 35% of the population, but make up 51% of the primary school children.

RELIGIOUS DISCRIMINATION AGAINST TEACHERS

Like Holland, Germany and the U.S.A., the Roman Catholic Church authorities prefer to educate the children in their own schools. The part upkeep of these schools is a very heavy burden on Roman Catholics, but the fact that they accept it is surely proof that they want things this way.

For educated Catholics schools present some of the few good employment opportunities in Ulster. There is a law in Northern Ireland, unlike the rest of Britain, which prohibits school teachers from being members of County Councils. We claim that this is discriminatory, and is solely to prevent this articulate group in the Roman Catholic community, the teachers, from speaking in local affairs on behalf of the under-privileged.

POST OFFICE

Control of the postal service is directly held by London and discrimination here is widespread. Our figures were collected in 1967.

Since the Post Office was divided into Regional Administrations in the mid 1930's there have been eight holders of the post of Director of the Northern Ireland Region. None have been Catholics. The Director heads a Board of Administration consisting of Postal Controller, Telecommunications Controller, Staff Controller and Finance Officer. None of these posts, all of which have changed hands several times in the past thirty years, has ever been held by a Catholic.

The other chief posts in the Service here, with a minimum salary of £2,000 plus p.a., are the Head Postmaster, Belfast; Assistant Head Postmaster, Belfast; the Telephone Manager; Deputy Telephone Manager; Three Area Engineers; The Area Accountant; Chief Sales Superintendent; Chief Traffic Superintendent. None of these posts have ever been held by a Catholic.

Outside Belfast, for example, there are thirteen Head Postmasterships. Going back forty years, the holders have never been Catholics with one exception many years ago. There are over 6,000 Post Office employees in Northern Ireland, practically all of whom are recruited locally. On a population basis it is reasonable to assume that at least 35% of these should be Catholic. As one progresses up the grades this percentage gets smaller.

Take the Belfast Head Post Office as an example. The basic clerical grade is that of Postal and Telegraph Officer and the rungs of the ladder upwards from that are:—Overseerships, Assistant Superintendents, Superintendents, Chief Superintendent. Allowing for mobility among the applicants there are Postmasterships and Head Postmasterships and some occasional transfers outside the manipulative work of the Service such as Welfare Officer Posts.

The following Table shows the trend:

Post	Total	Number of Catholics
Postal and Telegraph Officers	145	45
Overseerships	29	8
Superintendent	1	1
Assistant Superintendent	7	1
Chief Superintendent	1	—

Of the five Postmasterships of Crown Offices in the Belfast area, namely, Bangor, Holywood, Newtownards, Carrickfergus and Larne, none is held by a Catholic. There are approximately 190 sub-offices under the control of the Belfast Head Post Office and less than 10% of these are held by a Catholic.

The attention of two British Postmasters General, Mr. Edward Short and Mr. John Stonehouse was drawn to these facts. They denied there was any substance to our complaints, which is surely hypocritical ?

RELIGIOUS DISCRIMINATION IN THE TRADE UNIONS

The Northern Ireland Committee of Irish Congress of Trade Unions is the ruling body. Here the Chairman is a Catholic, but none of the other eleven members is.

Full-time Paid Trade Union Officials:

Protestants 62; Catholics 16; Catholic Percentage 20.

Craft Unions of Manual Skilled Workers:

Protestants 35; Catholics 5; Catholic Percentage 12.

These comprise the highly skilled and paid Unions. There is a traditional Protestant preponderance here.

Other Unions (white collar, professional and unskilled).

Protestants 27; Catholics 11; Catholic Percentage 29.

RELIGIOUS DISCRIMINATION IN RATING ABATEMENT

In 1966 the British Government introduced a Rate Rebate plan whereby the rates burden on houses occupied by the lower income groups was eased.

In Northern Ireland this rate rebate was spread over all domestic ratepayers otherwise it 'would benefit too many of the wrong sort' (meaning the poorer Roman Catholics).

Because most of the large firms, private and public, are controlled by Protestants, the bias is mainly anti-Catholic. It is very widespread. We give two examples only:

(1) In 1966 the Roman Catholic Bishop of the Belfast area, Dr. Philbin, claimed that in a specified engineering firm only three or four employees out of the total work force were Catholics (Belfast is 27.5% Catholic). The Bishop could not state the total labour force. Like ourselves in similar circumstances, there was no sympathetic person available to give him information. We estimate it at 3,000 for this factory.

The manager, in a letter to the Bishop, claimed the Catholics 'did not feel at home in a Protestant atmosphere.' As the Bishop pointed out to him, poorly-off discriminated-against Catholics are never in the position of choosing the atmosphere in which they work.

Although this factory is in receipt of Government grants the authorities have repeatedly refused to reveal the amounts, or to make a fair employment policy a condition for their continuance.

(2) In another town with approximately fifty-fifty Protestants and Catholics, there is a large textile factory with a pay-roll of about 2,500. In this factory-complex there is one Roman Catholic director (who was seconded from London); one Roman Catholic manager; one Roman Catholic under-manager; three Roman Catholic charge hands; one Roman Catholic mechanic; five Roman Catholic supervisors. In all, only 12 Roman Catholic persons above the lowest grade. There has never been, with possibly one or two exceptions, any Roman Catholics in the despatch department.

The rest are the 'hewers of wood and the drawers of water.'

How can it be done so thoroughly ? Because, as a matter of policy, this firm does not, nor never has, taken any pupils from the local Roman Catholic grammar school to train for the higher posts. All come from the Protestant grammar school. The academic records of both schools are similar.

SPECIAL POWERS ACT

In April 1963, the South African Minister of Justice, now the Prime Minister, introduced a new Coercion Bill by saying that he "would be willing to exchange all the legislation of that sort for one clause of the Northern Ireland Special Powers Act."

This Act, which has been continuously in operation since 1922, empowers the authorities to:

(1) Arrest without warrant.

(2) Imprison without charge or trial and deny recourse to habeus corpus or a court of law.

(3) Enter and search homes without warrant, and with force, at any hour of day or night.

(4) Declare a curfew and prohibit meetings, assemblies (including fairs and markets) and processions.

(5) Permit punishment by flogging.

(6) Deny claim to a trial by jury.

(7) Arrest persons it is desired to examine as witnesses, forcibly detain them and compel them to answer questions, under penalties, even if answers may incriminate them. Such a person is guilty of an offence if he refuses to be sworn or answer a question.

(8) Do any act involving interference with the rights of private property.

(9) Prevent access of relatives or legal advisers to a person imprisoned without trial.

(10) Prohibit the holding of an inquest after a prisoner's death.

(11) Arrest a person who "by word of mouth" spreads false reports or makes false statements.

(12) Prohibit the circulation of any newspaper.

(13) Prohibit the possession of any film or gramophone record.

(14) Arrest a person who does anything "calculated to be prejudicial to the preservation of peace or maintenance of order in Northern Ireland and not specifically provided for in the regulations."

(15) The Act allows the Minister of Home Affairs to create new crimes by Government Decree, e.g., he recently made it a crime to name a club a "Republican Club."

The Ulster Government has all the usual legal remedies at hand to maintain the peace. Some of these laws, like the new Public Order Act Amendments, are much more repressive than anything in Britain. Indeed, if the provisions are carefully studied it becomes apparent that what the Unionists are in fact doing is making these Amendments so penal that they may be enabled to drop the Special Powers Act at a later date.

We suggest that the Special Powers Act is retained in Northern Ireland by a nation of bullies to intimidate a subject people, since it applies to no other part of the United Kingdom.

HOUSING

APARTHEID IN NORTHERN IRELAND — GHETTO HOUSING

In towns where the Unionists have a slender majority they consolidate their position by the use of gerrymandered wards. They can convert a paper minority into a majority by this means.

This is how it is done

The town is divided into wards, frequently three in number. In the two smaller Unionist wards the electors are thinly spread and allocated the same number of councillors per ward as the anti-Unionists who are crammed into the third ward, and give the same number of councillors. Londonderry is the classical example and is detailed overleaf. This also happens in Dungannon, Omagh, Armagh, Enniskillen and many other places.

The most notorious single ghetto housing estate with regard to size is one owned by Belfast Corporation, called Turf Lodge, where there are 1,175 Catholic families and only 22 Protestant families (1967 figures).

There is another Government sponsored body in Northern Ireland, the Housing Trust, which builds homes for letting. It often mixes the religions, and we found in such estates that Protestants and Catholics live together in amity, and have a much healthier attitude to each other. The Trust usually selects better-off people since they make more stable tenants, the most needy being thereby passed over. However, in most towns the bigoted Unionist councils see to it that the balance of power is not upset, even obstructing the Housing Trust if too many Catholics are being accommodated, e.g., Enniskillen and Londonderry.

The Trust is not blameless of occasionally practising religious discrimination. It has refused enquiring opposition M.P.s information as to how it selects tenants. More often than not it re-lets to people of the same religion as the old tenants, and not solely on need.

VOTING INJUSTICES

In many areas, where they would be in danger from a simple majority, the Unionists manipulate electoral boundaries in a very undemocratic way known as 'gerrymandering', and thereby keep control. (Please see details of a classic example of Londonderry, pages 20-21)

In local government elections there is denial of 'one man, one vote.' Only householders and their wives have one vote each. This means that in all of Northern Ireland there are at present a quarter of a million people disfranchised out of a total electorate of less than one million. To prevent control passing from them Unionists refuse to allocate Catholics their fair share of local authority housing — built with public funds, denial of a house meaning denial of a voice in local affairs. Thus Catholics are not in a position to help their co-religionists who are forced to emigrate.

Catholics may be on housing waiting lists for up to twelve years or longer, whilst Protestants can often choose their council house and have it allocated before they are married.

Such a case was spotlighted in 1968 at Caledon in Co. Tyrone by Austin Currie, M.P., who, after he had exhausted all legal remedies available, himself squatted in a council house. This house had been allocated to a young unmarried stenographer of a Unionist candidate for a Westminster seat, Mr. B. McRoberts.

Housing injustices such as this cause great bitterness at local level, and our Campaign is deeply resentful of the unchristian way the least influential and articulate members of the Catholic population have been squeezed out over the past forty-eight years.

British political leaders like Prime Minister Wilson, Lord Butler, Lord Brooke, Sir Alec Douglas-Home and many others before them have been given full details of these injustices, but so far nothing concrete has been done.

Pressure from outside has recently compelled the Unionists to offer 'one man, one vote'. This will be useless unless each vote is of equal value, in other words if there is no gerrymander. It is something of a tragedy that there is no apparent groundswell of Protestant public opinion in favour of this course.

It would be hard to imagine the Unionists taking an honourable course in this vital field of public authority housing and voting.

'HE WHO PAYS THE PIPER CALLS THE TUNE' — the Tory claim exploded.

The Unionist excuse for denying those who are not householders a vote in local government elections is that they allege they are not paying domestic rates for the upkeep of the local council. But the Minister of Development revealed (30/1/67) that only 30% of local expenditure is raised from the rates. The remainder comes from central tax funds, to which all contribute.

Despite the fact that Northern Ireland receives more than ⅓ of its yearly upkeep from Britain, the Unionists will not allow Britain to press them to give the Ulster minority civil rights. For example, Viscount Brookborough, a previous Prime Minister, recently called on Unionists to unite in resisting all pressures from Whitehall (the London Parliament).

ELECTORAL IRREGULARITIES

There are many voting irregularities in elections. The adage 'vote early and often' is frequently quoted. A South African liberal, writing in the "Belfast Telegraph" 10:12:65, reports how she met an apparently respectable citizen who told her "I voted thirty-six times."

This Campaign sent a large dossier detailing electoral irregularities to an official enquiry by the London Parliament in 1965, but so far nothing has been done. We instanced dead people being voted for, a nun being voted for by a civilian, wholesale personation by Unionists, unopened ballot boxes from anti-Unionist areas having been found in an outhouse. Intimidation of anti-Unionist voters by a Presiding Officer. We detailed areas where anti-Unionist personating agents were afraid to attend the booths to check on the correct identity of the voters.

Ballot papers in Northern Ireland are numbered. A Unionist official records the voter's name as he votes. Even though the voting papers are stated to be destroyed after the count, people fear that some could be retrieved and persons who voted wrongly, subsequently discriminated against.

Postal votes are frequently alleged to be destroyed by unsympathetic postmen.

CALCULATED NEGLECT OF THE WEST

There are six counties in Northern Ireland, the eastern three, Antrim, Down and Armagh are predominantly Protestant; the western three, Londonderry, Tyrone and Fermanagh, predominantly Roman Catholic.

The natural capital of the eastern counties is Belfast, of the western counties, the city of Londonderry. Derry is the second city in size in Northern Ireland with a deep sea port and a naval base.

The Unionists have, through the years, continued to consolidate their position by strengthening the economy of the eastern half of the state and encouraging few industries to set up in the western counties.

To stimulate the setting up of industries the Government builds 'advance factories' for them. The following are the details of where they have been sited. (Official report, dated 11:3:69).

Co. Antrim	27	)		Co. Londonderry	10	)
Co. Armagh	10			Borough of London-		
Co. Down	17		Eastern	derry	1	Western
Borough of Belfast	5		half of	Co. Tyrone	3	half of
	—		Ulster	Co. Fermanagh	1	Ulster
	59	)			—	)
	—				15	)

The extremes to which Unionism will go is exemplified as follows:

The then Minister of Commerce, Mr. Brian Faulkner, who held the post for some years, announced, on 21st June 1967, the impending arrival of an East German firm to open a factory in Bangor, Co. Down, where, at that time, official figures gave unemployment as 245 persons. On the same date 20% of the people of Derry City were unemployed and, in Strabane, Co. Tyrone, the rate was 25%.

In the past few years even more determined attempts have been made to further weaken and depopulate the western three counties in the following ways:

1. There were two separate railway lines to Londonderry. In the interests of economy it became necessary to close one of them. The one to be 'axed' traversed the western region. This has left Fermanagh, Tyrone and practically all of the county of Londonderry with no railway whatever. The other three counties have two separate systems, one running north from Belfast, the other south.

2. In order to further strengthen the relatively prosperous east, the government of Northern Ireland is building a new city in Co. Armagh. As a further irritant to Catholics it was named after the most famous anti-Catholic bigot, 'Craigavon', Mr. Geoffrey Copcutt was engaged as its chief designer. He is an Englishman who came here after planning Cumbernauld New City near Glasgow. After one year's work he resigned saying, "I have become disenchanted with the Stormont scene." He suggested the abandonment of the New City and that the development of Londonderry should be concentrated upon in order to give the province a reasonable balance.

3. The government, in February 1965, accepted the Wilson Plan for economic development (H.M. Stationery Office, Belfast). This report outlined four centres for rapid industrial development, all within a 30-mile radius of Belfast, and in western counties virtually nothing.

4. In February, 1965, the government also accepted the Lockwood Report (H.M. Stationery Office, Belfast). Here, Londonderry was rejected as the site for a new university, in spite of the fact that Magee University College, a hundred year old institution, is at present providing the first two years of university education in certain subjects. Copcutt in his statement said "Londonderry is the obvious choice to expand as the centre for higher education outside Belfast. It could prove the most promising way of unifying the present populations and integrating future immigrant communities."

THE LEGAL POSITION WITH REGARD TO RELIGIOUS DISCRIMINATION

Because of a record of previous discrimation in Ireland, some half-hearted legal provisions to prevent it were incorporated in the Government of Ireland Act, 1920. Half-hearted, because those offered had been rejected in 1893* when they were proposed to safeguard Protestants in a previously united Ireland, where they were in a minority for the whole country. The Republic of Ireland is almost totally Roman Catholic. The relevant sections in the 1920 Act are Nos. 5 and 8. In effect these prohibit Stormont from making any law which would impose disability on any religious group. They are of no practical help, because the Government of Ulster never found it necessary to make laws to penalise Catholics. Using its permanent majority Stormont has always been able to discriminate as it wished.

In 1964, Sir Alec Douglas-Home, like others before him, claimed that the Roman Catholics, who felt they were discriminated against, could seek the protection of the courts, using the relevant sections of the 1920 Act.

This Campaign wrote to him telling him that we had consulted a senior barrister, who told us that the Act could not be used—that it would not even allow discriminated against people to get into court.

We wrote to Sir Alec, asking how this could be done. His unhelpful and evasive series of letters in reply are published by us as a pamphlet, obtainable on request, entitled, "Northern Ireland, Why Justice can not be done."

At a later stage, another Ulster senior barrister claimed that he had found a loophole in the law, which would at least permit aggrieved parties to get into court with a case of alleged discrimination in housing allocation. The barrister informed us that for the litigants to finance their own case up as far as the House of Lords, where their opponents would undoubtedly force it, were they to lose in a lower court, would cost up to £20,000.

Despite the fact that there is a Free Legal Aid scheme for people such as these penniless Roman Catholics, Aid was denied to the litigants.

Full documentation in the Campaign pamphlet "Northern Ireland, Legal Aid to oppose discrimination, not likely !"

WHAT LEGAL SAFEGUARDS DOES THE SITUATION DEMAND?

In 1968 Britain introduced anti-discrimination legislation, the Race Relations Act. Despite the efforts of a substantial lobby of British Labour and Liberal Members of Parliament, led by Mr. Ben Whittaker, the British Government refused to allow this Bill to apply to Northern Ireland, and to relate it to religious discrimination.

The Labour M.P.s belong to an 80 strong group of parliamentarians called the Campaign for Democracy in Ulster (President Lord Brockway, Chairman Paul Rose).

In the Stormont Parliament, Miss Sheelagh Murnaghan has been presenting a Human Rights Bill since 1967. She did so for the fifth time on 18:12:68. The Ulster Unionists have always rejected her attempts.

The anti-discrimation clauses of the Government of Ireland Act, 1920, though seen to be ineffective, have never been revised since they were first introduced. The British Prime Minister is well aware that there is continuing injustice, and it is entirely his Government's responsibility to strengthen the Act. Readers must draw their own conclusions, bearing in mind his promises as set out on the inside cover.

* "What Home Rule Means Now," a pamphlet issued in 1893 by the Irish Unionist Alliance.

THE LONDON GOVERNMENT HOLDS THE WHIP HAND OVER STORMONT

(a) Because of Section 75 of the Government of Ireland Act. (Please see inside front cover) (b) Because Britain subsidises the Stormont Government to the tune of £100 million per year, out of a total expenditure of £300 million per year—this figure was given by the former Ulster Prime Minister, Capt. O'Neill on a television broadcast at the end of 1968. This is probably the minimum amount, and does not include Northern Ireland's share towards the British National and diplomatic services, Royal Mint, National Debt and other Imperial expenditures.

(For comparison purposes, the projected income for the coming year in the independent Republic of Ireland will be £387 million. The expenditure will be £386 million. These figures are official Budget estimates released 6:5:69).

(c) Because 91% of Northern Ireland's trade is with Britain (Ulster Minister of Finance 15:11:68).

THE "CONVENTION" NOT TO INTERFERE

When complaints of Stormont Government injustices have been made in the London Parliament by Mr. Fitt, or other sympathetic British Labour or Liberal Members of Parliament, they are ruled out of order because of a "Convention" evolved by the British Conservative Party, which prevents discussion of Northern Ireland's affairs Yet the British Privy Council on 23rd July, 1968 ruled that the same "Convention" relating to Rhodesia had no legal force, and further, Britain did intervene in the past in Northern Ireland's domestic affairs. It did so when the Ulster Government tried to reduce the Childrens' Allowance for the third and subsequent child (in order to discriminate against Roman Catholics who have larger families). The Northern Ireland Government was compelled by London, in this instance, to drop this uncharitable scheme.

London again intervened in 1962 when the Unionists sought to modify the Government of Ireland Act, 1920, to allow them to seize lands belonging to the Church, which the 1920 Act forbids.

UNIONIST INTOLERANCE, HALF TRUTHS AND EXCUSES

Unionists claim that their opponents are out to destroy the State, whereas in fact they are merely striving for British standards of justice, as at present obtaining in the remainder of the United Kingdom.

The leader of the Parliamentary Opposition at Stormont has never been paid the extra salary his position merits. He is remunerated in the same way as ordinary Members of Parliament.

For the past forty eight years the Stormont Parliament has never allowed any Opposition Bill to become law, with the exception of the Wild Birds Act, in 1931.

It is not surprising, therefore, that many people think that progress will only be achieved by street demonstrations and civil disobedience.

Unionists claim that Roman Catholics are more bigoted than they. Surely with its monopoly of power the initiative for change must come from the ruling Unionist Party.

Instances of Roman Catholic tolerance are:—

1. In Armagh in the 1964 local council elections a Ratepayers group put up candidates. A Catholic was nominated in a Protestant ward. He came bottom of the poll, whereas a Protestant in the Catholic ward topped it.

2. In Dungannon at the last council elections a Protestant topped the poll in the Catholic ward.

3. In the recent Stormont elections, Ivan Cooper, a Protestant, won the seat against Roman Catholics in the mainly Catholic Constituency of Mid-Derry, and Claude Wilton, another Protestant, has just been elected to the Senate by Catholic M.P.s.

Regrettable though it is, it is not surprising that isolated acts of violence and sabotage do occur. It is not always, however, what it seems. Some time ago shots were fired into the house of an extreme Protestant member of Parliament, Mr. John McQuade. It was assumed widely that this was the work of Catholic extremists.

It came out at the trial of murdered Catholics, the Malvern Street trial, some time later, that the attack had been made by extreme Protestants themselves. Many riots in places like Londonderry during the past months have been wrongly attributed to the Civil Rights Movement by the Unionists. With the single exception of Newry, all properly pre-arranged and marshalled Civil Rights demonstrations have been non-violent.

THE PROPOSED "REFORMS"

The world publicity afforded by the police brutalities and subsequent riots in Londonderry on and after October 5th, 1968 compelled the Stormont Tories to do something to appease public opinion. They took the following steps:—

(1) The Derry City Corporation was suspended and a Commission set up to govern Londonderry. This is not a satisfactory substitute for ordinary democratic majority rule. The Chairman of this Commission was a Unionist member of the notorious Belfast Corporation, which has a well-known reputation for religious discrimination.

(2) A Commission of Enquiry was also set up to look into the causes of recent civil strife in Ulster. This Commission has the following serious shortcomings:

It has not the power to compel witnesses to attend. It is hearing evidence in secret. A member of the Stormont Government has said that its findings may never be made public. The Constitution of this Commission was not even discussed with the representatives of the minority, who comprise 35% of the population. The Chairman is a Scottish Judge, Lord Cameron. Another of its three members is a leading medical politician, Sir J. Biggart, the Dean of the Medical Faculty at Queen's University, Belfast, a past member of the Northern Ireland Hospitals Authority and Chairman of the Medical Advisory Committee to the Northern Ireland Ministry of Health. The third member of the Cameron Commission, Mr. J. J. Campbell, M.A., is a Catholic. He is a member of the Senate and Director of the Institute of Education of Queen's University. The Opposition is at a serious disadvantage in this Enquiry in that many facts are very difficult to obtain, whereas the Unionists, with control of the Civil Service, have easy access to all public records.

For example, (a) When we tried to obtain the names of the staff of the Housing Trust, we were met with a blank refusal from it's headquarters (17:4:69); (b) At a meeting in Omagh on 10th March, 1969, Tyrone County Council members, who are also members of the local Civil Rights Committee, were refused details of staff, salaries, etc., by the Unionist majority.

(3)   The Ulster Government proposed four Reforms.   These are minimal, and are widely regarded merely as window dressing. Should they become law (and at present there seems no indication of haste in the Stormont Parliament) they will not afford genuine safeguards to civil rights for all in Northern Ireland, nor will we be required to make more than marginal amendments to our publicity material, including this booklet.

The further ''reforms'' proposed are:

(i)   The withdrawal of the Special Powers Act, but not at present.

(ii)   An ''Ombudsman'' to be appointed. He will, however, have no power to investigate local authority injustices or police behaviour, two of the most important fields.

(iii)   The Government will recommend, but, not compel, local authorities to initiate a ''points scheme'' for fair housing allocation. In the details of the Government scheme, so far given, there is mention of provision for slum clearance cases, key workers, overcrowded dwellings but, significantly, no mention of 'new families.' In the past the Unionists have controlled the size of the opposition by not making proper provision for new families in their housing schemes.

(iv)   The franchise is to be reviewed. This item is dealt with under the heading of ''Enniskillen,'' overleaf.

Machinery to deal with grievances against Local Authorities has since been mentioned: although it was not included in the original reforms package.

It would be impossible to give all the glaring facts in a publication of this size.

Here are a few examples from widely scattered towns:

Londonderry

This is the second city in Northern Ireland. It was endowed by the City of London Companies after the British Plantation of Ulster in the sixteenth century. It has strong links with the Protestant ascendancy, so the Unionists have stooped to unbelievable depths to maintain control, as the following details show.

GERRYMANDER

(i)   Stormont Parliament:

There was a separate seat for the City of Londonderry in the early years of the Stormont parliament. Because of the preponderance of Catholics the constituency returned an anti-Unionist member (Nationalist). In order to neutralise the seat the electoral division was re-arranged. The city itself was cut in two, Foyle returning a Nationalist. The boundary of the ''City'' was stretched eight miles into the country. The map below illustrates the way this was done, and how the planners of the new boundary of the City constituency found it necessary to reach out to include pockets of Unionists voters, without reference to natural geographical features, in order to scrape together a Unionist majority.

LONDONDERRY PARLIAMENTARY CONSTITUENCIES

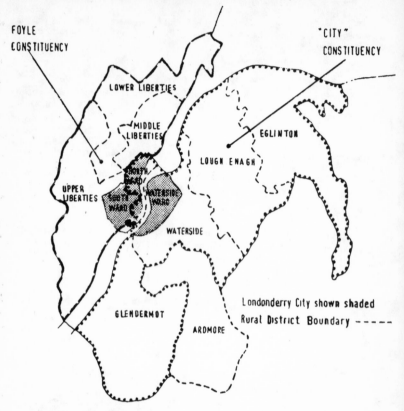

FOYLE
CONSTITUENCY

"CITY"
CONSTITUENCY

LOWER LIBERTIES

MIDDLE
LIBERTIES

EGLINTON

LOUGH ENAGH

NORTH
WARD

UPPER
LIBERTIES

SOUTH
WARD

WATERSIDE
WARD

WATERSIDE

Londonderry City shown shaded
Rural District Boundary - - - - -

GLENDERMOT

ARDMORE

(ii) Local Government:

Until the Commission took over in early 1969, Derry City was the textbook case of gerrymander in local government. The diagram over shows the extent of this. These figures only include the householders and wives. If all adults over 21 years had a vote, the position would be shown to be much worse.

In their attempt to contain the opposition, the Unionist Corporation determined not to build extra houses within the City boundary. They have not built a single house since 1966, and only 136 since 1958. Over 1,000 houses in Derry are occupied by more than one family and in several cases seven or eight families are occupying what was originally a single dwelling. There are over 1,500 families on the waiting list, nearly all Catholics. Even the Housing Trust, which has built large numbers of flats and dwellings, has been seriously hampered in its house-building efforts by the continued refusal of the Corporation to extend the City boundary. Many times each year proposals to this end by opposition councillors have been rejected.

THE WARDS SYSTEM IN <u>Londonderry</u>
(1966 REVISION)

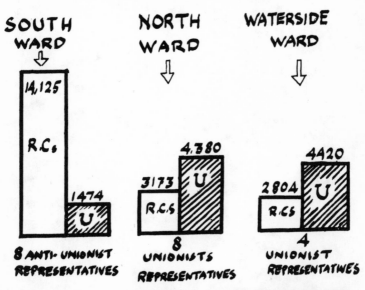

SOUTH WARD

NORTH WARD

WATERSIDE WARD

14,125 R.Cs

1474 U

8 ANTI-UNIONIST REPRESENTATIVES

3173 R.Cs

4,380 U

8 UNIONISTS REPRESENTATIVES

2804 R.Cs

4420 U

4 UNIONIST REPRESENTATIVES

20,102 VOTERS ELECT 8 ANTI-UNIONIST REPRESENT.

10,274 VOTERS ELECT 12 UNIONIST REPRESENTATIVES

8

12

☐ ROMAN CATHOLIC.

▨ UNIONIST

A private body, the Derry Housing Association, secured ground and applied for permission to build 700 houses. This permission was at first steadfastly refused and only lately a proportion of the number requested has been allowed after tedious appeals to the Central Authority, and a public hearing.

In Britain, Housing Associations, which build houses to supplement local authority enterprises, have full co-operation from councils. In Northern Ireland they encounter continuous obstruction. In Dungannon, for example, the Housing Association there had to cease functioning after being blocked in three different sites by Dungannon Urban District Council.

Until the Londonderry Commission was set up, all houses were let by one man, the Lord Mayor. The Derry Corporation Housing Committee did not function.

Omagh

Population 61.2% Catholic.

Gerrymander in Omagh:

39% of the people elect 12 Unionist Councillors.

61% of the people elect 9 anti-Unionist Councillors.

The Electoral Gerrymander:

The ghetto principle operates in Omagh urban area. There are three wards. The Unionist Wards are small, the anti-Unionist a large Catholic ghetto.

North.—Unionist voters 774; anti-Unionist voters 315 — 6 Councillors.

South — Unionist voters 709; anti-Unionist voters 473 — 6 Councillors.

West.—Unionist voters 369; anti-Unionist voters 1,759—9 Councillors.

The Register is, of course, on the restricted franchise of householders and their wives.

Urban Council Housing:

Since the last war, of the 197 houses built in the North Ward, 100% went to Protestants. In the South Ward, of the 116 houses built 95% went to Protestants. In the West Ward the number of houses built was 251 and the percentage allocated to Catholics was 98.

Housing Trust:

This body are in the West Ward where the Trust has 261 dwellings, only 13 Urban Council.

All schemes are in the West Ward where the Trust has 261 dwellings, only 13 going to Protestants. (Like in most Ulster towns, the Unionist Urban Council provides adequately for Unionist supporters, without the help of the Trust).

No matter how many houses are built in the West Ward, the balance of power will not be disturbed because the citizens can only be represented by their nine councillors.

Employment:

County Hall: Staff 100; Catholics 4.

Education Offices: Staff 70; Catholics 2.

Rural Council: Staff 35; Catholics 2.

We have succeeded in obtaining full details of one category, viz:

Staff of Tyrone County Council, whose appointments and salary are subject to the approval of the Ministry of Development

Name	Post	Remuneration
R. Parke	Secretary	£4,470 - £5,050
H. Martin	Accountant	£2,610 - £3,260
E. Diffin	Assistant Accountant	£1,780 - £2,170
T. Crawford	Assistant Accountant	£1,780 - £2,170
J. Eakin	Assistant Accountant	£1,780 - £2,170
T. Bowie	Local Taxation Officer	£1,715
S. C. Neely	County Surveyor	£3,590 - £4,010
J. McCleery	Deputy Co. Surveyor	£2,500 - £2,820
J. A. T. McCurdy	Senior Engineer	£2,005 - £2,610
R. W. D. Smith	Senior Engineer	£2,005 - £2,610
C. M. Henderson	Special Assistant Surveyor	£2,005 - £2,610
*G. P. McCaughey	Divisional Surveyor	£1,780 - £2,425
J. A. Clements	Divisional Surveyor	£1,780 - £2,425
M. Pollard	Divisional Surveyor	£1,780 - £2,425
B. Lambert	Divisional Surveyor	£1,780 - £2,425
G. H. Scott	Senior Assistant Engineer	£1,780 - £2,255
W. J. E. Dukeow	Senior Assistant Engineer	£1,780 - £2,255
J. Leitch	Assistant Surveyor	£1,265 - £2,085
R. A. Hale	Assistant Surveyor	£1,265 - £2,085
J. N. Robinson	Rate Collector	£440
J. Lecky	Rate Collector	£513
G. Little	Rate Collector	£1,207

* Of all these employees, only Mr. G. P. McCaughey is a Catholic.

Lurgan

Although the population, according to the 1961 Census, is 45.7% Catholic, there is no anti-Unionist (Catholic) representation on the 15 man Council. Though there are large religious ghettos operated by the Council, due to the 'block' system of voting these people have no council representatives. In all the central and local government employment in the town there is only one Catholic, holding a salaried, as against a labouring job, he being employed in the gasworks*. The present mayor, Councillor S. Gardiner, declared before the last local government election, in the presence of the present Minister of Development, Mr. Brian Faulkner†: "This is a Protestant country and it is up to us to keep it this way. We must keep Unionists in control, not only in Lurgan, but throughout the whole of Northern Ireland."

* Lurgan Borough Council: 156 employees; 131 Protestant; 25 Catholic. Of the 25 Catholics 23 are labourers.

† The new Minister of Development is Mr. Faulkner, who is in charge of the re-structuring of the local authorities.

Lurgan Hospital:

North Armagh Hospital Committee: 18 members; 3 Catholics.

Hospital Staff	Protestant	Catholic
Medical Consultants (Full Time)	9	0
Medical Consultants (Part Time	4	0
Medical Registrars	3	0
Radiographers*	1	4
X-ray Secretaries	2	0
Store Clerks	2	0
Physiotherapists*	2	1
Ward and Lab. maids	7	10
Porters	6	5
Pharmacist	1	0
Pharmacist's Assistant	1	0
Seamstresses	2	0
Ambulancemen	7	0
Matron	1	0
Assistant Matron	2	0
Ward Sisters	8	7
Dietician	1	0
Cooks	7	1
Kitchen Managers	1	0

Receptionists	4	0
Superintendents	1	0
Laundry Workers	6	5
Laboratory Technicians	10	0
Engineers	1	0
Electricians	2	0
Carpenters	2	0
Painters	2	1
Boilermen	4	0
Yardmen	2	0
Kitchen maids	9	2
Clerical Staff	14	0

* These two grades are in short supply in N. Ireland, as are nurses.

The Catholic-Protestant ratio of nurses in most hospitals is reasonable.

Fivemiletown

(1967 facts and figures)

Population: 435 adult Protestants and 123 adult Catholics.

Post Office—Postmaster and three counter hands; 8 Postmen. None are Catholic. As in Dungannon and elsewhere vacancies for postmen are never advertised.

Co-operative Creamery — Approximately one third of the milk suppliers are Roman Catholic. No Catholics on staff, the size of which we can only estimate as between 80 and 100 since we have no informants. Method of selection can be instanced. A local Catholic youth with training applied for a job in the laboratory. A Protestant aged 15, just finished in the intermediate school, was appointed.

High School.—550 on roll of which 140 are Roman Catholic.

	Protestants	Catholics
Permanent teachers	23	3
Part-time teachers	5	—
Bus drivers	5	—
Kitchen staff	6	—
Cleaners	6	—
Secretary to Principal	1	—
Assistant Librarian	1	—
Laboratory Assistant	1	—
Total	48	3

Ratio   16   1

Ballylurgan Co-operative Stores employs 16 Protestants and one Catholic.

Housing:

Approximately 91 houses have been built by Clogher Rural District Council. Of these 77 are let to Protestants and 14 to Catholics.

Armagh

The city was 53.5% Catholic at the 1961 Census. It has now been estimated that the number of Catholics has fallen to half in spite of a much higher Catholic birth rate.

Local Government Representation:

There were 3,449 adult Catholics and 3,050 adult Protestants in Armagh in 1968. Due to gerrymander and restricted franchise the Protestants (Unionists) are represented by 12 councillors whilst the Catholics have only 8.

Council Housing:

The religions are almost totally segregated in the housing estates, e.g., in the Catholic ghetto, of the 324 houses owned by the Council only two Protestant families are housed. In the Protestant ghettos, with 534 houses, the council has only allowed 31 Catholic families in.

Housing Trust:

Whilst in a Unionist ward there are 44 Catholic families in Trust houses out of a total of 186, the Housing Trust has allowed its other three estates in the opposition wards to become Catholic ghettos, permitting only nine Protestant familes to reside in them out of a total of 145 houses.

Employment:

Armagh County Council—Non-manual employees: Protestant 193; Catholic 8.

County Education Committee—Non-manual workers: Protestant 96; Catholic 3.

Welfare Committee Workers—Protestant 52; Catholic 7.

No Catholic holds any position of Principal Officer under the County Council.

The County Surveyor, the County Medical Officer, the County Dental Officer, County Librarian, the Director of Education, the County Agricuitural Officer and the County Planning Officer are all Protestants.

Armagh Urban Council:

Out of the 17 non-manual employees in the City Hall only one is a Catholic.

Dungannon

The population here is 50.3% Catholic.

The Electoral Situation:

Due to gerrymander, restricted franchise and the unequal size of wards, there is grossly unfair representation. There are three wards. They are East, which contains the Protestant ghettos, Central, mainly Protestant, and West, which is a Catholic ghetto. Each of the three wards is represented by seven councillors. On the restricted franchise of householders and wives only, here are the numbers of electors:

East Ward (7 Unionist Councillors); 1,729 electors; 543 Catholic, 1,186 Protestant.

Central Ward (7 Unionist Councillors); 659 electors; 143 Catholic; 516 Protestant.

West Ward (7 anti-Unionist Councillors); 1,031 electors; 844 Catholic; 187 Protestant.

(The number of people over 21 years in the three wards are: East 2,149; Central 804 and West 1,353).

Assuming that Protestants vote Unionist and Catholics anti-Unionist (which holds good almost to a man in Dungannon) it takes 147 voters in the West ward to elect one anti-Unionist councillor, whilst in the Central ward, 94 voters can elect a Unionist representative !

The Chairman of the Council is Senator William Stewart, Unionist member of the Upper House in the Northern Ireland Parliament.

HOW THE CIVIL RIGHTS MOVEMENT BEGAN

In 1963 there were upwards of 300 families on the housing waiting list, some for as long as 12 years, and not one new Catholic family had been allocated a permanant house for 34 years. Council houses had been allocated to a pharmaceutical chemist, the Council's own engineer, and several other comfortably off Protestant people. Other Protestants had sold good villa residences to move into Council houses.

Young Protestants were boasting to their Catholic workmates that they could, and did, select new council houses and move in as soon as, or shortly after, they were married.

The histograph over, describes the Urban Council's housing record.

The Housing Trust also owns a considerable number of houses in the town. Its letting record is much fairer, but, as elsewhere, the Urban Council maintains the balance of power.

The Dungannon Rural District Council has built 204 houses since 1944 in the area of Dungannon Roman Catholic parish. Only two have been given to new Catholic families.

Housing in Ghettos

The Urban Council owns five post-war housing estates. All the houses in the Unionist East Ward (180) are and have always been tenanted by Protestants. Only two out of 31 houses in the Central Ward have ever been occupied by Catholics.

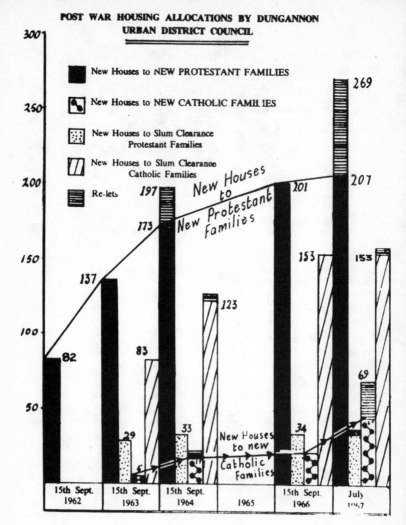

POST WAR HOUSING ALLOCATIONS BY DUNGANNON URBAN DISTRICT COUNCIL

New Houses to NEW PROTESTANT FAMILIES

New Houses to NEW CATHOLIC FAMILIES

New Houses to Slum Clearance Protestant Families

New Houses to Slum Clearance Catholic Families

Re-lets

When tenants were moved in the slum clearance operation from 50 prefabricated bungalows, the Council announced that these were to be knocked down to make way for further house building. Before the bungalows could be dismantled 30 Catholic families, who were living in single rooms in appalling conditions and paying up to half their incomes in rent, "squatted" overnight into the 'prefabs.' (27:8:63).

"The Homeless Citizens' League" was born from this operation, and its first discovery was that there were no plans submitted to the Minister to develop the area on which the prefabricated bungalows stood. The Unionist Council's only reason for wanting to demolish the bungalows was to keep the Catholic numbers down.

The League also discovered that the Council Chairman's wife owned slum property, which was not condemned, nor was a tenement belonging to a Unionist supporter, in which there were living eight families, consisting of 29 people, sharing one kitchen, one bathroom and two toilets.

Much better property owned by Catholics was condemned and the people forced to leave against their will.

Two Unionist councillors offered a substantial sum of money to a woman who had rented a shop with living accommodation from them, if she would give up her tenancy.

The offer was later withdrawn and the living accommodation condemned by the Sanitary Officer.

The Stormont Minister for Health and Local Government was informed of all these irregularities, but did nothing.

The protest marches and meetings of the League marked the beginning of the Civil Rights movement in Northern Ireland. The Campaign for Social Justice also developed as a fact-finding and publicity organisation.

Employment: Urban Council:

Fifteen employees from the Town Clerk down as far as the bricklayer, with no Catholics. Then ten Catholic and five Protestant labourers.

State Electricity Board:

Nineteen employees from the District engineer to the linesman charge-hand, with no Catholics. Linesmen: 5 Catholic; 4 Protestant; 5 Protestant and no Catholic drivers; 21 Catholic and 16 Protestant labourers; 1 Storekeeper and 1 H.T. Line Supervisor, both Protestants.

Post Office:

Discrimination seems to be worse here than anywhere else we know of. Representations to two British Postmasters-General have achieved nothing.

There are 53 persons working in the Head Post Office. Of these only five are Roman Catholics, and of the five, four are postmen.

County Fermanagh

(Including Enniskillen)

This town and county is the worst in Northern Ireland for job and housing discrimination. Reference to the graph will show that even more Catholics than the average for the province are forced to emigrate, e.g., since 1920, only twenty new houses have been allocated to new Catholic families by the Borough Council in the town of Enniskillen. The rest have all been slum clearance which merely shifts Catholics from old houses to new (1967 figures).

The Unionist party is run, according to the English Duke of Westminster who has a residence there, by "a dictatorship" . . . "of less than half a dozen people." (6:5:69).

Discrimination in Public Appointments:

It is most difficult to obtain figures because of obstruction by the authoritites. Fermanagh County Council has 166 employees of which 156 are Protestants.

The 156 Protestants earn between then £162,632, the ten Catholics earn £9,340. Fermanagh Education Committee employs 179. Of these 169 are Protestants earning £80,987 and ten Catholics earning £3,155. The Public Health and Welfare Committee employs 136 people, made up of 110 Protestants earning £108,704 and 26 Catholics receiving £27,151, e.g., of the 68 school coach drivers in County Fermanagh, 67 are Protestants.

The Mechanics of Gerrymander in County Fermanagh:

Population by religions according to Government Census 1961 (latest figure available): Roman Catholics 27,291; Protestants 24,322.

The representation on the various public bodies since the 1920's has been:

	Un.	A-Un.
Fermanagh County Council	20	6
Enniskillen Borough Council	14	7
Enniskillen, Irvinestown and Lisnaskea Rural Councils	54	30
	88	43

This was achieved by a combination of gerrymander, manipulation of boundaries and restricted local government franchise.

Projected reform of local Government:

Then, in 1966, with a great flourish, the Unionists announced that they were going to re-structure local government. They would therefore be seen to be acting to counter the injustices of the numerous public bodies whose record of housing and job injustices was notorious.

They selected County Fermanagh as the pilot scheme. The County Council was ordered to set up a steering Committee to arrange the amalgamation of local bodies. This ten man committee was composed of Unionists only (in a County with an anti-Unionist majority).

CO. FERMANAGH

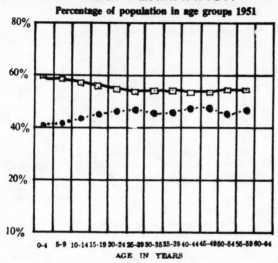

Percentage of population in age groups 1951

AGE IN YEARS

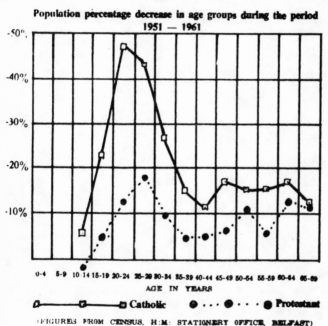

Population percentage decrease in age groups during the period 1951 — 1961

AGE IN YEARS

□————□————□ Catholic ● · · · ● · · · ● Protestant

(FIGURES FROM CENSUS. H.M. STATIONERY OFFICE, BELFAST)

THE RESULT OF RESTRUCTURING CO. FERMANAGH LOCAL AUTHORITIES (The New Gerrymander)

In 1967, the County was placed under one public authority on which there are 36 Unionists (including two co-options) and 17 anti-Unionists (including one co-option).

The Chairman and vice-Chairman are both Protestants (Unionists).

From this, undemocratic, re-organised Fermanagh County Council, sub-Committees have been set up. For full measure the Chairman and vice-Chairman have been made "ex-officio" members of all these sub-Committees, e.g., Education sub-Committee: 12 Protestants; 3 Catholics. Agricultural sub-Committee: 13 Protestants; 5 Catholics. Housing sub-Committee: 6 Protestants; 3 Catholics.

The new Prime Minister of Northern Ireland, Major J. Chichester-Clark, has announced that there will be one man, one vote, and a new local authority arrangement by the time the next local government elections take place in 1971. But if there is to be further gerrymander of the other areas in the way that Fermanagh has been manipulated, then one man, one vote will prove to be a useless concession to the minority.

If you suspect us of overstatement or even inaccuracy in this catalogue of repression and injustice, please remember that the Campaign for Social Justice in Northern Ireland has been pressing Westminister for years to set up a Judicial Enquiry composed of English lawyers, or a Royal Commission, to prove or disprove our contentions.

The Ulster Unionists, who are past masters in the art of the half-truth*, have steadily opposed this. Surely we are entitled to claim that they have much to hide ?

* The most recent example of Unionist half-truths may be cited viz:

On 12:6:69 the Prime Minister, Major Chichester-Clark, said:

"We have been in a position where some quite small grievances or alleged grievances have been magnified out of all proportion, and used to blacken the good name we have built up in the world over many, many years."

SIR JAMES CRAIG (later VISCOUNT CRAIGAVON). Prime Minister of Northern Ireland 1921-40.

"It is also from the ranks of the Loyal Orange Institution that our splendid 'Specials' have come." (Belfast Newsletter, 13th July, 1922)

"I have always said I am an Orangeman first and a politician and Member of this Parliament afterwards . . . all I boast is that we are a Protestant Parliament and Protestant State." (24th April, 1934. Parliamentary Debates, N.I. Vol. XVI, Cols. 1091-95).

Dame Enid Lyons, widow of Joseph A. Lyons, Prime Minister of Australia 1932-39, recalls in her memoirs ("So we take comfort," London 1965, p. 235) a famous gaffe illustrative of Craigavon's religious feelings.

"It was Lord Craigavon, the fiercely anti-Catholic Prime Minister of Northern Ireland, who knowing nothing of Joe's personal background, had asked him at a banquet, 'Lyons, have you got many Catholics in Australia ?' 'Oh, about one in five' Joe replied. 'Well watch 'em, Lyons, watch 'em', Craigavon had urged. 'They 'They breed like b———y rabbits'."

SIR BASIL BROOKE (later VISCOUNT BROOKEBOROUGH). Minister of Agriculture 1933-41, Minister of Commerce 1941-43, Prime Minister 1943-63.

"There were a great number of Protestants and Orangemen who employed Roman Catholics. He felt he could speak freely on this subject as he had not a Roman Catholic about his own place . . . He would appeal to Loyalists, therefore, wherever possible, to employ good Protesant lads and lassies.' (Fermanagh Times, 13th July, 1933).

'He made certain remarks regarding the employment of Roman Catholics which created a certain amount of controversy. He now wished to say he did not intend to withdraw a single word of what he then said.' (Fermanagh Times, 17th August, 1933).

"Thinking out the whole question carefully . . . I recommended those people who are Loyalists not to employ Roman Catholics, ninety-nine per cent of whom are disloyal . . . I want you to remember one point in regard to the employment of people who are disloyal. There are often difficulties in the way, but usually there are plenty of good men and women available, and the employers don't bother to employ them. You are disfranchising yourselves in that way. You people who are employers have the ball at your feet. If you don't act properly now before we know where we are we shall find ourselves in the minority instead of the majority." (Londonderry Sentinel, 20th March, 1934).

SIR DAWSON BATES. Minister of Home Affairs, 1921-43.

Mr. G. C. Duggan, a Protestant, who was a civil servant in Belfast (1921-39) and who returned after war service to become Comptroller and Auditor-General (1945-49), wrote as follows in the Irish Times (4th May, 1967):

"When it is remembered that the first Minister, Sir Dawson Bates, held that post for 22 years and had such a prejudice against Catholics that he made it clear to his Permanent Secretary that he did not want his most juvenile clerk, or typist, if a Papist, assigned for duty to his Ministry, what could one expect when it came to filling posts in the Judiciary, Clerkships of the Crown and Peace and Crown Solicitors ?"

EDWARD ARCHDALE (later Sir Edward Archdale). Minister of Agriculture 1921-33.

"A man in Fintona asked him how it was that he had over 50 per cent Roman Catholics in his Ministry. He thought that was too funny. He had 109 of a staff, and so far as he knew there were four Roman Catholics. Three of these were civil servants, turned over to him whom he had to take when he began." (Northern Whig, 2nd April, 1925).

SIR JOSEPH DAVISON, Orange Grand Master of Belfast, Senator 1935, Deputy Leader of Senate 1941, died 1948.

"When will the Protestant employers of Northern Ireland recognise their duty to their Protestant brothers and sisters and employ them to the exclusion of Roman Catholics . . . it is time Protestant employers of Northern Ireland realized that whenever a Roman Catholic is brought into their employment it means one Protestant vote less. It is our duty to pass the word along from this great demonstration and I suggest the slogan should be 'Protestants, employ Protestants.' " (Northern Whig, 28th August, 1933).

BRIAN FAULKNER, M.P. Minister of Home Affairs, 1959-63, Minister of Commerce, 1963-69, Minister of Development 1969:

"The Church of Rome, he warned, ran a world-wide organisation — the most efficient political undertaking in the world. It controlled newspapers, radio and television stations and a hundred and one other avenues of propaganda. It was able to give vigorous publicity to any cause it espouses . . . that it favours Irish Republicanism today as whole-heartedly as it has done for generations past is universally recognised." (Northern Whig, 13th July, 1954).

"There is no reason why Orangemen individually and collectively should not interest themselves in the economic welfare of the community. I mean by that statement we should be anxious to find employment for our brethern." (County Down, Spectator, 17th July, 1954).

'Of one thing, I for my part, have no doubt—if it should ever happen that Orangemen dissassociate themselves from the political life of Ulster, both Ulster and the Orange institution are doomed . . . I have said before and I repeat today — the Orange Order is the backbone of Ulster. (Irish News, 13th July, 1960).

ALEX. HUNTER, M.P.

Mr. Alex Hunter, M.P., said "he had been recently horrified to learn that a local authority within the combined Orange district had oppointed a Roman Catholic to represent them on the County Antrim Education Committee." (Northern Whig, 13th July, 1956).

E.C. FERGUSON, M.P. (Resigned from Parliament in October 1949 to become Crown Solicitor for Co. Fermanagh).

"The Nationalist majority in the county ,i.e., Fermanagh) notwithstanding a reduction of 336 in the year, stands at 3,684*. We must ultimately reduce and liquidate that majority. This county, I think it can be safely said, is a Unionist county. The atmosphere is Unionist. The Boards and properties are nearly all controlled by Unionists. But there is still this millstone around our necks." (Irish News, 13th April, 1948).

* At the present time the majority is down to about 200.

THOMAS LYONS, M.P.

Mr. Lyons said: "that in the Castlederg district they stood firmly for Orangeism, Protestantism and Unionism. They all mean the same thing. A man who was a Protestant and not a Unionist had a 'kink' in his make up. Such a person was not normal." (Belfast Newsletter, 14th July, 1947).

ALDERMAN GEORGE ELLIOT

"We are not going to build houses in the South Ward and cut a rod to beat ourselves later on.

"We are going to see that the right people are put into these houses and we are not making any apology for it." (At Enniskillen on 7th November, 1963). (Impartial Reporter, 14th Nov., 1963).

SENATOR J. E. N. BARNHILL

"Charity begins at home. If we are going to employ people we should give preference to Unionists, I am not saying that we should sack Nationalist employees, but if we are going to employ new men we should give preference to Unionists." (At Londonderry on 9th January, 1964).

CAPTAIN TERENCE O'NEILL. Prime Minister 1963-1969.

"Protestant girl required for housework. Apply to The Hon. Mrs. Terence O'Neill, Glebe House, Ahoghill, Co. Antrim." (Advertisement in Belfast Telegraph, November, 1959. Quoted by Sunday Times, London, 2nd March, 1969).

"It is frightfully hard to explain to Protestants that if you give Roman Catholics a good job and a good house, they will live like Protestants, because they will see neighbours with cars and television sets.

"They will refuse to have 18 children, but if a Roman Catholic is jobless, and lives in the most ghastly hovel, he will rear 18 children on National Assistance.

"If you treat Roman Catholics with due consideration and kindness, they will live like Protestants in spite of the authoritative nature of their Church." (Belfast Telegraph, 10th May, 1969).

MAJOR J. CHICHESTER-CLARK. Prime Minister, 1969:

"Indeed, I am proud to be in the (Orange) Order and those criticising it know nothing about it." (Irish Weekly, 31st May, 1969).

Appendix II

Northern Ireland

WHY JUSTICE CAN NOT BE DONE

THE DOUGLAS HOME CORRESPONDENCE

Issued by

THE CAMPAIGN FOR SOCIAL JUSTICE IN NORTHERN IRELAND
CASTLEFIELDS - DUNGANNON

Committee :

MRS. PATRICIA McCLUSKEY
MRS. MAURA MULLALLY
MRS. OLIVE SCOTT
MAURICE BRYNE, B.D.S.

J. J. DONNELLY
PETER GORMLEY, F.R.C.S.
CONOR GILLIGAN, F.R.C.S.
HUGH P. McCONVILLE, P.T.
BRIAN GREGORY, B.A., F.R.I.B.A.

CONN McCLUSKEY, M.B.
THOMAS McLAUGHLIN
SEAN McGIVERN
LEO SULLIVAN, B.SC.

The Campaign for Social Justice in Northern Ireland was inaugurated on 17th January, 1964, for the purpose of bringing the light of publicity to bear on the discrimination which exists in our community against the Catholic section of that community representing more than one-third of the total population.

We announced at a formal Press Conference in Belfast on the same date our intention to use all necessary means at our disposal for the dissemination of factual information about discriminatory practices exercised against our people in employment provided by central and local government agencies and also in housing provided by public funds. Accordingly, when the Prime Minister of the United Kingdom, the Right Hon. Sir Alec Douglas Home, M.P., visited Northern Ireland in the month of March this year and stated in reply to questions at a Belfast Press Conference, and later when interviewed on television, that recourse could be had to the courts in matters of complaint regarding religious discrimination, we felt compelled to give this important statement the fullest consideration.

We believed that the Prime Minister of the United Kingdom would not make such a statement without due consideration and knowledge. The Campaign Committee therefore immediately consulted eminent legal authority, only to be informed "that the discrimination practised by local authorities is not capable of review by the courts under the terms of the Government of Ireland Act 1920 or any other statutory provisions".

As this same Government of Ireland Act 1920 empowers the British Government to intervene decisively in the affairs of Northern Ireland, the committee felt that the British Prime Minister should be approached and asked to give the legal basis for his statement. We present herewith the correspondence which ensued.

(COPY)

CAMPAIGN FOR SOCIAL JUSTICE IN NORTHERN IRELAND
CASTLEFIELDS, DUNGANNON, CO. TYRONE

13th April, 1964

The Right Honourable Sir Alec Douglas Home, M.P.,
10 Downing Street,
LONDON.

Dear Prime Minister,

During your recent visit to Northern Ireland, you indicated that discrimination could be dealt with by law ; and that the rights of the minority could be protected by recourse to the courts, under the terms of the Government of Ireland Act, 1920.

This organisation has irrefutable evidence of discrimination by Local Authorities, in the allocation of houses and jobs in certain areas in Northern Ireland.

In the light of your remarks, we engaged the services of Solicitors and Counsel to investigate the possibility of having these acts of discrimination examined in a Court of Law.

We have now been advised by Senior and Junior Counsel : . . . . . "that the discrimination practiced by Local Authorities is not capable of review by the courts under the terms of the Government of Ireland Act, 1920, or any other Statutory Provisions".

We assume that your statement was made with some consideration of the legal position ; and in the circumstances, we would be obliged if you would refer us to the specific provisions which you had in mind.

Yours respectfully,

BRIAN GREGORY, Secretary.

Letter formally acknowledged 21st April, 1964

. . . .

10, DOWNING STREET,
WHITEHALL.

May 8, 1964

Dear Sir,

The Prime Minister has asked me to reply to your letter of April 13 asking for a reference to the provisions he had in mind in the course of some remarks made during his visit to Northern Ireland. The provisions are section 5 of the Government of Ireland Act 1920, which prohibits the Parliament of Northern Ireland from making laws interfering with religious equality, and section 8 (6), which prohibits religious discrimination in the exercise of the executive powers granted to the Governor of Northern Ireland. I should add, having regard to your letter, that these provisions were relevant in the context of the remarks made by the Prime Minister in the course of replies to questions put at a press conference.

Yours truly,

M. H. M. REID

The Secretary,
Campaign for Social Justice.

3

CAMPAIGN FOR SOCIAL JUSTICE IN NORTHERN IRELAND

CASTLEFIELDS, DUNGANNON, CO. TYRONE

2nd June, 1964

The Right Honourable Sir Alec Douglas Home, M.P.,
10 Downing Street,
LONDON.

Dear Prime Minister,

      Thank you for your letter of May 8 in which you state that Section 5 of the Government of Ireland Act provides against religious discrimination in enactments of the Northern Ireland Parliament and Section 8 (6) prohibits religious discrimination in the exercise of executive powers granted to the Government of Northern Ireland. This legislation does not, however, appear to prevent discrimination in the exercise of powers conferred or duties imposed by Acts of the Northern Ireland Parliament ; and in particular it does not appear to give any redress against discriminatory acts by local authorities in the exercise of their powers.

      It is this latter matter which is of most immediate concern in Northern Ireland. As we have stated in previous correspondence, we believe there is clear evidence that certain local authorities in exercising their functions have discriminated against people on the grounds of religion. We would be pleased to have your advice as to whether there is any existing legal process whereby persons in Northern Ireland can bring such cases of alleged religious discrimination before the Courts, and secure redress in the event of the allegations being established. If such provision is not at present available, we would like to know whether your Government would be prepared to initiate legislation, whether by way of amendment to the Government of Ireland Act or otherwise, which would enable cases of alleged religious discrimination by public authorities to be examined by the Courts and to be rectified where proved.

Yours respectfully,

BRIAN GREGORY, Secretary.

Letter formally acknowledged 4th June, 1964

4

CAMPAIGN FOR SOCIAL JUSTICE IN NORTHERN IRELAND
CASTLEFIELDS, DUNGANNON, CO. TYRONE

24th June, 1964

The Right Honourable Sir Alec Douglas Home, M.P.,
10 Downing Street,
LONDON.

Dear Prime Minister,

While appreciating the demands which are made upon a Prime Minister's time, may we state with all courtesy that we are most anxious to have a considered reply to our letter of the 2nd instant, which you acknowledged on the 4th instant.

We feel sure that you recognise the importance of the issues raised in our letter, and we trust that the delay in replying thereto is in some measure occasioned by the necessity of giving full consideration to these issues.

Yours respectfully,
BRIAN GREGORY, Secretary.

. . . .

10, DOWNING STREET,
WHITEHALL.
June 25, 1964

Dear Sir,

I write on behalf of the Prime Minister to acknowledge the receipt of your letter of June 24.

The Prime Minister has asked the Home Secretary to look into the points that you raised and a further reply will be sent to you in due course.

Yours truly,
M. H. M. REID

The Secretary,
Campaign for Social Justice.

. . . .

HOME OFFICE,
WHITEHALL,
LONDON, S.W.1.
30th June, 1964

Sir,

I am directed by the Secretary of State to reply to your letter of 2nd and 24th June which, as you know, have been forwarded to him.

The matters raised in these letters appear to the Secretary of State to be within the field of responsibility which the Government of Ireland Act, 1920, has entrusted to the Parliament and Government of Northern Ireland, and it would not be proper for him to comment upon them. Her Majesty's Government have no legislation in view to amend the 1920 Act.

I am, Sir,
Your obedient Servant,
A. J. LANGDON

The Secretary,
Campaign for Social Justice in Northern Ireland,
Castlefields,
DUNGANNON,
Co. Tyrone.

CAMPAIGN FOR SOCIAL JUSTICE IN NORTHERN IRELAND
CASTLEFIELDS, DUNGANNON, CO. TYRONE

13th August, 1964

The Right Honourable Sir Alec Douglas Home, M.P.,
10 Downing Street,
LONDON.

Dear Prime Minister,

As promised by you in your letter of June 25th, 1964, we have
received a letter from Mr. Henry Brooke, copy of which is enclosed.

It seems to us to leave our original questions to you, in our letters of
13th April 1964 and 2nd June 1964, unanswered.

Since there are upwards of half a million Roman Catholic people in Northern
Ireland who feel that they are suffering injustice by living their lives at a
disadvantage as compared with their Protestant fellow countrymen, and since,
in the final analysis, you and your Government are responsible for their welfare,
may I take the liberty of pressing you for precise answers to the questions posed.

Yours faithfully,
Mrs. PATRICIA McCLUSKEY, Chairman.

Letter formally acknowledged 14th August, 1964

. . . .

10, DOWNING STREET,
WHITEHALL.

August 20, 1964

Dear Madam,

The Prime Minister has asked me to reply to your letter of August 13,
referring to your previous letters, of April 13 and June 2, about allegations of
religious discrimination in Northern Ireland.

As explained in the Home Office letter of June 30, the matters you raise appear
to be within the field of responsibility of the Parliament and Government of
Northern Ireland, and are not, therefore, matters upon which the Prime Minister
can properly comment. Nor is it possible for the Prime Minister to advise on
the possibility of initiating legal proceedings in Northern Ireland.

Yours truly,
M. H. M. REID

The Chairman,
The Campaign for Social Justice in Northern Ireland.

6

CAMPAIGN FOR SOCIAL JUSTICE IN NORTHERN IRELAND
CASTLEFIELDS, DUNGANNON, CO. TYRONE

25th August, 1964

The Right Honourable Sir Alec Douglas Home, M.P.,
10 Downing Street,
LONDON.

Dear Prime Minister,

Thank you for your letter of 20th August, 1964, with reference to religious discrimination in Northern Ireland. We note your statement that the matters we raised "appear to be within the field of responsibility of the Parliament and Government of Northern Ireland" and that therefore you cannot properly comment upon them. If by this statement you seek to disclaim responsibility in the matter, we must refer you to Section 75 of the Government of Ireland Act, 1920, by which the British Government retained overall responsibility for Northern Ireland affairs "notwithstanding the establishment of the Parliament of . . . Northern Ireland".

You further state in your letter that it is not possible for you to advise on the possibility of initiating legal proceedings in Northern Ireland. May we refer you to your reply of 8 May, 1964 to our letter of 13 April, 1964 and the remarks made by you on your visit to Northern Ireland and referred to by you in the same reply. You actually quoted the sections of the Government of Ireland Act to which your remarks referred. If your remarks and your letter of May 8 do not advise legal proceedings in cases of discrimination what other meaning do they bear ?

As this is a matter of the highest constitutional importance, we should be grateful for a clear statement on it. Would you please tell us therefore :

1. Do you still hold to the opinion that charges of discrimination against local and central government in Northern Ireland are capable of being tested in court under the Government of Ireland Act ?
2. Are you now stating that the Government of Northern Ireland is the final judge in charges of discrimination brought against that government ?
3. Do you hold that the Government of Northern Ireland is the responsible authority to which charges of discrimination against local government authorities should be referred ?

We trust you will appreciate that our object in seeking clarification of these points is to eliminate causes of tension and frustration, and not to score points in an argument. We would urge upon you, therefore, the need for serious and immediate attention to the constitutional issues we have raised.

BRIAN GREGORY, Secretary,
Campaign for Social Justice.

10, DOWNING STREET,
WHITEHALL.

September 3rd, 1964

Dear Sir,

The Prime Minister has asked me to reply to your further letter of 25th August about allegations of religious discrimination in Northern Ireland.

Section 75 of the Government of Ireland Act, 1920, preserves the supreme authority of the Parliament of the United Kingdom — not of Her Majesty's Government in the United Kingdom — over all persons, matters and things in Northern Ireland. Section 5 of the Act already prohibits the enactment by the Parliament of Northern Ireland of laws interfering with religious equality : and the Prime Minister sees no reason for asking the United Kingdom Parliament to legislate further on this matter.

Yours truly,

The Secretary,
The Campaign for Social Justice in Northern Ireland.

CONCLUSION

To sum up, therefore, we have established with Sir Alec Douglas Home that :

(1) *The Parliament of the United Kingdom has the ultimate responsibility for discrimination in Northern Ireland, but the Prime Minister is unwilling to ask Parliament to intervene.*

(2) *Despite the fact that the British Prime Minister told us that allegations of discrimination could be dealt with by law, he is now either unable or unwilling to let us know how this can be done.*

We are left wondering if Sir Alec spoke in error, or if in fact he has no real interest in the problem of the minority and the facts of religious discrimination in Northern Ireland.

SUBSCRIPTIONS TO HELP OUR CAUSE GRATEFULLY RECEIVED

Select Bibliography

An asterisk denotes those most recommended as being sound, detailed and vivid, and, of these, most are written by Protestants or Englishmen.

Barritt, D.P. and C.F. Carter, *The Northern Ireland Problem*, OUP 1962.
*Boyd, Andrew, *Brian Faulkner*, Tralee: Anvil Books 1972.
Boyd, Andrew, *Holy War in Belfast*, Tralee: Anvil Books 1969.
Callaghan, James, *A House Divided*, London: Collins 1973.
Devlin, Bernadette, *The Price of my Soul*, London: Pan Books 1969.
Dillon, M. and D. Lehane, *Political Murder in Northern Ireland*, Harmondsworth: Penguin Books 1973.
Egan, B. *et al.*, *Burntollet*, London: L.R.S. Publishers 1969.
Fields, R.M., *A Society on the Run*, Harmondsworth: Penguin Books 1973.
*Hastings, Max, *Ulster 1969*, London: Gollancz 1970.
Howard, A. and R. West, *The Making of the Prime Minister*, London: Cape 1965.
*Jeffrey, J., *The Divided Province* (well illustrated), London: Orbis 1985.
Kelly, Henry, *How Stormont Fell*, Dublin: Gill and Macmillan 1972.
*Moloney, E. and A. Pollak, *Paisley*, Dublin: Poolbeg Press 1986.
Northern Ireland hearings by House of Representatives Committee on Foreign Affairs Washington U.S.A., U.S. Government Printing Office, Washington 1972.
O'Neill, Terence, *Autobiography*, London: Rupert Hart-Davis 1972.
Rose, Richard, *Governing without Consensus*, London: Faber 1971.
*'Sunday Times' Insight Team, *Ulster*, Harmondsworth: Penguin 1972.
Uris, Jill and Leon, *Ireland, A Terrible Beauty*, London: Corgi 1977.

Wallace, Martin, *Drums and Guns*, London: Geoffrey Chapman 1970.
Wallace, Martin, *Northern Ireland, Fifty Years of Self Government*, London: Rupert Hart-Davis 1971.
White, Barry, *John Hume*, Belfast: Blackstaff Press 1984.

Government Publications, H.M.S.O.
(all available from Government Bookshop, 80 Chichester Street, Belfast)
Special Powers Act.
Cameron Report.
Hunt Report on the Police in Northern Ireland.
Compton Report on Allegations of Brutality by the Security Forces.
Scarman Report on Violence and Civil Disturbances.
Widgery Report on Events in Londonderry 30 January 1972.
Parker Report: Committee of Privy Councillors on Procedures of Interrogation.

Index

239

243

244